MW00857109

Limitless Analytics with Azure Synapse

An end-to-end analytics service for data processing, management, and ingestion for BI and ML requirements

Prashant Kumar Mishra

BIRMINGHAM—MUMBAI

Limitless Analytics with Azure Synapse

Copyright © 2021 Packt Publishing

All rights reserved. No part of this book may be reproduced, stored in a retrieval system, or transmitted in any form or by any means, without the prior written permission of the publisher, except in the case of brief quotations embedded in critical articles or reviews.

Every effort has been made in the preparation of this book to ensure the accuracy of the information presented. However, the information contained in this book is sold without warranty, either express or implied. Neither the author, nor Packt Publishing or its dealers and distributors, will be held liable for any damages caused or alleged to have been caused directly or indirectly by this book.

Packt Publishing has endeavored to provide trademark information about all of the companies and products mentioned in this book by the appropriate use of capitals. However, Packt Publishing cannot guarantee the accuracy of this information.

Group Product Manager: Kunal Parikh

Publishing Product Manager: Sunith Shetty

Senior Editor: David Sugarman

Content Development Editor: Nathanya Dias

Technical Editor: Arjun Varma

Copy Editor: Safis Editing

Project Coordinator: Aparna Ravikumar Nair

Proofreader: Safis Editing

Indexer: Manju Arasan

Production Designer: Nilesh Mohite

First published: June 2021

Production reference: 1210521

Published by Packt Publishing Ltd.

Livery Place

35 Livery Street

Birmingham

B3 2PB, UK.

ISBN 978-1-80020-565-9

www.packt.com

Foreword

I would like to start by saying that data is the new currency for all enterprises across all industries as well as in the government sector. Digital transformations are rampant across every customer segment and data-first modernization is critical, whether for business transformation or legacy modernization. Microsoft's data products and the Azure platform are being widely used for true digital transformation as they provide a single pane of glass to store, analyze, and get better insights into data. For Azure Synapse Analytics, the emphasis on it being a platform rather than a product is key to underscore, as Azure Synapse is an amalgamation of big data analytics with an enterprise data warehouse that enables you to perform limitless analytics on your data at scale without worrying about any infrastructure management overhead.

In this book, Prashant Kumar Mishra, an engineering architect and my colleague at Azure Data Product Engineering, leads you on a journey to learn Azure Synapse from scratch. He explains dedicated SQL pools, serverless SQL pools, and Spark pools in detail. He has also covered data integration, visualization, and machine learning operations with Azure Synapse in this book.

This book is a step-by-step guide for beginners. You will find easy-to-understand guidance on the features available in Azure Synapse. You will also learn how to secure the data stored in Azure Synapse and how to perform backup and restore operations for high availability as well as disaster recovery solutions.

I have been in the industry for more than 20 years now and I have never seen people be as keen on digital modernization as they are now. In this era, Microsoft has done a great job of introducing Azure Synapse to the world as the best analytics solution. I moved to Microsoft approximately 7 years ago, but I have always been an avid admirer of Microsoft's data services, and I take immense pride in saying that Microsoft provides you with all the solutions you need for your data-related problems.

On this note, I would like to thank Prashant for writing this book. This book will definitely give you the full picture of how all of Microsoft's data services are stitched together by Azure Synapse.

Mukesh Kumar
Principal Group Engineering Architect Manager, Microsoft

Contributors

About the author

Prashant Kumar Mishra is an engineering architect at Microsoft. He has more than 10 years of professional expertise in the Microsoft data and AI segment as a developer, consultant, and architect. He has been focused on Microsoft Azure Cloud technologies for several years now and has helped various customers in their data journey. He prefers to share his knowledge with others to make the data community stronger day by day through his blogs and meetup groups.

I wish to thank those people who have been close to me and supported me, especially my wife, Saranya, who inspired me to write this book, my parents (Mr. Mohan Mishra and Mrs. Uma Devi), my in-laws (Mr. Ravichander T and Mrs. Kalai Ravi), and my sisters (Supriya and Diya), who have always stood by me in all my decisions and endeavors.

I can't end this note without mentioning my small, cute Maltese, Toffee, who brings joy to our lives every day.

About the reviewer

Amit Navgire is a computer science postgraduate, a Microsoft Certified Trainer, and a Microsoft Certified Azure Data Engineer. He currently works as a data architect and brings with him 13+ years of extensive experience in designing, architecting, and implementing enterprise-scale data warehouse solutions using Azure, SQL Server, MSBI, and so on. He is quite popular in the world of Azure training, with more than 25,000 students enrolled in his courses, which are published on various online platforms, including Udemy and Coursera, as well as on his website.

About the contributor

Saranya Ravichander is a senior cloud solution architect at Microsoft and also a Microsoft Certified Trainer. She has been working on the Microsoft technology stack for more than 10 years, with a large part of this time devoted to Microsoft Azure, focusing on designing, architecting, and implementing enterprise-scale application development and DevOps workloads.

Table of Contents

Section 2: Data Ingestion and Orchestration

3

Bringing Your Data to Azure Synapse

4

Using Synapse Pipelines to Orchestrate Your Data

5

Using Synapse Link with Azure Cosmos DB

Section 3: Azure Synapse for Data Scientists and Business Analysts

6
Working with T-SQL in Azure Synapse

7
Working with R, Python, Scala, .NET, and Spark SQL in Azure Synapse

8
Integrating a Power BI Workspace with Azure Synapse

9

Perform Real-Time Analytics on Streaming Data

10

Generate Powerful Insights on Azure Synapse Using Azure ML

Section 4: Best Practices

11

Performing Backup and Restore in Azure Synapse Analytics

12

Securing Data on Azure Synapse

13

Managing and Monitoring Synapse Workloads

14
Coding Best Practices

Other Books You May Enjoy

Index

Preface

Azure Synapse Analytics is an analytics platform offered by the Microsoft Azure cloud platform. This book will help you understand the basic concepts of Azure Synapse and get you familiar with how it works in practice, step by step. This book has been written in simple language and with plenty of diagrams to make it easier for you to understand the concepts.

Each main topic has a whole chapter dedicated to it, such that even the minor concepts are explained in detail. You just need to have a basic knowledge of SQL Data Warehouse and Azure generally to follow the topics in this book.

To fully understand Azure Synapse, you need to understand a few other technologies as well, such as Power BI, Azure Data Factory, and Azure Machine Learning. I have tried to cover these services and how they are integrated together with Azure Synapse. Overall, this book should leave anyone well equipped to start working on Azure's analytics platform within a week.

Who this book is for

This book is a must-buy for anyone who works with Azure's data services. However, anyone working with or studying big data will also find it helpful. AWS or Google data architects will also find this book very helpful in terms of comparing Synapse with their own big data analytics platforms. You need to have a basic knowledge of dedicated SQL pool and be familiar with Azure to understand all the concepts in this book. Some of the chapters are specific to data orchestration, Azure Machine Learning, and Power BI, so if you have prior knowledge of these topics, it will be easier for you to learn all the concepts covered in this book.

What this book covers

Chapter 1, Introduction to Azure Synapse, provides an overview of all the components that make up the Synapse workspace: dedicated SQL pool, Spark pools, Synapse pipelines, Azure Machine Learning, and Power BI. In this chapter, you will learn the basics of Synapse and how to create your first Synapse workspace.

Chapter 2, *Considerations for Your Compute Environment*, focuses on the compute environments of Synapse. This chapter will focus mainly on dedicated SQL pool, serverless SQL pools, and Spark pools. It will help you choose the correct environment for your business problem.

Chapter 3, *Bringing Your Data to Azure Synapse*, covers multiple options to bring your data from various sources to Azure Synapse. You will learn how to use different services to set up a connection with Azure Synapse.

Chapter 4, *Using Synapse Pipelines to Orchestrate Your Data*, focuses on Synapse pipelines, which are very similar to Azure Data Factory pipelines; however, you don't need to create a separate Data Factory pipeline for orchestration. Instead, you can perform all the operations you need to do directly within Synapse Studio.

Chapter 5, *Using Synapse Link with Azure Cosmos DB*, is where you will learn how you can perform analytics operations directly on Cosmos DB data without moving data. This chapter will help you understand how Synapse Link has reduced the total time required for running an analytics operation on Cosmos DB data by removing the need for data movement from Cosmos DB to Azure Synapse.

Chapter 6, *Working with T-SQL in Azure Synapse*, teaches you how to query data using T-SQL on Azure Synapse. This chapter will cover the pre-requisites and provide the details for sample data that can be used to perform some simple operations on Azure Synapse using T-SQL.

Chapter 7, *Working with R, Python, Scala, .NET, and Spark SQL in Azure Synapse*, covers how to query data using various coding languages on Azure Synapse. This chapter will cover the pre-requisites and provide details on sample data that can be used to perform simple operations on Azure Synapse using R, Python, Scala, .NET, and Spark SQL.

Chapter 8, *Integrating a Power BI Workspace with Azure Synapse*, explores how to integrate a Power BI workspace with Azure Synapse and how you can connect Azure Synapse data to Power BI Desktop.

Chapter 9, *Perform Real-Time Analytics on Streaming Data*, looks at how to perform real-time analytics on streaming data. This chapter focuses on bringing streaming data to Synapse and performing operations on this data using various languages.

Chapter 10, *Generate Powerful Insights on Azure Synapse Using Azure Machine Learning*, shows you how to integrate Azure Machine Learning with Azure Synapse. You will also learn how to use different languages to pair Azure Machine Learning with Azure Synapse.

Chapter 11, Performing Backup and Restore in Azure Synapse Analytics, is where you will learn how to use backup and restore in Azure Synapse SQL pools. You will learn about automatic and user-defined restore points. This chapter covers how a user can perform cross-subscription restores and geo-redundant restores as well.

Chapter 12, Securing Data on Azure Synapse, talks about how to secure customer data on Azure Synapse. It is very important to understand how you can keep your data safe. This chapter guides you on how you can enable all the best security measures in your Synapse workspace.

Chapter 13, Managing and Monitoring Synapse Workloads, focuses on manageability and monitoring resource utilization and query activity in Azure Synapse Analytics.

Chapter 14, Coding Best Practices, helps you to understand the best practices for performance and management. In this chapter, you will also learn about the best practices for dedicated SQL pools, serverless SQL pools, and Spark pools.

To get the most out of this book

Now let's look at the technical requirements for this book:

Software/hardware covered in the book	OS requirements
SQL Server Management Studio	Windows
Azure Data Studio	Windows
Power BI Desktop	Windows
SQL Server on-premises	Windows
Self-Hosted Integration Runtime	Windows
Visual Studio	Windows

If you are using the digital version of this book, we advise you to type the code yourself or access the code via the GitHub repository (link available in the next section). Doing so will help you avoid any potential errors related to the copying and pasting of code.

Having the following pre-requisites will mean you can follow the book and understand the concepts covered:

- You must have a basic knowledge of the Azure portal.

- It would be helpful if you had prior knowledge of SQL Data Warehouse, Azure Data Factory, Power BI, and Azure Machine Learning.

- You should have an Azure subscription or access to any other subscription with contributor-level access.

Download the example code files

You can download the example code files for this book from GitHub at
`https://github.com/packtPublishing/Limitless-Analytics-with-Azure-Synapse/`. In case there's an update to the code, it will be updated on the existing GitHub repository.

We also have other code bundles from our rich catalog of books and videos available at `https://github.com/PacktPublishing/`. Check them out!

Download the color images

We also provide a PDF file that has color images of the screenshots/diagrams used in this book. You can download it here:

`https://static.packt-cdn.com/downloads/9781800205659_ColorImages.pdf`.

Conventions used

There are a number of text conventions used throughout this book.

`Code in text`: Indicates code words in text, database table names, folder names, filenames, file extensions, pathnames, dummy URLs, user input, and Twitter handles. Here is an example: "We will use the following T-SQL code to create a `UserData` table in Synapse SQL."

A block of code is set as follows:

```
CREATE TABLE UserData (
  UserID INT,
  Name     VARCHAR(200),
  EmailID  VARCHAR(200),
  State   VARCHAR(50),
  City VARCHAR(50)
)
```

When we wish to draw your attention to a particular part of a code block, the relevant lines or items are set in bold:

```
[default]
exten => s,1,Dial(Zap/1|30)
exten => s,2,Voicemail(u100)
exten => s,102,Voicemail(b100)
exten => i,1,Voicemail(s0)
```

Any command-line input or output is written as follows:

```
$ SubscriptionName="<YourSubscriptionName>"
$ ResourceGroupName="<YourResourceGroupName>"
```

Bold: Indicates a new term, an important word, or words that you see onscreen. For example, words in menus or dialog boxes appear in the text like this. Here is an example: "For the **Use existing data** property under **Data source**, select **Backup**."

> **Tips or important notes**
> Appear like this.

Get in touch

Feedback from our readers is always welcome.

General feedback: If you have questions about any aspect of this book, mention the book title in the subject of your message and email us at customercare@packtpub.com.

Errata: Although we have taken every care to ensure the accuracy of our content, mistakes do happen. If you have found a mistake in this book, we would be grateful if you would report this to us. Please visit www.packtpub.com/support/errata, selecting your book, clicking on the Errata Submission Form link, and entering the details.

Piracy: If you come across any illegal copies of our works in any form on the Internet, we would be grateful if you would provide us with the location address or website name. Please contact us at copyright@packt.com with a link to the material.

If you are interested in becoming an author: If there is a topic that you have expertise in and you are interested in either writing or contributing to a book, please visit authors.packtpub.com.

Reviews

Please leave a review. Once you have read and used this book, why not leave a review on the site that you purchased it from? Potential readers can then see and use your unbiased opinion to make purchase decisions, we at Packt can understand what you think about our products, and our authors can see your feedback on their book. Thank you!

For more information about Packt, please visit packt.com.

Section 1:
The Basics and
Key Concepts

The objective of this section is to introduce you to the key concepts, download supporting data, and introduce you to example scenarios.

This section comprises the following chapters:

- *Chapter 1, Introduction to Azure Synapse*
- *Chapter 2, Considerations for Your Compute Environment*

1

Introduction to Azure Synapse

Azure Synapse Analytics, formerly known as Azure SQL Data Warehouse, is not a mere data warehouse anymore. Azure Synapse is an amalgamation of big data analytics with an enterprise data warehouse. It provides two different types of compute environments for different workloads: one is the SQL compute environment, which is called a SQL pool, and the other one is the Spark compute environment, which is called a Spark pool. Now developers can choose their compute environment as per their business needs. Azure Synapse also provides a unified portal called Synapse Studio for developers that creates a workspace for data prep, data management, data exploration, data warehousing, big data, and AI tasks.

This chapter covers an introduction to **Azure Synapse** and guides you on starting to use Synapse Studio. You will learn how to create an Azure Synapse workspaces and get acquainted with the components of Azure Synapse. You can start using Synapse with the sample data and queries provided in the Azure portal itself.

In this chapter, our topics will include the following:

- Introducing the components of Azure Synapse
- Creating a Synapse workspace
- Understanding Azure Data Lake
- Exploring Synapse Studio

Technical requirements

In this chapter, you are going to learn how to create your first Synapse workspace in the Azure portal. In order to do this, there are certain prerequisites before you start working on Azure Synapse.

It would be beneficial to have basic knowledge of the Azure portal, as well as an understanding of SQL and Spark. Knowledge of Azure Data Factory and Power BI would be helpful but not essential.

You must have your own Azure subscription or access to an Azure subscription with appropriate permissions. If you are new to Azure, you can go through the following link to create a free Azure account: `https://azure.microsoft.com/en-us/free/`.

Once you have your Azure subscription created, you can proceed further with the main topics of this chapter.

Introducing the components of Azure Synapse

Azure Synapse is a **limitless analytics service** on the Azure platform. It bundles together data warehousing and big data analytics with deep integration of **Azure Machine Learning** and **Power BI**. Azure Synapse brings together relational and non-relational data and helps in querying files in the data lake without looking for any other service.

One of the best features that has been introduced with Azure Synapse is code-free data orchestration where you can build ETL/ELT processes to bring data to Synapse from various sources.

> **Important note**
> Synapse provides various layers of security for the data stored; however, you need to follow the security guidelines to keep your data secured. For example, do not expose the username and password in any publicly accessible place – you will invite the biggest threat to your data by doing so. It is important to understand that Azure gives you the power to secure your data, but it is in your hands to best use that power.

What happens when we embrace a new technology in an organization?

We need to look out for a resource that already has knowledge of it, which brings extra costs on top of the cost of the technical implementation. However, Azure Synapse supports various programming languages, such as T-SQL, Python, Scala, Spark, SQL, and .NET, making it easy for people who are already familiar with those languages to learn. In this chapter, we will show a demo for T-SQL, but we will cover examples for other languages in upcoming chapters.

The following diagram represents all the components of Azure Synapse and how all these components are tied together within Synapse Analytics:

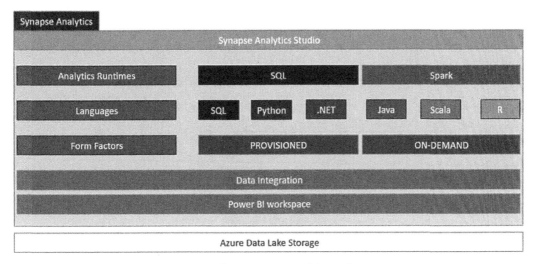

Figure 1.1 – The components of Azure Synapse

The preceding diagram represents all components of Azure Synapse, which includes Analytics runtimes, supported languages, form factors, data integration, and Power BI workspaces. We will cover all these topics in upcoming chapters.

> **Important note**
>
> Although Azure Synapse is deeply integrated with Spark, Azure ML, and Power BI, you do not need to pay for all these services. You will pay only for the features/services that you use. If you are using an Azure Synapse workspace only for enterprise data warehousing, you will be charged only for that. You can find out complete pricing details in Microsoft's documentation: `https://azure.microsoft.com/en-us/pricing/details/synapse-analytics/`.

Creating a Synapse workspace

Synapse workspace provides an integrated console to manage, monitor, and administer all the components and services of Azure Synapse Analytics. In order to get started with Azure Synapse Analytics, we need to create an Azure Synapse workspace, which provides an experience to access different features related to Azure Synapse Analytics.

You can create a Synapse workspace in the Azure portal just by providing some basic details. Follow these steps to create your first Azure Synapse workspace:

1. Go to `https://portal.azure.com` and provide your credentials.

2. Click on **Create a resource**:

Figure 1.2 – A screenshot of the Azure portal

3. Search for `Azure Synapse` using the search bar.

4. Select **Azure Synapse Analytics (Workspaces preview)** from the search drop-down and click on **Create**:

Figure 1.3 – A screenshot of the Azure Synapse Analytics page in Azure Marketplace

5. You need to provide basic details to create your Synapse Analytics workspace:

• **Subscription**: You need to select your subscription. If you have many subscriptions in your Azure account, you need to select a specific one that you are going to use to create a Synapse workspace.

> **Important note**
> All resources in a subscription are billed together.

• **Resource group**: A **Resource group** is a container that holds all the resources for the solution, or only those resources that you want to manage under one group. Select a Resource group for the Synapse workspace. If you do not already have a Resource group created, click on **Create new** right below the text field for **Resource group**:

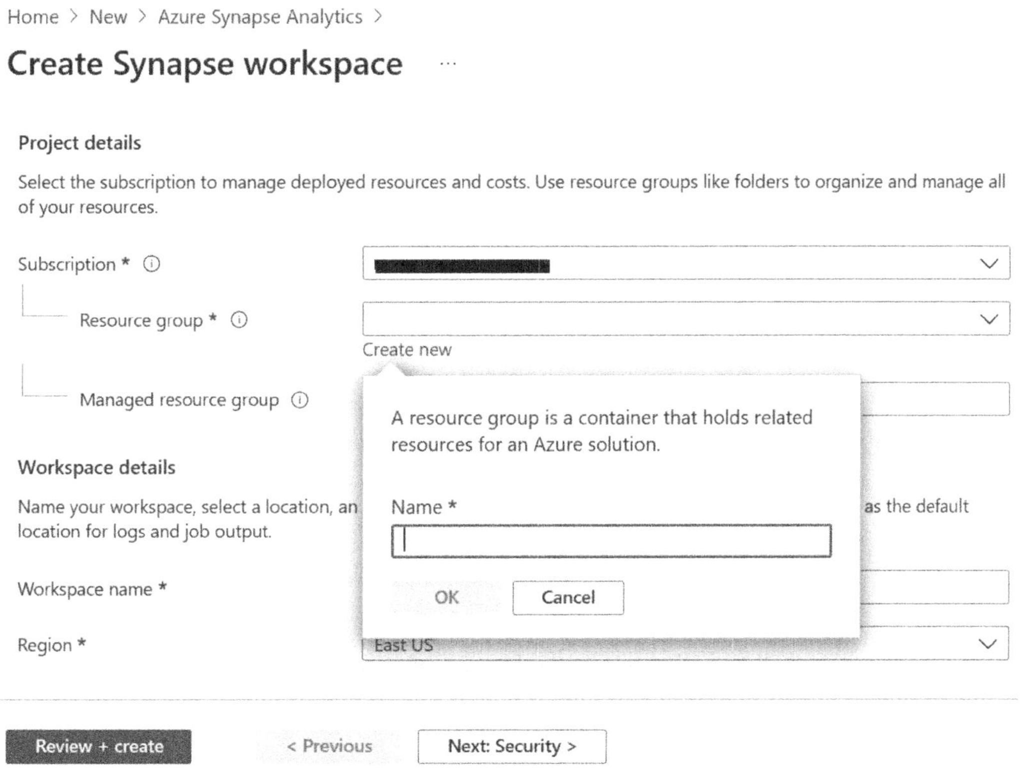

Home > New > Azure Synapse Analytics >

Create Synapse workspace   ...

Project details

Select the subscription to manage deployed resources and costs. Use resource groups like folders to organize and manage all of your resources.

Subscription * ⓘ	▆▆▆▆▆▆▆▆▆▆▆▆▆▆ ⌄
Resource group * ⓘ	⌄
	Create new

Managed resource group ⓘ

A resource group is a container that holds related resources for an Azure solution.

Workspace details

Name your workspace, select a location, an   as the default
location for logs and job output.

Name *

[   ]

Workspace name *

OK   Cancel

Region *   East US   ⌄

[Review + create]   < Previous   [Next: Security >]

Figure 1.4 – A screenshot highlighting the field to provide a Resource group name

- **Workspace name**: Provide an appropriate name for the workspace that you are going to create.

> **Important note**
> This name must be unique, so it is better to keep it specific to your team/ project.

- **Region**: You can see many options in the dropdown. Select the most appropriate region for your Synapse Analytics workspace:

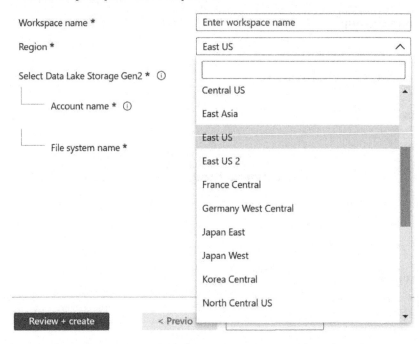

Figure 1.5 – A screenshot of regions appearing in a drop-down list

- **Select Data Lake Storage Gen2**: This will be the primary storage account for the workspace, holding catalog data and metadata associated with the workspace:

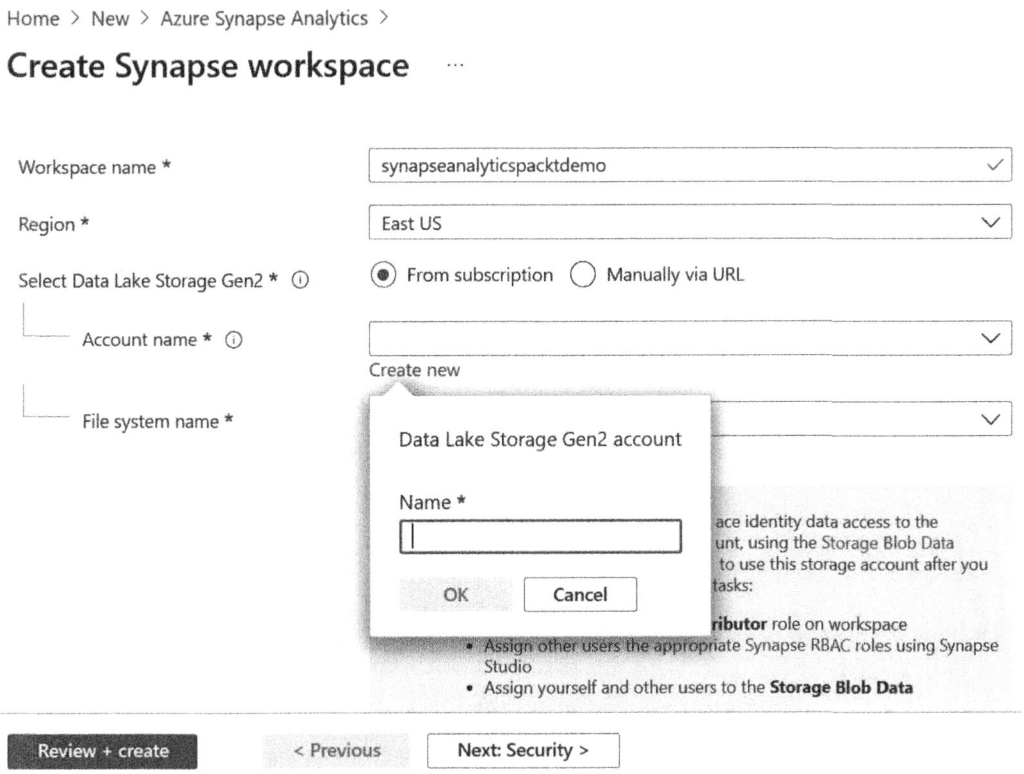

Home > New > Azure Synapse Analytics >

Create Synapse workspace   ⋯

Workspace name *	synapseanalyticspacktdemo ✓
Region *	East US ⌄

Select Data Lake Storage Gen2 * ⓘ   ● From subscription   ○ Manually via URL

Account name * ⓘ

[dropdown ⌄]

Create new

File system name *

[dropdown ⌄]

Data Lake Storage Gen2 account

Name *

[   ]

OK   Cancel

ace identity data access to the
unt, using the Storage Blob Data
to use this storage account after you
tasks:

ributor role on workspace
• Assign other users the appropriate Synapse RBAC roles using Synapse Studio
• Assign yourself and other users to the **Storage Blob Data**

Review + create   < Previous   Next: Security >

Figure 1.6 – A screenshot highlighting fields of Select Data Lake Storage Gen2

- **Account name**: You can select from the dropdown or you can create a new one. Only Data Lake Gen2 accounts with a hierarchical namespace enabled will appear in the dropdown. However, if you click on **Create new**, then it will create a Data Lake Gen2 account with hierarchical namespace enabled.

Important note

A storage account name must be between 3 and 24 characters in length and use numbers and lowercase letters only.

- **File system name**: Again, you can select from the dropdown or you can create a new one. To create a new file system name, click on **Create new** and provide an appropriate name for it. A file system name must contain only lowercase letters, numbers, or hyphens:

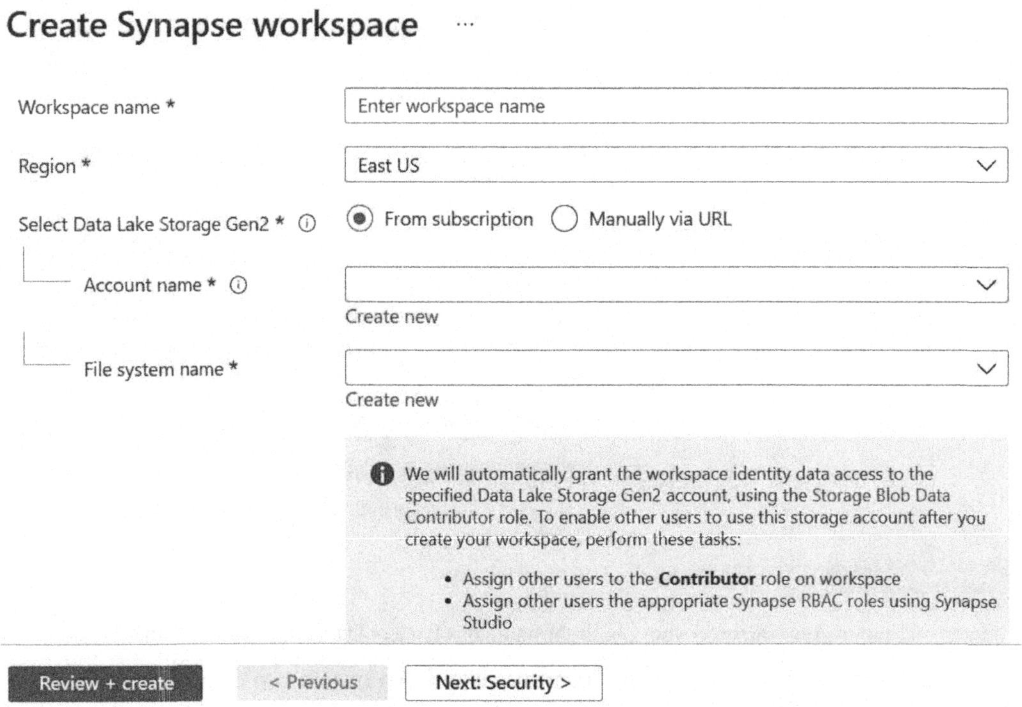

Create Synapse workspace   ...

Workspace name *	Enter workspace name
Region *	East US ∨
Select Data Lake Storage Gen2 * ⓘ	⦿ From subscription ◯ Manually via URL
└── Account name * ⓘ	∨
	Create new
└── File system name *	∨
	Create new

ⓘ We will automatically grant the workspace identity data access to the specified Data Lake Storage Gen2 account, using the Storage Blob Data Contributor role. To enable other users to use this storage account after you create your workspace, perform these tasks:

- Assign other users to the **Contributor** role on workspace
- Assign other users the appropriate Synapse RBAC roles using Synapse Studio

Review + create   < Previous   Next: Security >

Figure 1.7 – A screenshot highlighting assignment of the Storage Blob Data Contributor role

6. Click on **Security + networking** to configure security options and networking settings for your workspace, as seen in *Figure 1.8*.

    Provide SQL administrator credentials that can be used for administrator access to the workspace's SQL pools. We will talk about SQL pools in future chapters:

Home > Create a resource > Azure Synapse Analytics >

Create Synapse workspace   ...

* Basics   * Security   Networking   Tags   Review + create

Configure security options for your workspace.

SQL administrator credentials

Provide credentials that can be used for administrator access to the workspace's SQL pools. If you don't provide a password, one will be automatically generated. You can change the password later.

Admin username *	sqladminuser
Password	Enter server password ✓
Confirm password	Confirm the above password ✓

Workspace encryption

⚠ Double encryption configuration cannot be changed after opting into using a customer-managed key at the time of

[Review + create]   [< Previous]   [Next: Networking >]

Figure 1.8 – A screenshot of the Security + networking form for Azure Synapse

7. Click on **Tags** to provide a name-value pair to this resource.

8. Go to the next page to review the summary and click on **Create** after verifying all the details on the summary page.

9. In your Azure Synapse workspace in the Azure portal, click **Open Synapse Studio**:

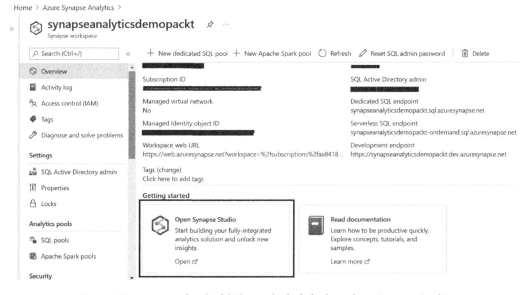

Figure 1.9 – A screenshot highlighting the link for launching Synapse Studio

This deployment takes just a couple of minutes and creates a workspace that bundles Synapse analytics, ETL, reporting, modeling, and analysis together under one umbrella. Now you are ready to build your enterprise-level solution!

Understanding Azure Data Lake

A data lake is a storage repository that allows you to store your data in native format without having to first structure the data at any scale.

Azure Data Lake Storage provides secure, scalable, cost-effective storage for big data analytics. There are two generations of Azure Data Lake, Gen1 and Gen2; however, we will focus on Gen2 only throughout this chapter. Azure Data Lake Gen2 converges the capabilities of **Azure Data Lake Gen1** with the capabilities of **Azure Blob Storage** with the addition of a **Hierarchical Namespace** to Blob Storage. Because of Azure Blob Storage's capabilities, you get a high availability/disaster recovery solutions for your data lake at a low cost.

The new **Azure Blob File System** (**ABFS**) driver is available within **Azure HDInsight**, **Azure Databricks**, and **Azure Synapse Analytics**, which can be used to access the data in a similar way to **Hadoop Distributed File System** (**HDFS**).

To use Data Lake Storage Gen2's capabilities, you need to create a storage account that has a hierarchical namespace. You can go through the following steps to create your Azure Data Lake Storage Gen2 account:

1. Log in to the Azure portal: `https://portal.azure.com`.

2. Click on the + **Create a Resource** link and select **Storage account** from the list of all available resources.

3. Select the **Resource group** where you want to create your storage account. If you don't have a **Resource group** created, click on the **Create new** link below the drop-down list.

4. Fill in the fields for **Storage account name** and **Location**.

5. Select **Standard** or **Premium Performance** as per your business need. If you are new to Data Lake, then it would be better to begin with **Standard**.

6. Select an appropriate value for **Account kind** and **Replication** as per the business need. Again, the recommendation would be to leave the default selected values in these fields if you are performing this operation just for your learning purposes:

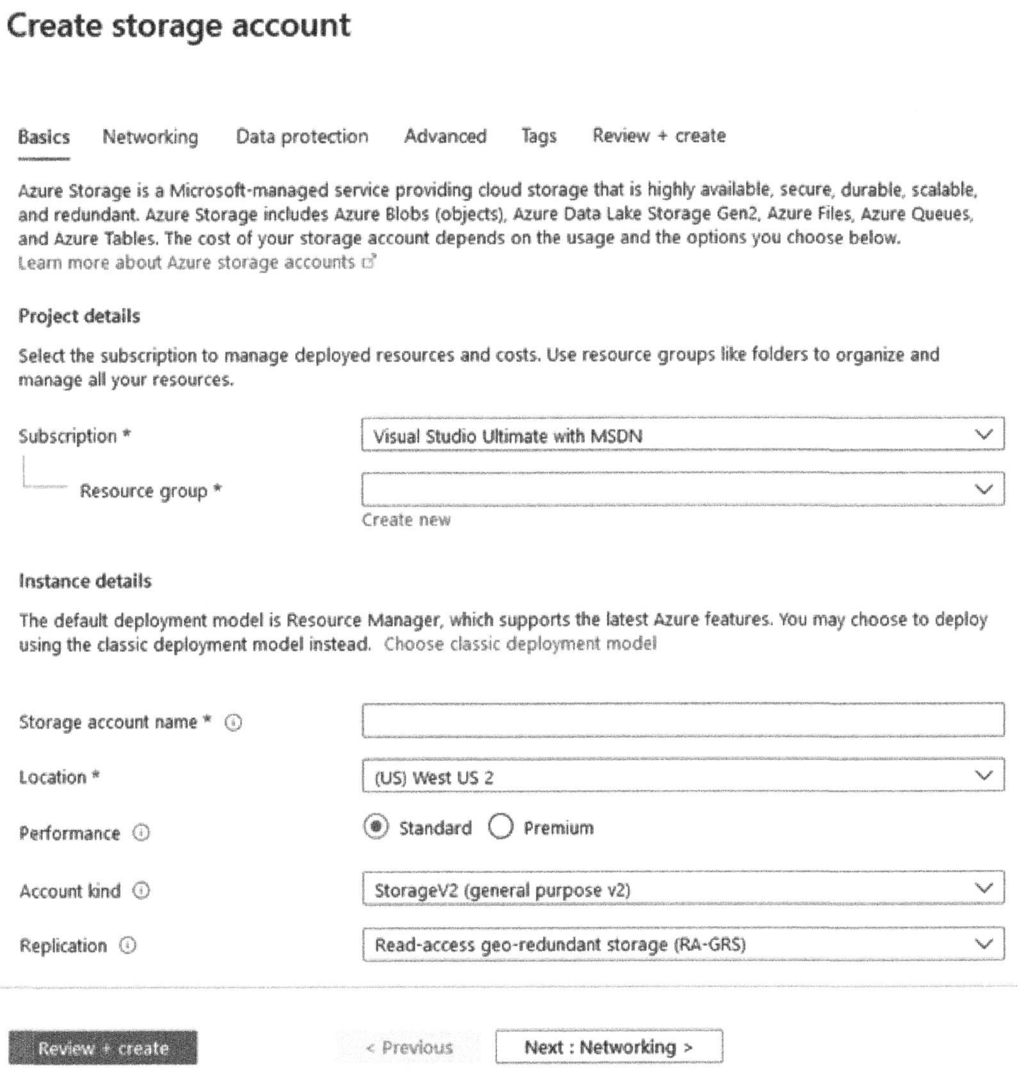

Create storage account

Basics   Networking   Data protection   Advanced   Tags   Review + create

Azure Storage is a Microsoft-managed service providing cloud storage that is highly available, secure, durable, scalable, and redundant. Azure Storage includes Azure Blobs (objects), Azure Data Lake Storage Gen2, Azure Files, Azure Queues, and Azure Tables. The cost of your storage account depends on the usage and the options you choose below. Learn more about Azure storage accounts ◻

Project details

Select the subscription to manage deployed resources and costs. Use resource groups like folders to organize and manage all your resources.

Subscription * | Visual Studio Ultimate with MSDN   ⌄ |

     └──── Resource group * | ⌄ |
                                 Create new

Instance details

The default deployment model is Resource Manager, which supports the latest Azure features. You may choose to deploy using the classic deployment model instead. Choose classic deployment model

Storage account name * ⓘ | |

Location * | (US) West US 2   ⌄ |

Performance ⓘ   ⦿ Standard ◯ Premium

Account kind ⓘ | StorageV2 (general purpose v2)   ⌄ |

Replication ⓘ | Read-access geo-redundant storage (RA-GRS) ⌄ |

[Review + create]   < Previous   [Next : Networking >]

Figure 1.10 – Creating Azure Data Lake Gen2 in Azure

7. For now, we can skip the **Networking** and **Data protection** tabs and move directly to the **Advanced** tab.

8. Click on the **Enabled** radio button for the **Hierarchical namespace** property under the **Advanced** tab:

Create storage account

| Basics | Networking | Data protection | Advanced | Tags | Review + create |

Security

Secure transfer required ⓘ   ◯ Disabled ⦿ Enabled

Allow shared key access ⓘ   ◯ Disabled ⦿ Enabled

Minimum TLS version ⓘ   [Version 1.2   ⌄]

Infrastructure encryption ⓘ   ⦿ Disabled ◯ Enabled

ⓘ Sign up is currently required to enable infrastructure encryption on a per-subscription basis. **Sign up for infrastructure encryption** ☐

Blob storage

Allow Blob public access ⓘ   ◯ Disabled ⦿ Enabled

Blob access tier (default) ⓘ   ◯ Cool ⦿ Hot

NFS v3 ⓘ   ⦿ Disabled ◯ Enabled

ⓘ Sign up is currently required to utilize the NFS v3 feature on a per-subscription basis. **Sign up for NFS v3** ☐

Data Lake Storage Gen2

Hierarchical namespace ⓘ   ◯ Disabled ⦿ Enabled

Azure Files

Large file shares ⓘ   ⦿ Disabled ◯ Enabled

ⓘ The current combination of storage account kind, performance, replication and location does not support large file shares.

Tables and Queues

| Review + create | | < Previous | | Next : Tags > |

Figure 1.11 – Enabling Hierarchical namespace for Data Lake Storage Gen2 on the Advanced tab

9. Leave the default values for all other fields and click on **Review + create**.

10. After reviewing all the details, click on **Create** and your Azure Data Lake Gen2 account will be created in a couple of minutes.

Now that you have already created your Azure Data Lake Gen2 account, you can use this account with Azure Synapse Analytics. We will learn how to read data from Data Lake in later chapters, but for now, we will learn about Azure Synapse Studio, and how it provides a unified experience when working with various resources under one roof.

Exploring Synapse Studio

Synapse Studio is a unified experience for data preparation, data management, data warehousing, and big data analytics. Synapse Studio is a one-stop-shop for developers, data engineers, data scientists, and report analysts.

Before we start exploring more about Synapse Studio, we should know how we can get to Synapse Studio from the Azure portal. There are a couple of ways to navigate to Synapse Studio, but for that, first we need to navigate to our **Synapse workspace** on the Azure portal. In *Figure 1.12*, you can see **Workspace web URL**, which is highlighted. You can either click on that URL or copy that URL and paste it in your browser to access Synapse Studio:

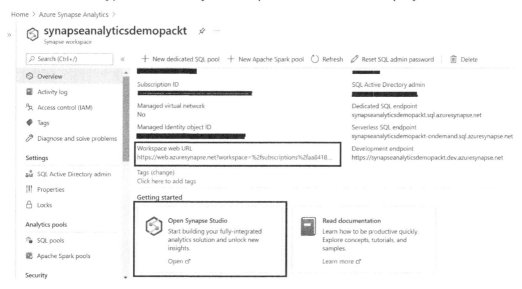

Figure 1.12 – A screenshot of a Synapse workspace in the Azure portal highlighting the links to access Synapse Studio

Another simple approach is to just click on the **Open Synapse Studio** link under the **Getting started** section of the Synapse workspace.

You will need to provide credentials to access Synapse Studio. After successful authentication, you will see Synapse Studio opened in a new tab. You will find a direct link to various hubs integrated in Synapse Studio:

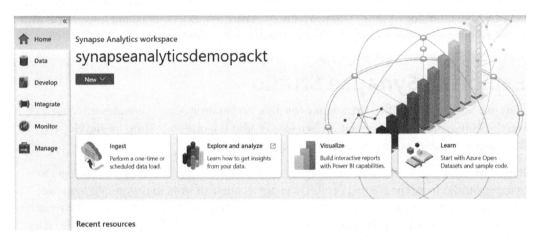

Figure 1.13 – A screenshot of the Synapse Studio Home page

As you can see in *Figure 1.13*, Synapse Studio has six different hubs. We will learn about all these hubs in brief here:

- **Home**: The **Home** hub provides you with a direct link to ingest, explore, or visualize your data. You can also access your recent resources without wasting your time searching across all the resources available on your Synapse Studio. In fact, you can click on the **New** button at the top of the Synapse Studio screen to create a new SQL script, notebook, data flow, Apache Spark job definition, or pipeline. You do not need to be worried about any of these if you are new to Azure Synapse; we are going to cover all these topics in detail in other chapters:

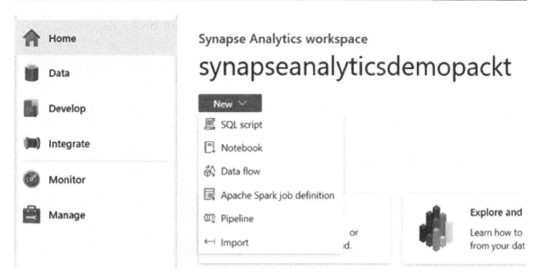

Figure 1.14 – Synapse Studio highlighting the New button at the top of the screen

- **Data**: The **Data** hub provides a simple way to organize your workspace databases and analytical stores for SQL as well as Spark. You can see two tabs in the **Data** hub: one is **Workspace**, which shows your SQL and Spark databases created and managed with your Azure Synapse workspace. The other tab is **Linked**, which shows connected services such as Data Lake Gen2, operational stores in Azure Cosmos DB, and so on:

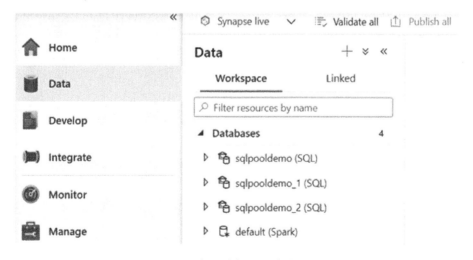

Figure 1.15 – A screenshot of the Data hub on Synapse Studio

- **Develop**: The **Develop** hub contains your SQL scripts, notebooks, data flows, and Spark job definitions. You can also find all your Power BI reports created in your Power BI workspace if you have already connected your Power BI workspace with the Synapse workspace. We will learn more about this in *Chapter 8, Integrating a Power BI Workspace with Azure Synapse*:

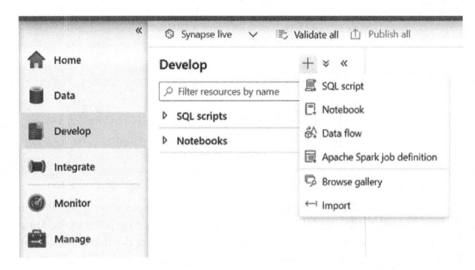

Figure 1.16 – A screenshot of the Develop hub on Synapse Studio

- **Integrate**: You will find a lot of similarities between the **Integrate** hub of Synapse Studio and Azure Data Factory if you are familiar with Azure Data Factory already. You can create new data pipelines to perform one-time or scheduled data ingestion from 90+ data sources. We will learn more about this in *Chapter 4, Using Synapse Pipelines to Orchestrate Your Data*:

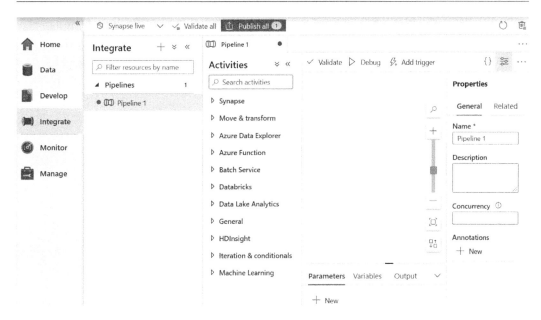

Figure 1.17 – Creating a pipeline in the Integrate hub of Synapse Studio

- **Monitor**: The **Monitor** hub enables you to see the statuses of all your **Integration** resources, activities, and pools in one place:

Figure 1.18 – A screenshot of the Monitor hub in Synapse Studio

- **Manage**: From the **Manage** hub, you can manage your SQL pools, Spark pools, linked services, triggers, and integration runtimes. The **Manage** hub also provides you with the ability to manage access control and credentials for your Synapse workspace. Recently, they added Git configuration to the **Manage** hub as well:

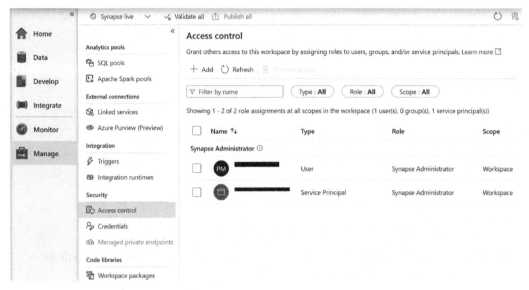

Figure 1.19 – A screenshot of the Manage hub on Synapse Studio

In this section, we got an introduction to Synapse Studio, however, in the following chapters, we are going to explore more about Synapse Studio.

Summary

In this chapter, we covered an introduction to Azure Synapse and how can you create your first Azure Synapse workspace. After going through the sample scripts, you should have a fairly good idea about how Azure Synapse Studio works, and some of the different languages supported by Azure Synapse. We also discussed the differences between Azure SQL Data Warehouse and Azure Synapse. You learned about pausing and resuming a SQL pool, as well as automatic pausing of a Spark pool, which will save you some money if implemented.

In the next chapter, we will begin to look at specific analytics runtimes you need to understand and create your first Spark and SQL pool.

2
Considerations for Your Compute Environment

This chapter covers the analytics runtimes available with Azure Synapse. You will learn about the concepts of **SQL Pool**, **SQL on-demand**, and **Spark pool**. After completing this chapter, you will be able to decide which analytics runtime will be suitable for solving your business problem.

SQL Pool and SQL on-demand are both part of the **Structured Query Language** (SQL) engine, but they differ in terms of provisioning. When you create a SQL pool, you will provision databases under a logical server in your subscription; this means you will be paying for running the SQL engine all the time until SQL pool is paused. However, SQL on-demand is created when you want to leverage the SQL engine for running your workloads only for a short duration.

On the other hand, Spark pool works with the Apache Spark engine, deeply integrated with Azure Synapse. This gives you the option to configure your Spark pool with just a few clicks, along with an option to auto-pause after a certain time of being idle. We have covered this information in detail in this chapter.

In this chapter, our topics will include the following:

- Introducing SQL Pool
- Understanding Synapse SQL on-demand
- Understanding Spark pool

Technical requirements

In order to follow the instructions in the following sections, you need to have met certain prerequisites before we proceed, outlined here:

- You need to have your Azure subscription, or access to any other subscription with contributor-level access.
- You need to have your Synapse workspace on this subscription. You can follow the instructions from *Chapter 1, Introduction to Azure Synapse*, to create your Synapse workspace.

Introducing SQL Pool

SQL Pool uses a scale-out, node-based architecture with one **control node** and multiple **compute nodes** for distributed computational processing. Control nodes are a single point of contact for end users to interact with all compute nodes. The control node runs the **Massively Parallel Processing** (**MPP**) engine, which passes an operation to multiple compute nodes to do their work in parallel. MPP databases are optimized for analytical workloads, such as aggregating and processing large datasets. In this type of architecture, each compute node (which are also called processing units) works independently, with its own operating system and dedicated memory.

In this section, you will learn about the architecture of SQL Pool, which will help you in understanding data distribution across various nodes in SQL Pool. We will cover how to create a SQL pool using both the Azure portal and Synapse Studio in the following section.

Creating a SQL pool

In this section, you will learn how to create a SQL pool in a Synapse workspace using the Azure portal and Synapse Studio. You need to make sure that you have already created an **Azure Synapse workspace** in your subscription.

Using the Azure portal

First, let's look at how to set up the Azure portal. Follow these steps:

1. Log in to the Azure portal, at `https://portal.azure.com`.

2. Navigate to the **Synapse workspace** by typing the service name (or resource name) directly into the search bar, as highlighted in the following screenshot:

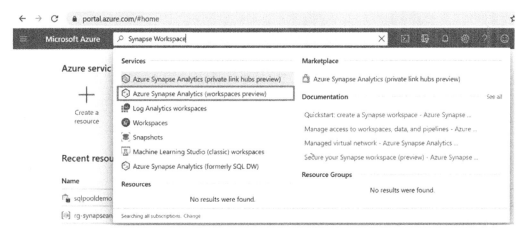

Figure 2.1 – A screenshot of the Azure portal, highlighting Synapse Workspace in the search bar

3. In the Synapse workspace, click on **New SQL pool**, as highlighted in the following screenshot:

Figure 2.2 – A screenshot of the Azure portal, highlighting the link to create a new SQL pool

4. Provide an appropriate name for your SQL pool and select **Data Warehouse Units** (**DWUs**) by sliding the **Performance level** bubble under the **Basics** tab. For the purpose of adding some examples, I am using DW1000c, which will give me one control node and six compute nodes, as highlighted in the following screenshot:

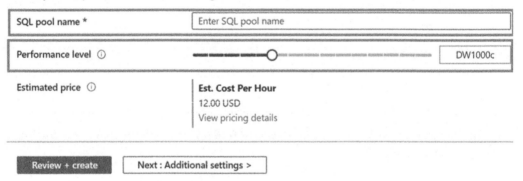

Create SQL pool

Synapse

| * **Basics** | * Additional settings | Tags | Review + create |

Create a SQL pool with your preferred configurations. Complete the Basics tab then go to Review + Create to provision with smart defaults, or visit each tab to customize. Learn more ☐'

SQL pool details

Name your SQL pool and choose its initial settings.

SQL pool name *	Enter SQL pool name
Performance level ⓘ	⸺⸺○⸺⸺ DW1000c

Estimated price ⓘ   **Est. Cost Per Hour**
12.00 USD
View pricing details

[Review + create]   [Next : Additional settings >]

Figure 2.3 – A screenshot of the form to create a SQL pool

5. Next, you can go to **Additional settings**. However, you can leave this tab unchanged and move to the next tab, **Tags**.

> **Important note**
> We will cover backup and restore in *Chapter 11, Performing Backup and Restore in Azure Synapse Analytics*.

6. You can provide an appropriate name-and-value pair if needed; otherwise, you can leave this field empty for now and go to the **Review + create** tab. After reviewing all the details, click on **Create**. You may need to wait a couple of minutes to start using it. The process is illustrated in the following screenshot:

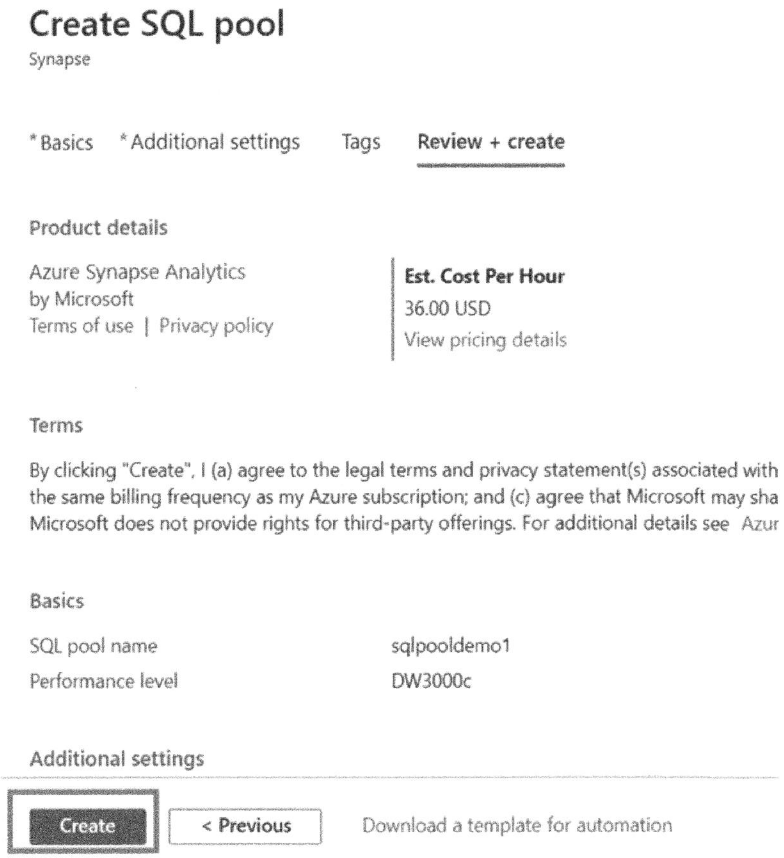

Create SQL pool

Synapse

*Basics   *Additional settings   Tags   **Review + create**

Product details

Azure Synapse Analytics
by Microsoft
Terms of use | Privacy policy

Est. Cost Per Hour
36.00 USD
View pricing details

Terms

By clicking "Create", I (a) agree to the legal terms and privacy statement(s) associated with
the same billing frequency as my Azure subscription; and (c) agree that Microsoft may sha
Microsoft does not provide rights for third-party offerings. For additional details see Azur

Basics

SQL pool name   sqlpooldemo1

Performance level   DW3000c

Additional settings

| Create | | < Previous | Download a template for automation |

Figure 2.4 – A screenshot of the Review + create page to create a SQL pool

---

Important note

You may need to add your client **Internet Protocol (IP)** address in the
Firewalls setting of the Azure Synapse workspace in order to connect to your
Synapse SQL pool using any client tool.

Similarly, we can create a Synapse-dedicated SQL pool using Synapse Studio.

Using Synapse Studio

Now, let's see how to use Synapse Studio. Follow these steps:

1. Log in to the Azure portal at `https://portal.azure.com`.

2. Navigate to the **Synapse workspace** by typing the service name (or resource name)
   directly into the search bar.

3. Click on the workspace where you want to create your SQL pool.

4. Click on **Open Synapse Studio**, as highlighted in the following screenshot:

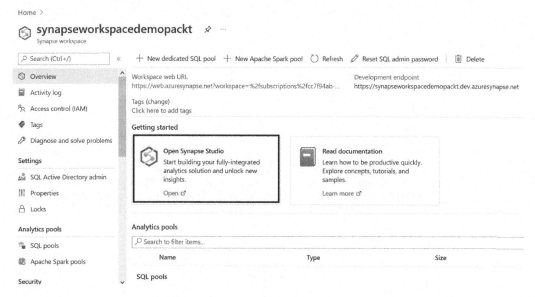

Figure 2.5 – A screenshot of the Azure portal, highlighting the link to launch Synapse Studio

5. Go to the **Manage** tab on the Synapse Studio home page, as highlighted in the following screenshot:

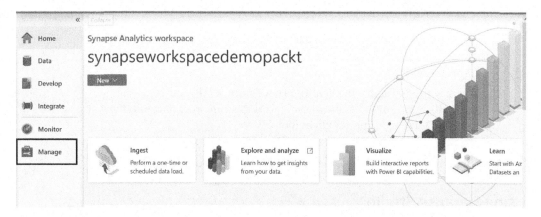

Figure 2.6 – A screenshot of the Synapse Studio home page, highlighting the Manage link

6. Click on the **+ New** link under the **SQL pools** section to create a new SQL pool, as highlighted in the following screenshot:

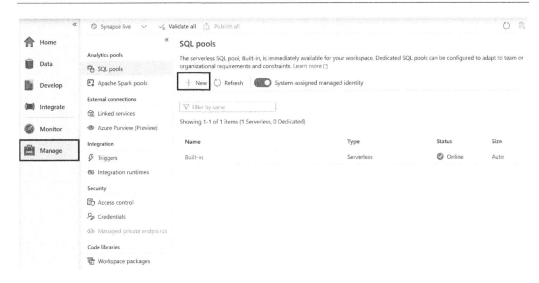

Figure 2.7 – A screenshot of Synapse Studio, highlighting the + New link to create a SQL pool

7. Provide an appropriate name for your SQL pool, and select DWUs by sliding the **Performance level** bubble under the **Basics** tab. As with the previous section, I am using DW1000c, which will give me one control node and six compute nodes, as illustrated in the following screenshot:

Create SQL pool

Synapse

* Basics   * Additional settings   Tags   Review + create

Create a SQL pool with your preferred configurations. Complete the Basics tab then go to Review + Create to provision with smart defaults, or visit each tab to customize. Learn more ☐

SQL pool details

Name your SQL pool and choose its initial settings.

SQL pool name *	Enter SQL pool name
Performance level ⓘ	DW1000c

Estimated price ⓘ   **Est. Cost Per Hour**
12.00 USD
View pricing details

Review + create   Next : Additional settings >

Figure 2.8 – A screenshot of the form to create a SQL pool

8. Next, you can go to **Additional settings**. However, you can leave this tab unchanged and move to the next tab, **Tags**.

9. You can provide the appropriate **Tags** details if needed, and go to the **Review + create** tab.

10. After reviewing all the details, click on **Create**. You may need to wait a couple of minutes to start using it. The process is illustrated in the following screenshot:

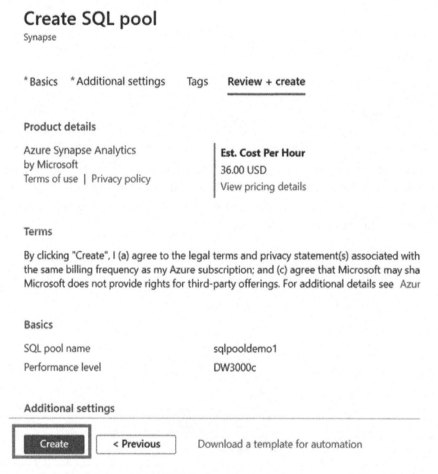

Create SQL pool
Synapse

| *Basics | *Additional settings | Tags | Review + create |

Product details

Azure Synapse Analytics
by Microsoft
Terms of use | Privacy policy

Est. Cost Per Hour
36.00 USD
View pricing details

Terms

By clicking "Create", I (a) agree to the legal terms and privacy statement(s) associated with the same billing frequency as my Azure subscription; and (c) agree that Microsoft may sha Microsoft does not provide rights for third-party offerings. For additional details see Azur

Basics

SQL pool name   sqlpooldemo1
Performance level   DW3000c

Additional settings

Create   < Previous   Download a template for automation

Figure 2.9 – A screenshot of the Review + create page to create a SQL pool

That concludes our initial dive into SQL Pool. Next we will learn about the architecture and components of Synapse SQL Pool.

Understanding Synapse SQL Pool architecture and components

The **Synapse SQL Pool** architecture has many components that work together to make it a unique Azure resource. This architecture is the same as it used to be for **SQL Data Warehouse** (**SQL DW**) and leverages an **MPP engine** to distribute computational processing across multiple compute nodes.

Compute nodes are used for computational work on a cluster to execute any business logic. The capacity of compute nodes is defined by the **performance level** of the SQL pool that you can set while creating the SQL pool, or you can change the value after the pool is created, as per the business demand. However, data is not stored on compute nodes in the case of a SQL pool; instead, there are separate nodes to store data, which are called **storage nodes**.

Compute nodes are separate from storage nodes, so you get the flexibility to scale your compute up or down without impacting the storage of your data warehouse.

The following architecture diagram represents how all the components are tied together in Azure Synapse SQL pool:

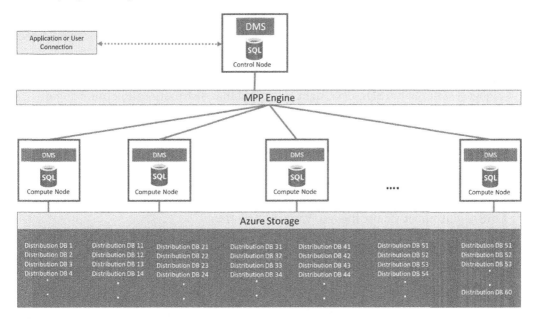

Figure 2.10 – Architecture of Synapse SQL pool

Now that we have learned about the architecture, let's try learning about the following components individually in brief:

- **Control node**: When an end user tries to run a **Transact-SQL (T-SQL)** query, the control node utilizes each distribution to run these queries in parallel. When you submit a query to a SQL pool, the control node leverages an MPP engine to run these queries against each distribution in parallel. We will learn about distributions further on in this chapter. There is only one control node associated with a SQL pool under a logical server. All the applications and connections can only interact with the control node; however, the control node interacts with all the compute nodes via the MPP engine whenever needed.

- **Compute node**: Compute nodes are computers or machines that are used for computational purposes. In an MPP architecture, various compute nodes run in parallel to process a query faster. A SQL pool can have a maximum of 60 compute nodes determined by the service level. Each compute node is identified by a unique node ID that can be seen in the system views.

- When you select DWUs to create a SQL pool or when you decide to change the DWU, distributions are mapped to compute nodes accordingly.

- **Data Movement Service (DMS)**: The DMS is a system-level internal service that shuffles data across various nodes to run queries in parallel and return consolidated results back to the MPP engine.

- **Azure Storage**: Synapse SQL stores your data in Azure Storage. When you ingest your data to SQL Pool, data is sharded into distributions to optimize the performance of the system. The sharding pattern can be defined while creating the table. You can create or choose Azure Storage while creating your Synapse workspace; however, only **Data Lake Storage Gen2** accounts with **Hierarchical Name Space** enabled are listed under the **Storage Account** dropdown. There are various tools available to access Azure Storage; I like using **Azure Storage Explorer**. You can connect to Azure Storage using access keys, a **Shared Access Signature (SAS)** token, or via the login to your subscription.

You can use the following query to get a count of the control and compute nodes available for your Synapse SQL pool:

```
SELECT * FROM sys.dm_pdw_nodes
GO
SELECT type,COUNT(1)
FROM sys.dm_pdw_nodes
GROUP BY type
```

The following screenshot displays the count of **control nodes** and **compute nodes** available in my Synapse SQL pool:

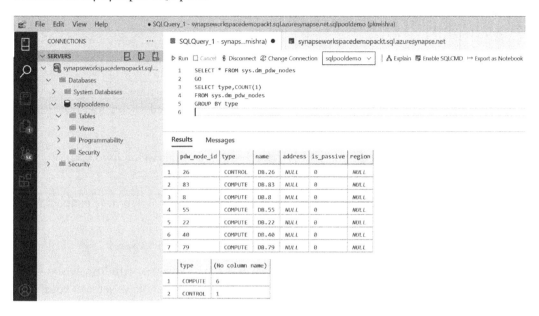

Figure 2.11 – A screenshot of Azure Data Studio showing the query results

You can decide how many compute nodes you need for your SQL pool by choosing DWUs while creating your Synapse SQL pool. However, you can scale it later as well, based on your business needs. So, let's try to understand a little more about DWUs.

Examining DWUs

When you purchase **DWUs** for SQL Pool, you basically purchase several analytical resources bundled together, such as the **Central Processing Unit** (**CPU**), memory, and **Input/Output** (**I/O**). You can change the DWUs even after creating a Synapse account. However, distributions will remap to compute nodes after you change DWUs for your Synapse account.

You can use the following query to view the current DWU setting:

```
SELECT   db.name [Database]
,        ds.edition [Edition]
,        ds.service_objective [Service Objective]
FROM     sys.database_service_objectives   AS ds
JOIN     sys.databases  AS db ON ds.database_id = db.database_id
```

You have already seen in the previous chapter how to select DWUs while creating your Azure Synapse SQL pool. Many customers prefer to scale down their SQL pool when not in use for cost savings, so it will be worth knowing how you can change DWUs in the existing SQL pool.

Changing DWUs

You can change DWUs directly on in the Azure portal. The following steps will show you how to change DWUs, but before you make any changes, you need to consider how this change will have a direct impact on performance:

1. Go to `portal.azure.com` and provide your credentials to log in to your Azure subscription.

    This may ask you for **Multi-Factor Authentication (MFA)** if you have enabled MFA for your subscription.

2. Go to your resource group and click on **Azure Synapse workspace**.

3. Click on **SQL pool** in the left blade. This will take you to a new window, as shown in the following screenshot. Click on **Scale** and slide the bubble to set it to your desired compute:

Figure 2.12 – A screenshot of the Azure portal, highlighting the link to Scale

Many people tend to scale up the compute whenever they face performance issues in their SQL pool. However, it is important to notice the table distribution type because it has a major impact on your query performance.

Understanding distributions in Synapse SQL Pool

All queries from end users are handed over to compute nodes from control nodes for parallel query execution. Each compute node can manage one or more (maximum 60) distributions.

You can use the following **Dynamic Management Views** (**DMVs**) to know more about your nodes and distributions:

```
SELECT distribution_id, pdw_node_id FROM sys.pdw_nodes_
partitions
GO
SELECT distribution_id,pdw_node_id FROM sys.pdw_distributions
GO
```

Each query from the end user gets divided into 60 parallel queries to be run on each of the 60 distributions. If there is just one compute node, this node will manage all 60 distributions; however, if you have 60 compute nodes to run in parallel, each compute node will manage one distribution.

The following diagram provides an example of distributions across various nodes if the performance level of your SQL pool is 3,000 DWUs:

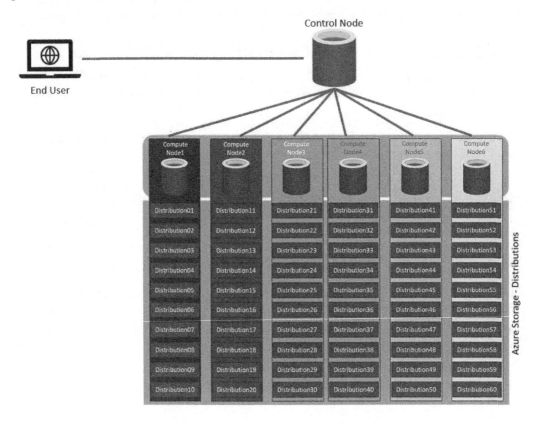

Figure 2.13 – Architecture for 3,000 DWUs

Now that we know how distributions play an important role in the architecture of a Synapse SQL pool, it will be worth learning about the usage of different types of distributions.

Hash distributed tables

Large fact tables are the best candidates for hash distributed tables. A hash distributed table uses a hash function to distribute table rows across the available compute nodes. This type of distribution is created to minimize data movement across various distributions because similar values tend to fall within the same distribution.

Tables that are more than 2 **Gigabytes (GB)** in size on disk and tables having more frequent INSERT, UPDATE, and DELETE operations are the best candidates for hash distributions.

The following code snippet provides an example of how to create a hash distributed table:

```
CREATE TABLE FactSales (
  SalesID INT IDENTITY(1, 1) NOT NULL,
  SalesDate DATETIME NOT NULL,
  SalesItemId INT,
  Description VARCHAR(500)
) WITH ( CLUSTERED INDEX (SalesID), DISTRIBUTION =
HASH(SalesDate) );
```

You cannot change a distribution once it has been created. If you wish to change a distribution, you may need to create another table using the **CREATE TABLE AS SELECT (CTAS)** command, as illustrated in the following code snippet:

```
CREATE TABLE [dbo].[FactSales_new]
WITH
(
  DISTRIBUTION = ROUND_ROBIN
  ,CLUSTERED COLUMNSTORE INDEX
)
AS
SELECT  *
FROM    [dbo].[FactSales];
```

When the table size is not very large, we can consider using **round-robin distributed tables** instead of a hash distributed table. We will learn about round-robin tables in the following section.

Round-robin distributed tables

The default distribution type for a table in SQL Pool is **round-robin** distribution, whereby data is divided evenly across all the distributions. Similar records are not guaranteed to fall within the same distribution, which slows down performance while retrieving records across various nodes. Sometimes, rows need to be reshuffled when you perform joining operations on round-robin distributed tables.

The following is an example of how to create a round-robin distributed table:

```
CREATE TABLE DimSalesItem (
  SalesItemID INT IDENTITY(1, 1) NOT NULL,
  Description VARCHAR(500)
) WITH ( CLUSTERED INDEX (SalesItemID), DISTRIBUTION = ROUND_
ROBIN );
```

If you use the following script to create a new table, it does not give you the flexibility to choose the distribution type. However, it will create a ROUND_ROBIN distribution by default, but you can use CTAS to define the distribution of the table data:

```
SELECT * INTO DimSalesItem_New FROM DimSalesItem
```

Temporary staging tables and tables with no obvious joining key are the best candidates for ROUND_ROBIN distributed tables.

Replicated tables

Replicated tables must only be used for small dimension tables. This replicates the table data across all distributions so that the data becomes local to each compute node and accessibility becomes easier. There is no need to move the data across various compute nodes for a running query, and this helps to return results very quickly. Small dimension tables with a size less than 2 GB are the best candidates for replicated tables.

The following snippet shows the code used for creating replication distributed tables in SQL Pool. You can use CTAS for this distribution type as well:

```
CREATE TABLE [dbo].[DimSalesRegion]
(
    RegionID INT IDENTITY(1,1) NOT NULL,
    Region VARCHAR(50) NOT NULL
)
    WITH ( CLUSTERED COLUMNSTORE INDEX, DISTRIBUTION =
REPLICATE )
```

This code will help you to find data skew for a distributed table:

```
DBCC PDW_SHOWSPACEUSED('dbo.FactSales');
```

When you are dealing with billions of records and your data tends to grow exponentially, you may need to take a few extra measures to ensure good performance. You may consider partitioning your data based on data volume and certain other circumstances. The following topic will help you understand more about **partitions** in a SQL pool.

Understanding partitions in Synapse SQL Pool

Table partitions are used to create smaller groups of records within a table. Partitioning not only helps to enhance the efficiency and performance of loading data but also benefits data maintenance and query performance. Partitioning is supported on columnstore indexes, clustered indexes, and heap indexes.

As we understand now that partitioning helps in various ways, we must be aware that creating a table with too many partitions can affect performance in certain circumstances.

There is no defined set of rules for deciding the number of partitions in a table, but for optimal compression and performance of clustered Columnstore tables, we need to have a minimum of 1 million rows per distribution and partition. In order to understand the concept of a clustered Columnstore index, it is recommended to have a look at the following link: https://docs.microsoft.com/en-us/sql/relational-databases/indexes/columnstore-indexes-overview.

A SQL pool proactively creates 60 distributions for each table, so adding a partition on these tables will multifold the total number of data groupings. Keeping 1 million records in mind, we need to have at least 60 million records in a table without any partition in order to get optimal performance. However, if you have 10 partitions created on your table, then you need to have a minimum of 60 distributions X 10 partitions X 1 million records (that is, 600 million records) in order to gain better results.

Usually, partitions are created on the **Date** column so that data gets equally distributed among all the partitions evenly as per the data loading date. However, you can choose any other column as your partition key where data grouping could be helpful. It would not be a good idea to create partitioning on unique key columns because you may end up creating a large number of partitions, and that could possibly kill the query performance.

The following code snippet provides an example of using partitions along with distributions:

```
CREATE TABLE [dbo].[FactSales] (
    [SalesID] int NOT NULL,
    [OrderDateKey] int NOT NULL,
    [CustomerKey] int NOT NULL,
    [PromotionKey] int NOT NULL,
```

```
    [SalesOrderNumber] nvarchar(20) NOT NULL,
    [OrderQuantity] smallint NOT NULL,
    [UnitPrice] money NOT NULL,
    [SalesAmount] money NOT NULL
) WITH (
CLUSTERED COLUMNSTORE INDEX,
DISTRIBUTION = HASH([ProductKey]),
PARTITION (
  [OrderDateKey] RANGE RIGHT FOR
  VALUES
    (
        20000101, 20010101, 20020101, 20030101,
        20040101, 20050101
    )
  )
);
```

> **Important note**
>
> If you are using a clustered Columnstore index in your table, it is recommended to have a minimum of 1 million rows per distribution and partition in order to get optimal compression and performance.

The following query will give you details about all the nodes, distributions, and partitions. If you have not created any partitions manually, then there will be only one partition created by default:

```
SELECT B.distribution_id,A.pdw_node_id,A.[type] AS node_type,A.
name AS node_name,C.partition_number,C.[rows]   FROM sys.dm_
pdw_nodes A
LEFT JOIN sys.pdw_distributions B ON A.pdw_node_id=B.pdw_node_
id
LEFT JOIN sys.pdw_nodes_partitions C ON B.distribution_id=C.
distribution_id AND A.pdw_node_id=C.pdw_node_id
ORDER BY B.distribution_id
GO
```

The following screenshot depicts Azure Data Studio displaying results for the preceding query on my Synapse SQL pool:

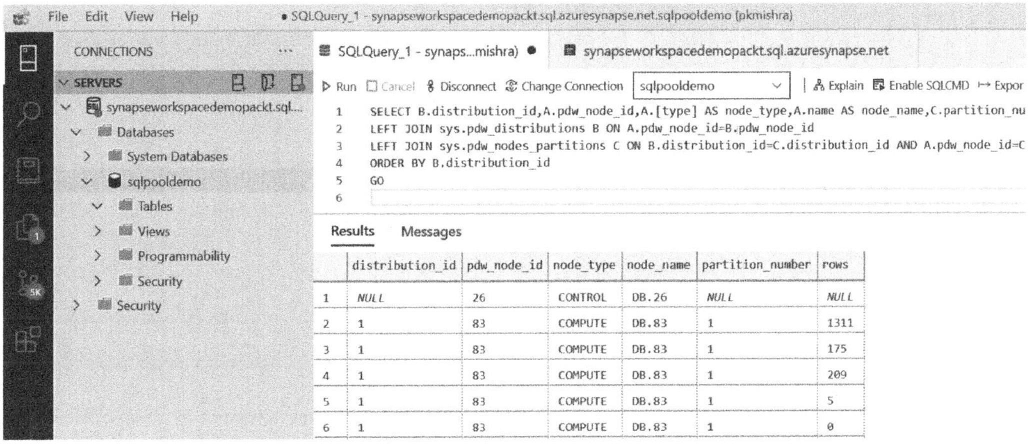

Figure 2.14 – A screenshot of Azure Data Studio showing the result of the preceding query

The syntax of partitioning in Synapse SQL Pool is slightly different from SQL Server, as partitioning functions and schemes are not used in Synapse SQL Pool in the same way they are in SQL Server.

To conclude the subject of table partitioning, it's time to learn about temporary tables in Synapse SQL pools. Synapse SQL allows you to create temporary tables as well, which you may sometimes need in stored procedures for better performance. However, there are a couple of differences from how you use them with SQL databases. Let's have a look at their usage and implementation in Synapse SQL.

Using temporary tables in Synapse SQL Pool

In SQL Pool, temporary tables exist at the session level. In the SQL pool, temporary tables are written on local rather than remote storage, resulting in better performance. In SQL Pool, temporary tables can be created in the same way as in a SQL database; however, they can also be created with a CTAS command, as illustrated in the following code snippet:

```
IF OBJECT_ID('tempdb..#tempFactSales') IS NOT NULL
BEGIN
    DROP TABLE #tempFactSales
END
GO
```

```
CREATE TABLE #tempFactSales
WITH
(
    DISTRIBUTION = HASH([SalesID])
,    HEAP
)
AS
(
SELECT SalesId,SalesItemId, Description
FROM FactSales
);
SELECT * FROM #tempFactSales
```

> **Important note**
> Global temporary tables are not yet supported in Synapse SQL.

Discovering the benefits of Synapse SQL Pool

The more you learn about Synapse SQL Pool, the more you will appreciate the features that it includes. There are many benefits that we will discover throughout this book; here are a few of them:

- It is easy to create a new SQL pool or scale your existing pool as per your business needs.

- Storage is kept separate from compute, so you can scale your compute without worrying about the storage. This gives you the flexibility to pause the compute when not in use without losing your data when you resume the compute.

- On your Azure Synapse SQL pool system, demands can come from different directions, such as Azure Databricks, Azure Data Factory, reporting layers, cube refreshes, and custom apps.

- Synapse SQL pool uses columnar storage to store data in relational tables. Columnar storage stores data by column (field), keeping all data associated with that column together in memory. This format significantly helps in data compression, which ultimately reduces data storage costs and improves query performance. They are optimized to read data more efficiently.

- Synapse SQL supports T-SQL, so you do not need to learn any new language to perform any sort of operation on your data. You will learn more about this in *Chapter 6, Working with T-SQL in Azure Synapse*.

Now that we have learned various concepts around a dedicated SQL pool, it would be worth taking a look at a serverless SQL pool in Synapse.

Understanding Synapse SQL on-demand

SQL on-demand is a serverless distributed data processing system that enables you to analyze your big data faster. There is no need to set up infrastructure or maintain a cluster to start using SQL on-demand, so you can start querying data as soon the workspace is created.

In this section, we are going to talk about the architecture and components of Synapse SQL on-demand, the benefits of using SQL on-demand, and how you can query files in your Azure Storage accounts using SQL on-demand.

SQL on-demand architecture and components

SQL on-demand is serverless, so scaling automatically accommodates the resource requirements for any query. The SQL on-demand architecture also has a control node, a compute node, DMS, and Azure Storage, but it does not have an MPP engine; instead, it uses a **Distributed Query Processing** (**DQP**) engine.

The architecture, as illustrated in the following screenshot, explains how a **control node** leverages a DQP engine to distribute a query across various computes as per the requirement. **Compute nodes** will reach out to the storage to fetch the required data as requested and send it back to the control node:

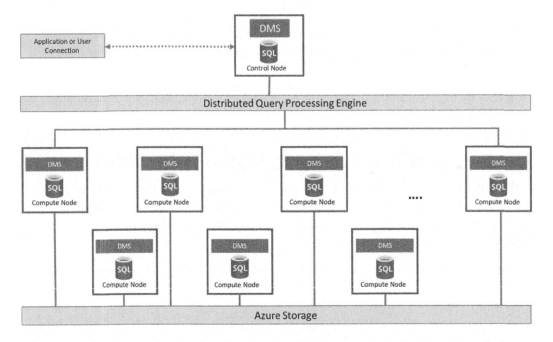

Figure 2.15 – Architecture of SQL on-demand

Most of the components in the SQL on-demand architecture are the same as in SQL pool. However, the functionalities are a little different. Let's go through all the components and their roles in this architecture, as follows:

- **Control node**: The control node utilizes the **DQP engine** to split user queries into smaller queries that will be executed on compute nodes. Each smaller chunk of a query is called a distributed query unit.

- **Compute node**: In Synapse SQL on-demand, you do *not* have control over the number of compute nodes through DWUs. In this case, compute nodes will be made available as per the resource requirement. The data is stored in **Azure Storage**, and the compute nodes run parallel queries against this data with the help of **DMS**.

- **Azure Storage**: Synapse SQL leverages Azure Storage to keep your data safe, irrespective of the analytics runtime that you choose for either SQL Pool or SQL on-demand. Azure Synapse supports both Azure Blob Storage and Data Lake Storage. You can create a Data Lake Storage Gen2 account just by enabling **Data Lake Storage Gen2** while filling in the form to create a storage account in the Azure portal, as seen in the following screenshot. With the SQL on-demand runtime, you can query your files from the data lake in a read-only manner:

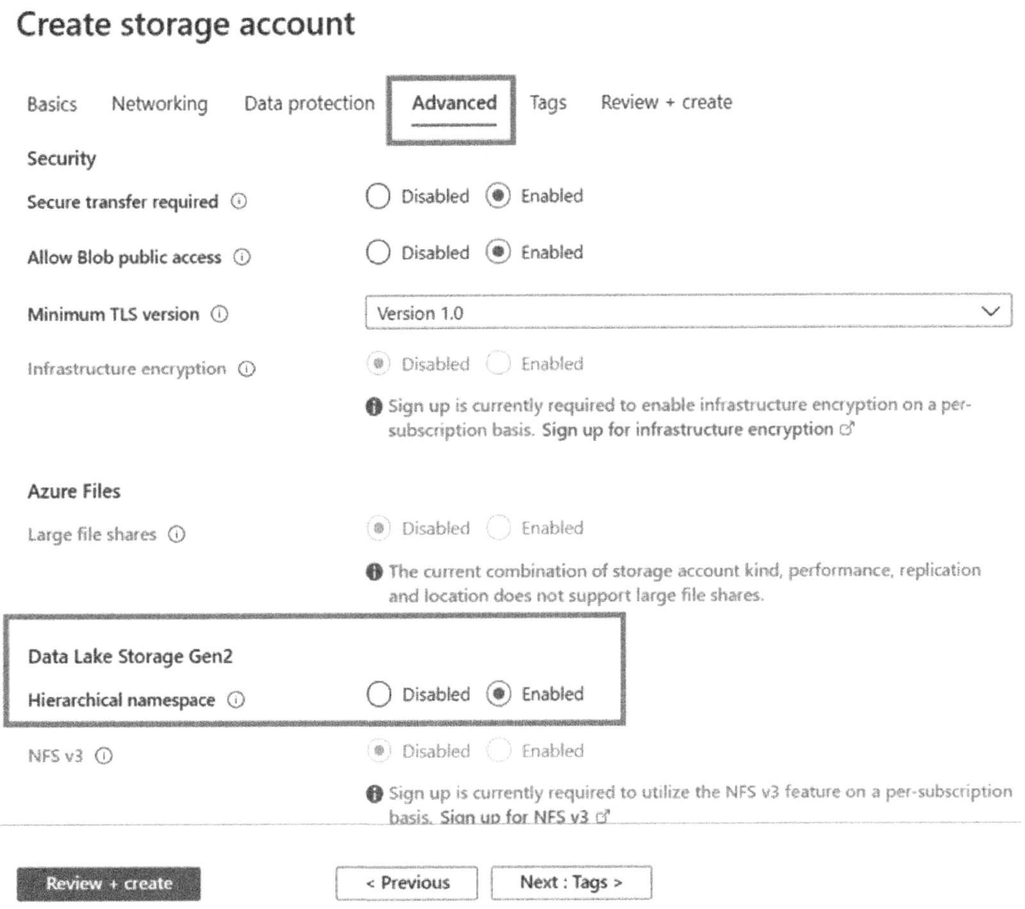

Figure 2.16 – A screenshot of creating an Azure Storage Data Lake Gen2 account in the Azure portal

> **Important note**
> DMS works the same with SQL on-demand as with SQL Pool.

Learning about the benefits of Synapse SQL on-demand

Many customers who already have some sort of experience with **Amazon Web Services** (**AWS**) ask whether Azure has any service that is similar to **Athena**. Now, we can tell them that Azure has that feature available and, moreover, it is integrated with an **Enterprise Data Warehouse** (**EDW**). There are many other benefits of using SQL on-demand, too. You can see a few of them here:

- It is very easy to discover and explore data in various formats (Parquet, **Comma-Separated Values** (**CSV**), and **JavaScript Object Notation** (**JSON**)) directly from your data lake.

- You can save money by using the compute only when required.

- There is no need to worry about infrastructure and managing clusters.

- You can easily explore and transform data in a simple, scalable, and performant way using T-SQL, and save the results back in a data lake to be visualized further through Power BI reports.

- You can build logical data warehouses by providing a relational abstraction on raw data without moving it anywhere. This saves the overhead of additional data ingestion steps and the cost of using Azure resources or any other tool for data movement. However, more importantly, it saves a lot of time by avoiding data movement and trying to keep it updated.

The following section outlines the concept of a Synapse Spark pool, and we will also learn how the Spark pool architecture is different from the Synapse SQL pool architecture.

Understanding Spark pool

Apache Spark is a very fast unified analytics engine for **big data** and **machine learning**.

Synapse Spark Pool is one of Microsoft's implementations of **Apache Spark** in Azure. Synapse Analytics workspace has a Spark engine built in, along with Notebook support. Because Synapse Spark supports C#, we can write Spark .NET directly within notebooks. You can also write your code in **Python**, **Scala**, **C#**, and **SQL**.

One Spark pool can be accessed by multiple users, but for every user, one new Spark instance will be created. A Spark instance is also dependent on the Spark pool capacity: if there is enough capacity in the pool to run multiple queries, the existing instance will be able to process the job; otherwise, a new instance will be created to process the job.

The following diagram displays different components of Apache Spark on Azure Synapse:

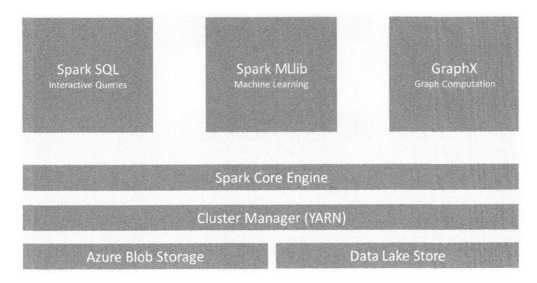

Figure 2.17 – Apache Spark in Azure Synapse Analytics

Let's try to dive into the architecture of Synapse Spark pool to understand how all the components are integrated with each other within the Azure Synapse workspace.

Spark pool architecture and components

Apache Spark works on a master-slave architecture, with one master and multiple worker nodes. During runtime, a Spark application maps to a single driver process and a set of executors distributed across the multiple worker nodes in a cluster.

The following diagram showcases the different layers of communication within Apache Spark and how worker nodes are interacting with the cluster manager in the Spark pool:

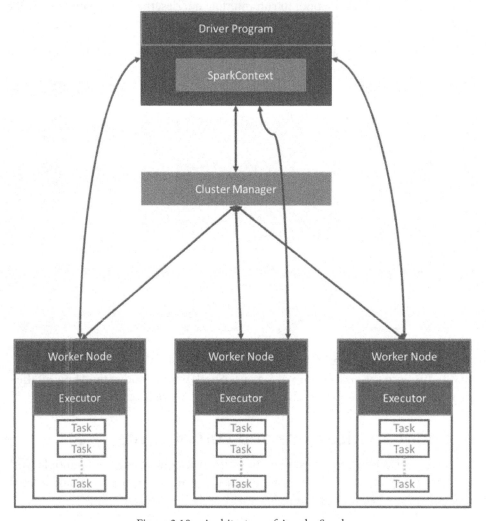

Figure 2.18 – Architecture of Apache Spark

Let's try to understand the different components of Apache Spark, as follows:

- **Driver Program**: The driver program is the heart of a Spark application and it is responsible for maintaining information about the Spark application during its lifetime, responding to a user's programming or input, and analyzing, distributing, and scheduling work across the executors.

- **SparkContext**: SparkContext is the entry gate of Apache Spark. Most of the functions that we might use in Spark—such as accumulators, broadcast variables, parallelize, and so on—come from SparkContext. Spark applications run as independent sets of processes on a cluster, coordinated by the driver program. Generating SparkContext is the most important step of any Spark driver application.

- **Cluster Manager** (**YARN**): **Yet Another Resource Negotiator** (**YARN**) is one of the cluster managers that control physical machines and allocate required resources to Spark applications. The cluster manager in Synapse Spark is **Apache Hadoop YARN**. YARN is mainly used to split up the functionalities of resource management and job scheduling into separate daemons.

- **Worker Node**: Worker nodes execute tasks assigned by the cluster manager and return them back to SparkContext.

- **Executor**: Executors are responsible for executing work in the form of tasks, as well as for storing any data that you cache.

Creating and managing an Apache Spark cluster is a tedious job. However, Apache Spark's implementation on Azure Synapse has made it very easy for users to create a Spark pool and start using it without worrying about managing the cluster. Let's learn how to create a Synapse Spark pool on Azure.

Creating a Synapse Spark pool

You can create your Synapse workspace without creating a Spark pool. However, you can go to the Azure portal anytime to create a Spark pool on your Synapse workspace, but you cannot create a Spark pool without already having a Synapse workspace.

Using the Azure portal

You can take the following steps to create your Spark pool, but don't forget to have all the prerequisites in place, as mentioned at the beginning of this chapter:

1. Log in to the Azure portal, at `https://portal.azure.com`.

2. Navigate to the **Synapse workspace** by typing the service name (or resource name) directly into the search bar.

3. Click on the Synapse workspace where you want to create your **Spark pool**.

4. Click on **Apache Spark pools** from the **Synapse workspace** blade in the Azure portal and click on **+ New** to create your **Spark pool**, as illustrated in the following screenshot:

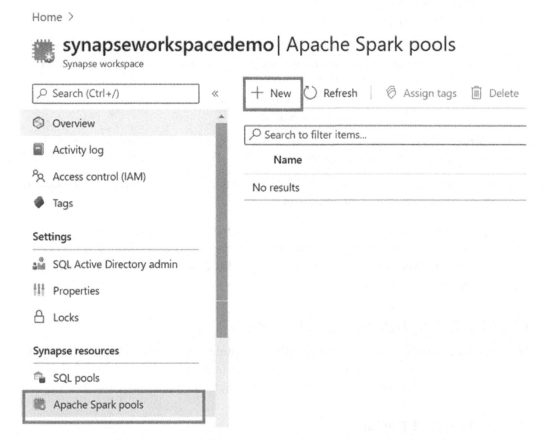

Figure 2.19 – A screenshot of the Synapse workspace blade, highlighting the link to create Spark pools

5. Under the **Basics** tab, you need to provide an appropriate name for your Apache Spark pool; select the required **Node size family** option from the dropdown; keep the **Autoscale** option set to **Enabled** or **Disabled** as per your business needs; and, finally, choose the **number of nodes** required for your Spark pool.

After filling in all the required details, you can move to the **Additional settings** tab by clicking the **Next: Additional settings >** button at the bottom of the screen, as illustrated in the following screenshot:

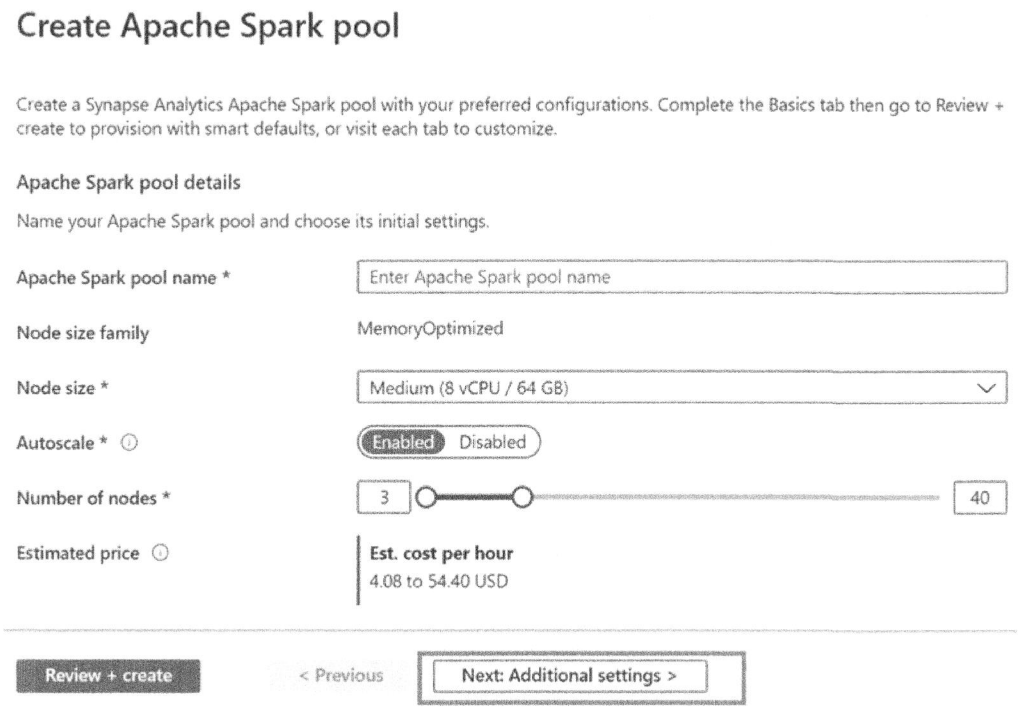

Create Apache Spark pool

Create a Synapse Analytics Apache Spark pool with your preferred configurations. Complete the Basics tab then go to Review + create to provision with smart defaults, or visit each tab to customize.

Apache Spark pool details

Name your Apache Spark pool and choose its initial settings.

Apache Spark pool name *	Enter Apache Spark pool name
Node size family	MemoryOptimized
Node size *	Medium (8 vCPU / 64 GB) ⌄
Autoscale * ⓘ	(**Enabled** Disabled)
Number of nodes *	3 ⟡——○—————————— 40
Estimated price ⓘ	**Est. cost per hour** 4.08 to 54.40 USD

Review + create   < Previous   Next: Additional settings >

Figure 2.20 – A screenshot of the Basics tab to create a Synapse Spark pool

> **Important note**
> If the **Autoscale** option is set to **Enabled**, your Apache Spark pool will automatically scale up and down based on the amount of activity.

6.   Under the **Additional settings** tab, you have the option to set the duration for idle time before auto-pause kicks in. It is always better to keep it set to **Enabled** so that you do not waste your money on unnecessary resource consumption.

So, I am going to keep it set to **Enabled** and set the **Number of minutes** idle time to 30.

7. You can install the required packages by uploading the environment configuration file using the file selector in the **Packages** section of the page, as illustrated in the next screenshot:

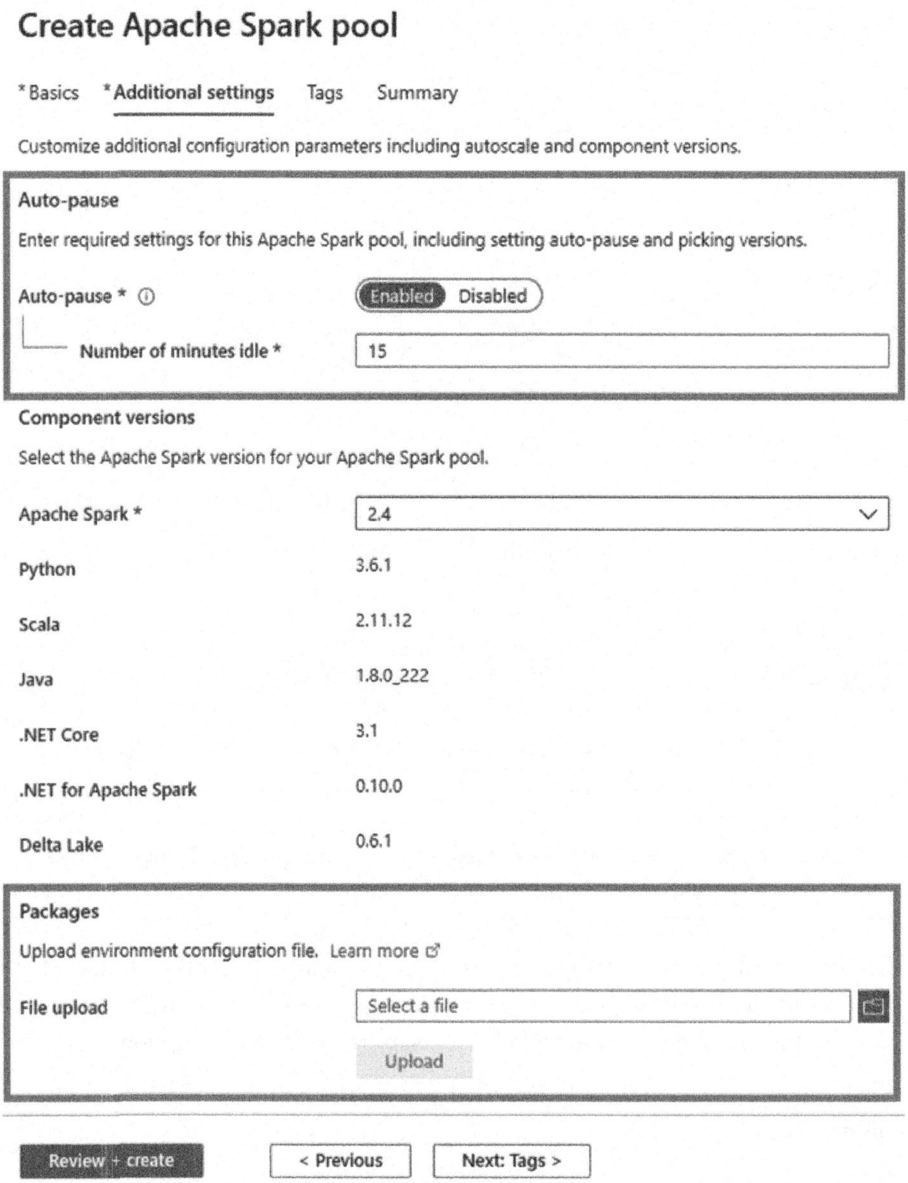

Create Apache Spark pool

*Basics　*Additional settings　Tags　Summary

Customize additional configuration parameters including autoscale and component versions.

Auto-pause

Enter required settings for this Apache Spark pool, including setting auto-pause and picking versions.

Auto-pause * ⓘ　　　　　　　　(Enabled　Disabled)

　└── Number of minutes idle *　　15

Component versions

Select the Apache Spark version for your Apache Spark pool.

Apache Spark *	2.4　⌄
Python	3.6.1
Scala	2.11.12
Java	1.8.0_222
.NET Core	3.1
.NET for Apache Spark	0.10.0
Delta Lake	0.6.1

Packages

Upload environment configuration file. Learn more ⬀

File upload　　　　Select a file　　　📁

　　　　　　Upload

[Review + create]　　[< Previous]　[Next: Tags >]

Figure 2.21 – A screenshot of the Additional settings page to create a Synapse Spark pool

> **Important note**
>
> Apache Spark in Azure Synapse Analytics already has a full Anaconda install, plus additional libraries that are included automatically when a Spark instance starts up. However, you have the option to update existing or install new libraries during or after pool creation.

8. Next, you can fill the **Tag** details on the next page, and finally, after reviewing all the details, click on **Create** to create a Synapse Spark pool.

Now that you have learned how to create a Spark pool using the Azure portal, it will be worth learning how to create a Spark pool on Synapse Studio itself so that you do not need to go back to the Azure portal if you need to run a Spark application.

Using Synapse Studio

The following instructions will help you learn how to create a Synapse Spark pool using Synapse Studio:

1. Log in to the Azure portal at `https://portal.azure.com`.

2. Navigate to the Synapse workspace by typing the service name (or resource name) directly into the search bar.

3. Click on the workspace where you want to create your SQL pool.

4. Click on **Launch Synapse Studio**.

5. Go to the **Manage** tab on the **Synapse Studio** home page.

6. Click on the **+ New** link under the **Apache Spark pools** section to create a new SQL pool.

Next, you can follow the same instructions as mentioned in *Steps 5* through *8* in the previous section.

Learning about the benefits of a Synapse Spark pool

There are many advantages to using Apache Spark by itself. However, integration with Azure Synapse Analytics adds even more value to Spark, including the following benefits:

- Spark comes packaged with higher-level libraries, including support for SQL queries, streaming data, machine learning, and graph processing.

- Spark notebooks can be created not just in Python, Scala, and SQL but also in C#, which is highly beneficial for C# developers.

- It is just a matter of clicking to create and trigger a Spark job through pipelines.

- There is a simple **Graphical User Interface (GUI)** to configure a Spark pool and notebooks.

- You can benefit from integration with IntelliJ IDEA to create Apache Spark applications.

That concludes our second chapter.

Summary

In this chapter, we covered the concepts of Synapse SQL and Synapse Spark. After going through this chapter, you have learned how to create your SQL pool, how to use SQL on-demand, and how to use Spark pool, as well as learning how to change DWUs for your SQL pool using both the Azure portal and Synapse Studio.

You can refer to other books to learn more about Apache Spark. In this chapter, we have tried to cover the Apache Spark concepts that are most relevant to Synapse.

We have used **Azure Data Studio** in a couple of places, to give you an idea of how it works. We will be seeing Azure Data Studio again, later on. I personally like to use Azure Data Studio because it offers a very smooth SQL coding experience with built-in features such as multiple tab windows, a rich SQL editor, code navigation, and source control integration.

In the next chapter, we are going to talk about various ways to bring your data to Azure Synapse.

Section 2: Data Ingestion and Orchestration

The objective of this section is to introduce you to the various ways of ingesting data to or from Azure Synapse and orchestrating data using various transformation techniques offered by Azure Synapse.

This section comprises the following chapters:

- *Chapter 3, Bringing Your Data to Azure Synapse*
- *Chapter 4, Using Synapse Pipelines to Orchestrate Your Data*
- *Chapter 5, Using Synapse Link with Azure Cosmos DB*

3
Bringing Your Data to Azure Synapse

Data has been the backbone of many top enterprises over the past few decades. Now, you can bring your data from various sources to Azure Synapse through various means and start analyzing your data immediately.

So far, you have learned about the Synapse workspace, as well as the architecture and components of Synapse SQL and Synapse Spark. You can create your SQL or Spark pool on Azure Synapse. So now, it's time to take the next step and bring your data to Azure Synapse.

The following topics will be the focus of this chapter, along with the various concepts that you must be aware of before you decide which method to use:

- Using Synapse pipelines to import data
- Using Azure Data Factory to import data
- Using SQL Server Integration Services to import data
- Using a COPY statement to import data

Technical requirements

To comply with the instructions in the following sections, there are a number of prerequisites that need to be fulfilled before we proceed:

- You should have your Azure subscription, or access to any other subscription with contributor-level access.

- Create your Synapse workspace on this subscription. You can follow the instructions from *Chapter 1*, *Introduction to Azure Synapse*, to create your Synapse workspace.

- Create your SQL pool and Spark pool on Azure Synapse. This has been covered in *Chapter 2*, *Consideration for Your Compute Environment.*

- You must have created a storage account or must have the requisite permission to access Data Lake. You can go to the following link, `https://azure.microsoft.com/en-us/resources/videos/creating-your-first-adls-gen2-data-lake/`, to create a new storage account if you are creating one for the first time.

- You must have SQL Server installed on your machine to follow this chapter. If you do not have a SQL Server license, you can download the Developer Edition of SQL Server from the following location, `https://go.microsoft.com/fwlink/?linkid=866662`, to your local machine and follow the instructions to install it.

- You should have Visual Studio installed on your machine along with the data tools required to create an Integration Services project.

- You will also need to create a DimEmployee and UserData table in Synapse SQL. You can copy the script from the following GitHub URL: `http://bit.ly/sql-chapter03`.

Now that you have all the prerequisites in place, it's time to dive into multiple options for bringing the data to **Azure Synapse**.

Using Synapse pipelines to import data

Data ingestion is one of the most critical aspects of data analytics, and there are many tools available for data movement. The challenge is to decide which tool is more efficient for your environment. In this section, we are going to show how can you use inbuilt orchestration tools available in Synapse for data ingestion. There are two options available under the **Orchestrate** tab: the first one is **Pipeline**, which can be used for data ingestion, but also allows you to add transformation logic. The second option is to use **Copy Data tool**, which gives you the option to only move data without implementing any data transformation logic. So, in a nutshell, you can use **Copy Data tool** if you require a pipeline just for data ingestion, but you have the option to use **Pipeline** if you need to add business logic to your data.

The following screenshot shows the **Integrate** hub of Synapse Studio, where we are going to use the **Copy Data tool** or **Pipeline** options to copy data from various sources to Azure Synapse Analytics:

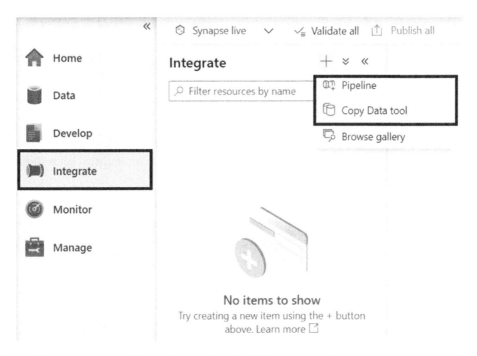

Figure 3.1 – A screenshot of Azure Synapse Studio highlighting the links to create Synapse pipelines

Let's now try to learn how to use **Copy Data tool** to bring data from our on-premises **SQL Server** to a **Synapse SQL pool**.

Bringing data to your Synapse SQL pool using Copy Data tool

Copy Data tool makes it very easy to bring your data to Azure Synapse. This is not that different to using the Copy activity of Azure Data Factory, except you do not have to spin up another service for data ingestion in Azure Synapse. You need to make sure you have applied all of the technical requirements before you start following these steps:

1. Click on **Copy Data tool** as highlighted in *Figure 3.1*. This will open a new window where you need to provide the source and destination connection details.

2. Provide an appropriate name for your pipeline, along with a brief description.

3. You can choose to run this pipeline once only, or you can schedule it to run regularly. For this example, we are going to schedule our pipeline to run on a daily basis.

   Click on **Run regularly on schedule** and select the **Schedule** trigger type.

4. Provide an appropriate value for **Start Date (UTC)**. This is auto populated with the current date and time by default, but you can change this value to any later date and time.

5. Choose the trigger type as per your business requirements. Let's select **Schedule** for this example.

6. Define **Recurrence** for this pipeline. You have the option to select the recurrence in minutes or hours. We want to schedule this pipeline to run daily, so keep 24 hours as the recurrence value.

7. I want this pipeline to run every day without any end date, so I have selected the **No End** radio button for the **End** field. However, if you do need to set an end for your pipeline, you can click on the **On Date** radio button:

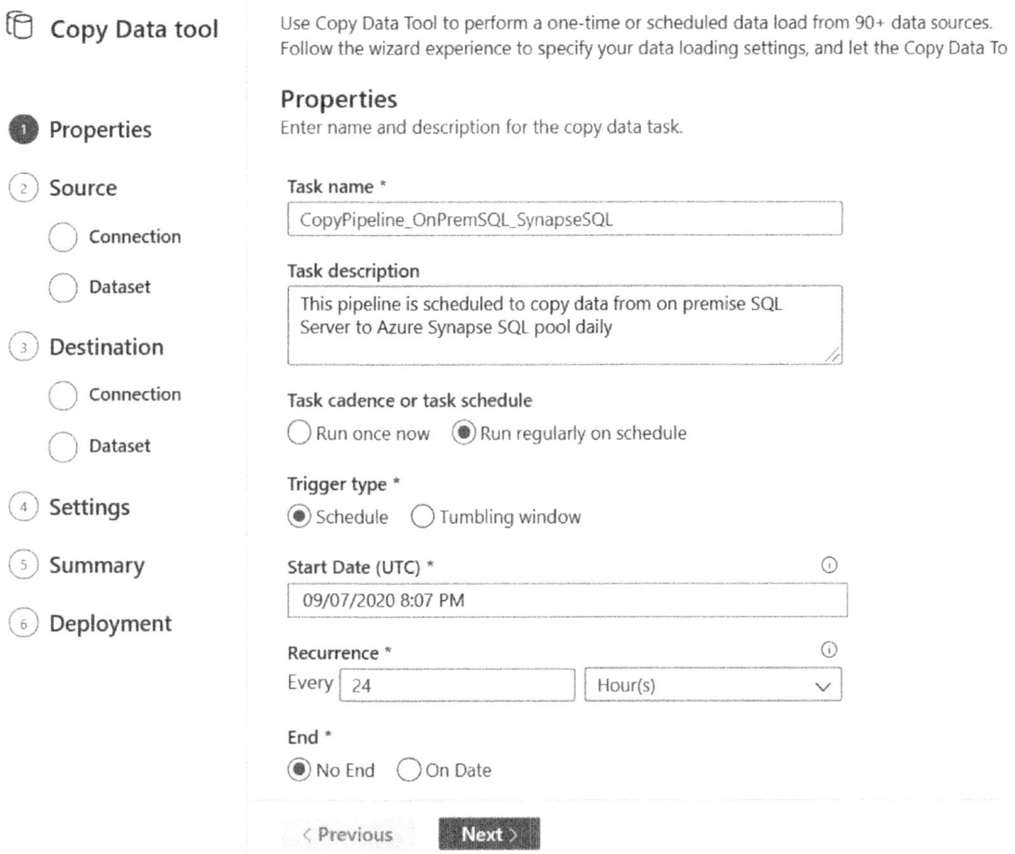

Copy Data tool

Use Copy Data Tool to perform a one-time or scheduled data load from 90+ data sources. Follow the wizard experience to specify your data loading settings, and let the Copy Data To

1 Properties

2 Source

○ Connection

○ Dataset

3 Destination

○ Connection

○ Dataset

4 Settings

5 Summary

6 Deployment

Properties

Enter name and description for the copy data task.

Task name *

CopyPipeline_OnPremSQL_SynapseSQL

Task description

This pipeline is scheduled to copy data from on premise SQL Server to Azure Synapse SQL pool daily

Task cadence or task schedule

○ Run once now   ● Run regularly on schedule

Trigger type *

● Schedule   ○ Tumbling window

Start Date (UTC) *   ⓘ

09/07/2020 8:07 PM

Recurrence *   ⓘ

Every | 24 | | Hour(s)   ∨ |

End *

● No End   ○ On Date

< Previous   **Next >**

Figure 3.2 – A screenshot of the Properties screen under Copy Data tool

After completing all the details on the **Properties** screen, click on **Next** to define the source.

8. On the next screen, you need to create a new connection for your data source. Click on + **Create new connection**:

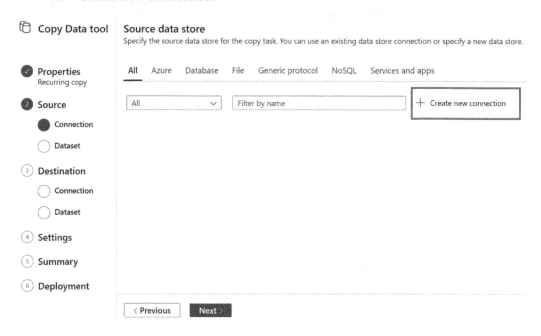

Figure 3.3 – A screenshot of Copy Data tool defining the source connection

9. In this section, we are going to use an on-premises SQL Server (SQL Server installed on your local machine or on-premises server) as our data source, so let's select **SQL Server** from the list of all the available sources. However, you can select the source as per your business requirements.

10. Search for and select the relevant data source and then click on **Continue**:

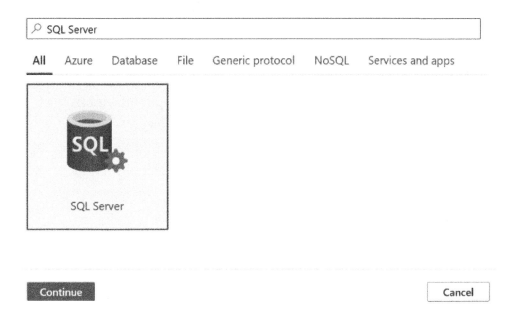

New linked service

🔍 SQL Server

All   Azure   Database   File   Generic protocol   NoSQL   Services and apps

SQL Server

Continue   Cancel

Figure 3.4 – A screenshot of the search results to create a linked service for the source

11. Now, you need to provide details to create a linked service for the data source. Give a meaningful name to the linked service and add the description.

12. Next, you need to set up an integration runtime to connect the pipeline to the on-premises SQL Server. Integration runtime is the compute infrastructure used by **Azure Data Factory** or **Synapse pipelines** to provide data movement, data flow, activity dispatch, and **SQL Server Integration Services (SSIS)** package execution capabilities across different network environments. There are two types of integration runtimes, **Self-Hosted** and **Azure** integration runtimes. We will learn about both options in *Chapter 5, Using Synapse Pipelines to Orchestrate Your Data*. In this section, we are going to use the self-hosted integration runtime, which is mainly used for running activities in an on-premises or private network. Click on **+New**:

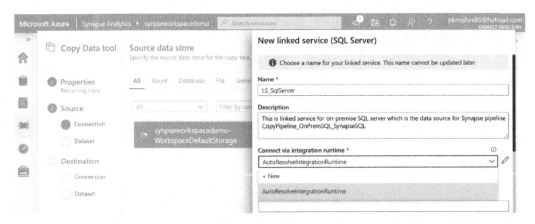

Figure 3.5 – A screenshot of the window for creating a new linked service for the source

13. Select **Self-Hosted** and then click on **Continue**. This will open a new form to provide a name and description for the integration runtime:

Integration runtime setup

Network environment:

Choose the network environment of the data source / destination or external compute to which the integration runtime will connect to for data flows, data movement or dispatch activities:

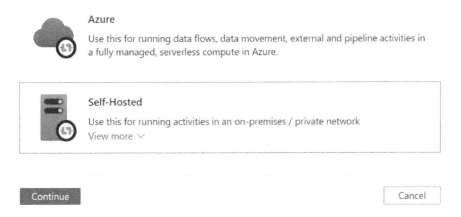

Azure

Use this for running data flows, data movement, external and pipeline activities in a fully managed, serverless compute in Azure.

Self-Hosted

Use this for running activities in an on-premises / private network
View more ⌄

Continue   Cancel

Figure 3.6 – A screenshot showing options for the integration runtime setup

14. Provide a name and description under the **Integration runtime setup** window and then click on **Continue**:

Integration runtime setup

Private network support is realized by installing integration runtime to machines in the same on-premises network/VNET as the resource the integration runtime is connecting to. Follow below steps to register and install integration runtime on your self-hosted machines.

ⓘ Choose a name for your integration runtime. This name cannot be updated later.

Name *   ⓘ

| IntegrationRuntimeOnPremSQLServer |

Description

| This IR is created for on premise SQL Server |

Type

| Self-Hosted |

Create   Back   Cancel

Figure 3.7 – A screenshot of the Integration runtime setup window

15. Next, you get the option to select the integration runtime setup. We are going to select **Manual setup** in this section. However, you can go with option 1 for the express setup:

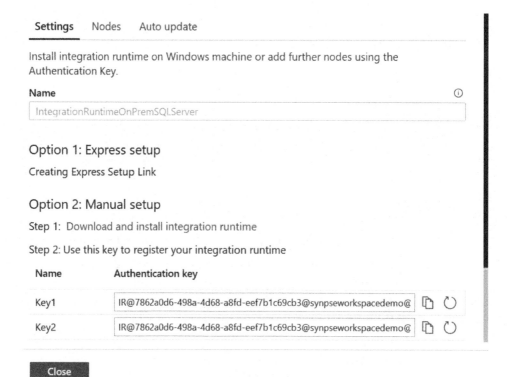

Figure 3.8 – A screenshot showing the options to set up the integration runtime

16. Click on the **Download and install integration runtime** link provided in option 2. This link will take you to a new URL to download the integration runtime.

17. After downloading the file, double-click on the file to start the installation wizard on your server. Follow the instructions on the wizard to complete the setup:

Figure 3.9 – A screenshot of Microsoft Integration Runtime Setup Wizard

18. This setup process will take a couple of minutes before your integration runtime setup is complete. After that, you can copy **Key1** and **Key2**, as shown in *Figure 3.8*, and paste them in the integration runtime window to complete the setup.

> **Important note**
> If you are following these instructions on a different machine from your source server, you need to install the integration runtime on your source machine and follow the further instructions.

In the following screenshot, an integration runtime can be seen running on a local machine where we have pasted **Key1**, copied from the Synapse pipeline:

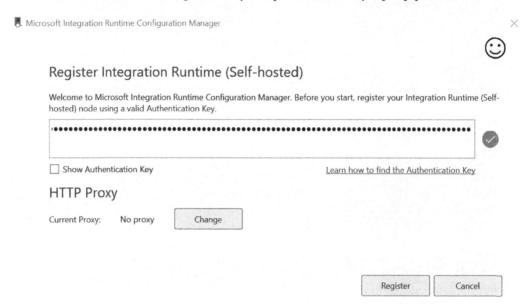

Figure 3.10 – A screenshot of Microsoft Integration Runtime Configuration Manager

19. Now, you can return to **Copy Data tool** to provide connection details for your on-premises SQL Server. Fill in the information for **Server name**, **Database name**, and credentials to access the database and then click on **Create**:

Edit linked service (SQL Server)

(Connection string)   (Azure Key Vault)

Server name *

[███████████████]

Database name *

[AdventureWorksDW2019]

Authentication type

[Windows authentication   ∨]

User name *

[████████████████]

(Password)   (Azure Key Vault)

Password *

[   ]

Additional connection properties

＋ New

Apply   ⌀ Test connection   [Cancel]

Figure 3.11 – Server details to create a linked service

20. Click on **Next** to go to the next screen.

21. Select a table/view to copy the data from the dropdown or you can use your custom query and click on **Next**:

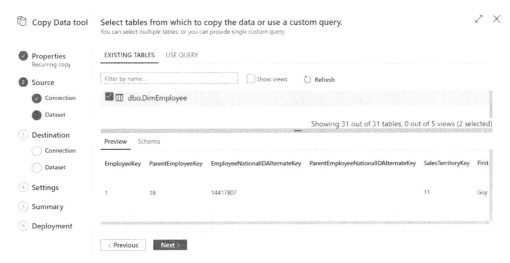

Figure 3.12 – A screenshot of dataset windows for selecting a table

22. On the next screen, you get the option to add a filter to your dataset, but we will skip this step and move to the next step to define the connection for the target:

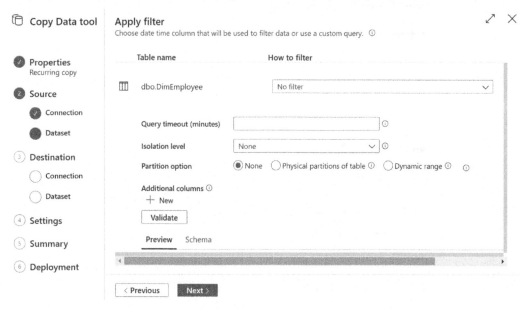

Figure 3.13 – Options to apply a filter to your data source

23. Now, you need to create linked services for the target. Search for *Synapse* in the search bar, select **Synapse Analytics** from the results, and then click on **Next**.

> **Important note**
>
> Make sure that you already have a SQL pool created in Azure Synapse and that you have the table schema already created in that pool before you proceed to the following step. You can go through *Chapter 2, Considerations for Your Compute Environment*, to learn how to create a SQL pool.

24. Provide the SQL pool details of your version of Azure Synapse, along with the server name, database name, username, and password. After filling in the details, click on **Create**, as seen in *Figure 3.14*:

> **Important note**
> You can use **Azure Key Vault** to provide a password instead of entering the password directly here. Instead of using SQL authentication, you have two more options available: – **Managed Identity** and **Service Principal**. You can choose either of these options as per your business requirements.

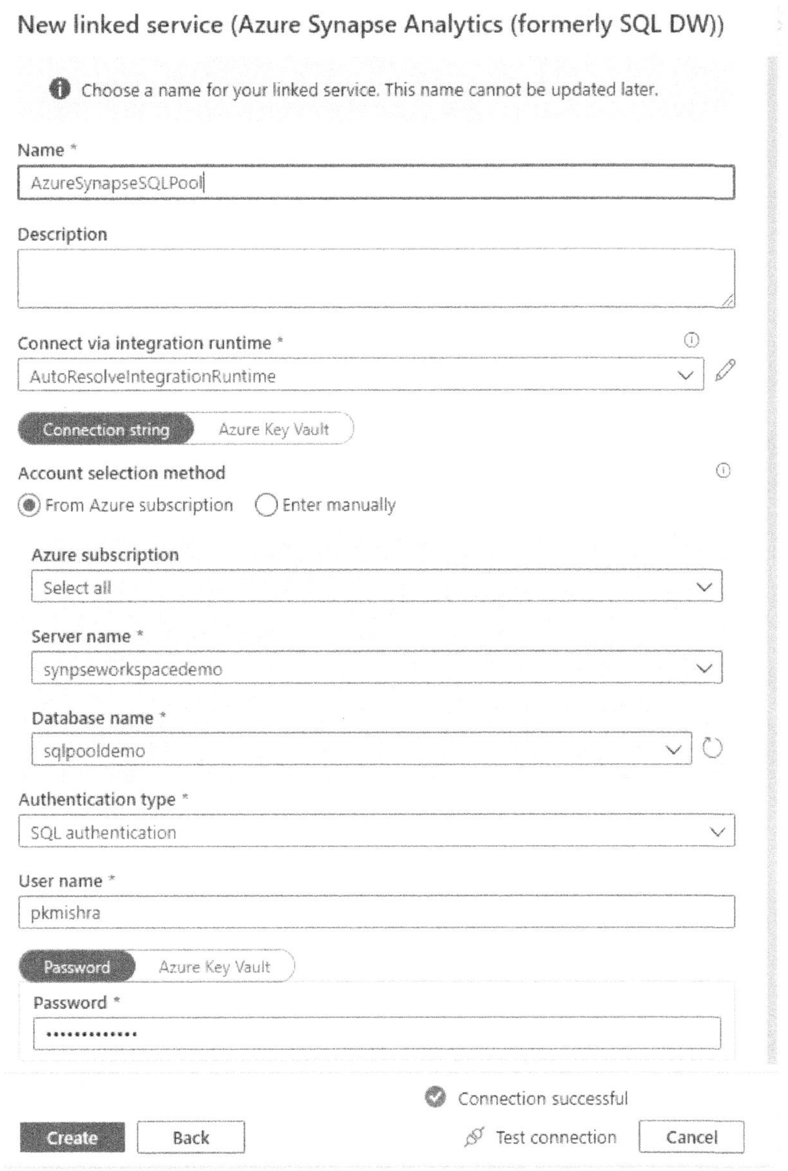

New linked service (Azure Synapse Analytics (formerly SQL DW))

ⓘ Choose a name for your linked service. This name cannot be updated later.

Name *

AzureSynapseSQLPool

Description

Connect via integration runtime *

AutoResolveIntegrationRuntime

(**Connection string**   Azure Key Vault)

Account selection method

◉ From Azure subscription   ◯ Enter manually

Azure subscription

Select all

Server name *

synpseworkspacedemo

Database name *

sqlpooldemo

Authentication type *

SQL authentication

User name *

pkmishra

(**Password**   Azure Key Vault)

Password *

••••••••••••

✓ Connection successful

Create   Back   ✏ Test connection   Cancel

Figure 3.14 – A screenshot of creating a linked service for AzureSynapseSQLPool

25. Click on **Next** to define a table mapping between the source and target. If you do not have a table available on your target, you can click on the **Auto-create a destination table with the source schema** link and then click on **Next** for column mapping:

Figure 3.15 – Screen to define a table mapping between the source and target

26. Map all the columns from the source to the columns available at the destination. If you have the same schema in both the source and destination, you will see that the column mappings populate automatically.

27. You can add type conversion settings and sink properties if your business demands this. We will leave these fields without making any changes. However, we will talk about these settings in our next chapter *Chapter 4, Using Synapse Pipelines to Orchestrate Your Data*. After filling in all the required details, click on **Next**:

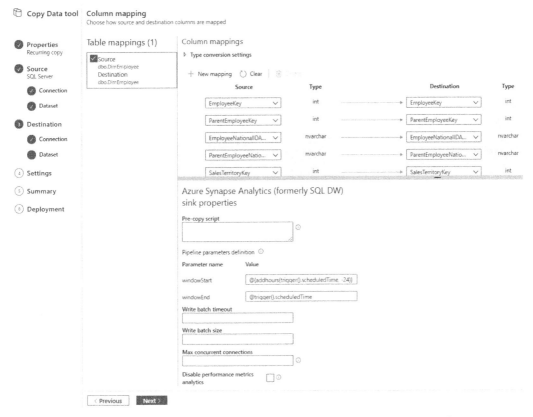

Figure 3.16 – Defining column mappings and other settings for the destination dataset

28. Click on the **Bulk insert** radio button under **Performance settings**, leave the other fields as their default values, and then click on **Next** to go to the **Summary** page. We will talk about other performance settings in detail in future chapters:

Settings
More options for data movement

Data consistency verification ☐ ⓘ

Fault tolerance   [∨] ⓘ

▲ Performance settings

Enable staging   ☐ ⓘ

▲ Advanced settings

Copy method   ○ PolyBase ⓘ   ○ Copy command (Preview) ⓘ   ◉ Bulk insert

Data integration unit   [Auto   ∨] ⓘ
                        ☐ Edit
                        You will be charged # **of used DIUs** * **copy duration** * **$0.25/DIU-hour.** Local currency and separate discounting may apply per subscription type.
                        Learn more

Degree of copy parallelism [   ] ⓘ
                        ☑ Edit

Figure 3.17 – Settings screen to select the Copy method

29. Review all the details on the **Summary** page and then click on **Next** to deploy your pipeline. In a couple of minutes, your pipeline will be created, and you will be ready to run the pipeline to bring your data to Synapse.

Although there is not much difference between **Synapse** pipelines and **Data Factory** pipelines, it is still worth taking a peek at that option, too.

Using Azure Data Factory to import data

Data Factory pipelines and **Synapse** pipelines have almost identical features. The only major difference lies in how you create your pipeline: you need to spin up another resource in Azure if you want to use Data Factory for data ingestion, whereas you can create pipelines within Synapse directly without leaving your Synapse workspace.

As we have already covered **Copy Data tool** in Synapse, which is exactly like **Copy Data tool** in **Data Factory**, in this section, we will create a pipeline to bring the data to Synapse. Make sure you have already satisfied all the prerequisites mentioned in the *Technical requirements* section:

1. Log in to the Azure portal, at https://portal.azure.com.

2. Click on **Create a resource** on the Azure home page and search for **Data Factory** in the **Search Marketplace** bar.

3. Select **Data Factory** from the search results and then click on **Create**.

4. Select the subscription and resource group where you want to create your **Data Factory**.

5. Select a region for your Data Factory instance, provide an appropriate name for the instance, and then select **V2** for **Version**:

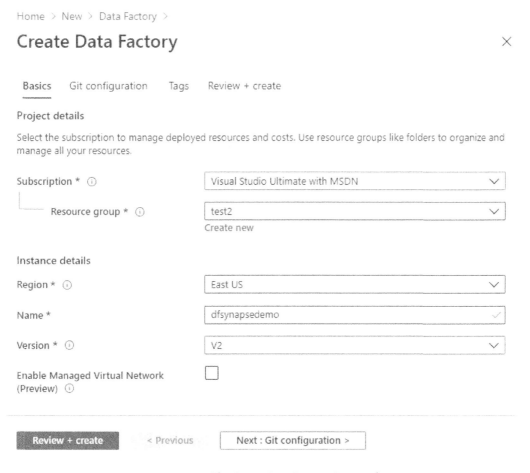

Figure 3.18 – The Create Data Factory Basics tab

6. Next, you can provide details regarding your Git configuration. However, let's skip this part for this example. Click on the checkbox for **Configure Git later** under the **Git configuration** tab.

7. So, click on **Review + create** to review the details and then click on **Create**. This will take couple of seconds while your Data Factory instance is created:

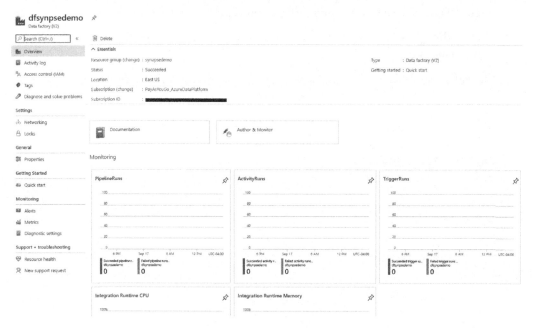

Figure 3.19 – A screenshot of a Data Factory instance on the Azure portal

8. Click on **Author + Monitor**. This will take you to a new window that looks like Synapse Studio.

9. Now, click on the **Create pipeline** link to create factory resources and activities:

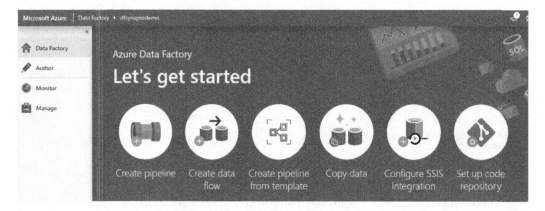

Figure 3.20 – A screenshot of Azure Data Factory

10. Provide an appropriate name for the pipeline under the **Properties** tab appearing on the right-hand side of the window.

11. Expand the **Move & transform** toggle under the **Activities** section and drag the **Copy data** activity to the canvas.

12. Click on the **Copy data** activity on your canvas and go to the **General** tab right below the canvas. Change the name to *CopyActivityDataLakeToSynapseSQL*. You can leave the other values as their default settings for now under the **General** tab:

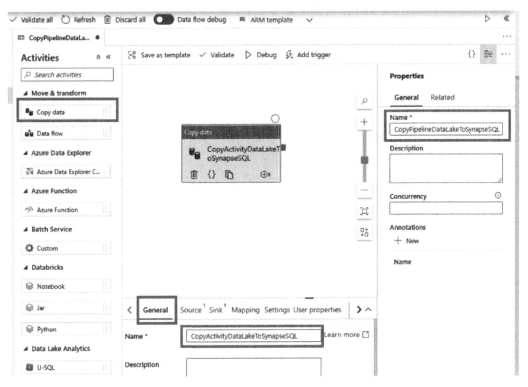

Figure 3.21 – Pipeline for copying data from Azure Storage Data Lake Gen2 to Synapse SQL

13. Click on the **Source** tab next to **General** and select the source dataset if you already have one. Otherwise, click on **+New** to create a new linked service for your source dataset. Do not forget to click on **Publish All** to save your changes.

14. Select **Azure Data Lake Storage Gen2** from the list of available data stores under the **New dataset** pane and then click on **Continue**.

15. You can see multiple options to **select a format** for your data source. We are going to select **Parquet** for this example. **Parquet** is an open source columnar storage format of the Apache Hadoop ecosystem. Click on **Continue** after selecting the format as per your requirements:

Select format

Choose the format type of your data

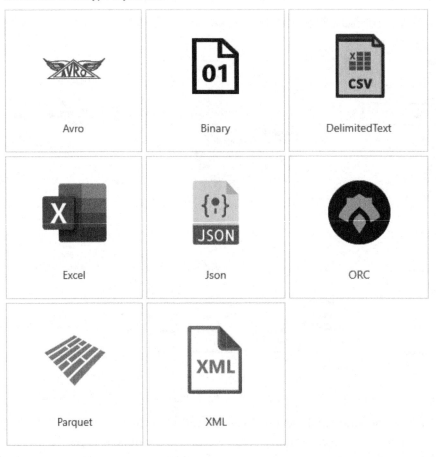

Figure 3.22 – Options to select the format for the file available on Azure Date Lake Storage Gen2

16. Provide an appropriate name for your dataset and select the linked service from the dropdown if you have already created it, otherwise create a new linked service by clicking on +**New**, which appears in the linked services drop-down list:

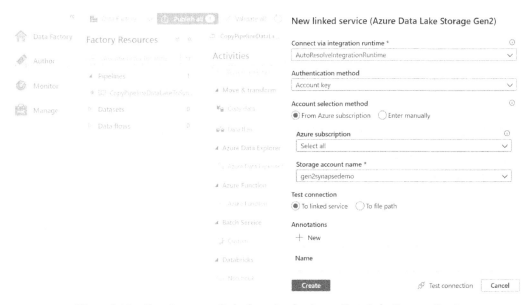

Figure 3.23 – Creating a new linked service for Azure Data Lake Storage Gen2

17. Select the storage account from the dropdown. However, if your storage account is not in the same subscription as your data factory, select the **Enter manually** radio button to enter the details manually for the storage account.

After filling in the details, click on **Create**.

18. On the next screen, define the file path either by entering the directory and filename manually, or by clicking on the folder to select your file. In this example, select the **demoparquetfiles** container. Click on **OK** after defining the file path:

Set properties

Name

| SrcParquetFiles |

Linked service *

| SrcAzureDataLakeStorageSynapseDemo |

File path

| File System | / | Directory | / | File |

Import schema

⦿ From connection/store   ◯ From sample file   ◯ None

▷ Advanced

Figure 3.24 – Defining the file path for the data source

19. When you return to the Data Factory canvas, make sure that the **Recursively** checkbox under the **Source** tab is checked if you want to copy the data from all the files available on the selected file path. However, you can uncheck this box if you want to copy data from just one file:

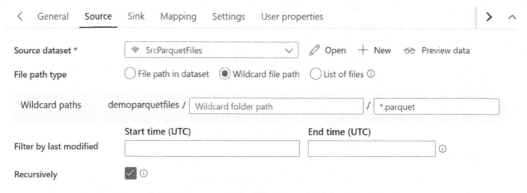

Figure 3.25 – A screenshot of the Source tab in Data Factory

20. After coming back to the Data Factory canvas, select **Wildcard file path** for **File path type**.

21. Now that you have defined the source in your pipeline, it's time to define **Sink**. Click on the **Sink** tab next to **Source**.

22. Click on **+New** to create the sink dataset. Select **Azure Synapse Analytics** from the list of all available data stores in the **New dataset** window and then click on **Continue**.

23. Click on **+New** from the drop-down list for **Linked service**.

24. Provide an appropriate name for your destination linked service, and then select the **Server name** and **Database name** values from the dropdown if **Synapse SQL** is in the same subscription. Otherwise, you can enter these details manually by selecting the **Enter manually** radio button.

25. Provide a username and password to access the server and then click on **Create**.

26. Select a **table name** from the dropdown and then click on **OK**:

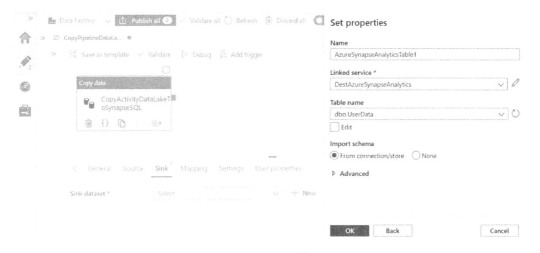

Figure 3.26 – Selecting a table name in the Azure Synapse SQL pool

27. Make sure you have selected **Bulk insert** for **Copy method** in the **Sink** tab. Instead of using the **Bulk insert** option, we can also use **PolyBase**. If the data is stored in Azure Blob storage or Azure Data Lake Storage, we can access this data directly using PolyBase technology via the T-SQL language:

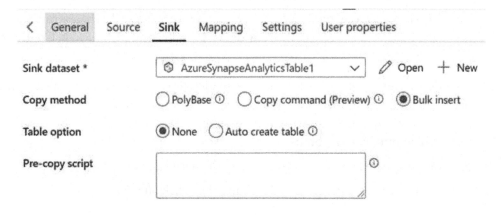

Figure 3.27 – Sink tab in the Data Factory pipeline

28. Now your pipeline is created and ready to run, click on **Add trigger** and then select the **Trigger now** option to run the pipeline to ingest the records to the Synapse SQL pool:

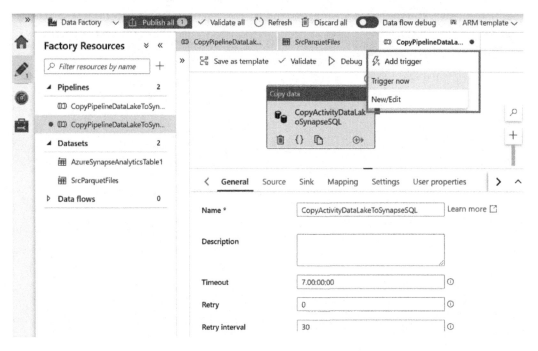

Figure 3.28 – Triggering the option to run the pipeline

You can run the following SQL query to view the results in **Synapse Studio**. Make sure you are connected to the correct server and database while running this query in Synapse Studio:

```
SELECT * FROM dbo.UserData
```

This should produce the following result:

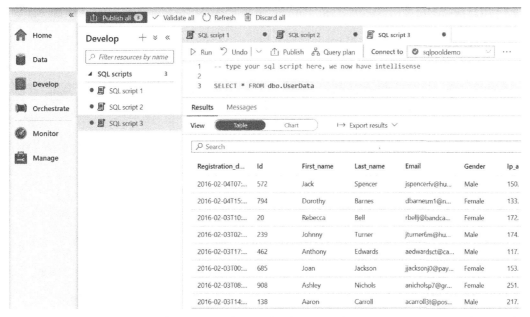

Figure 3.29 – A screenshot showing the results of the preceding query in Synapse Studio

Data Factory and Synapse pipelines are both Azure services where you do not require any tool on your local machine or server. However, you also have the option to use an SSIS tool for bringing data to Azure Synapse. You get integration services along with the SQL Server license, so, if you already have a SQL Server license, you are all set to create an integration services project in **Visual Studio** for your ETL operation.

Using SQL Server Integration Services to import data

SSIS is an **ETL** tool that is used for data ingestion and orchestration purposes. This tool comes with the SQL Server license, so, if you already have a **SQL Server** license, you may want to use SSIS as your ETL tool instead of spending money on any other ETL services. However, it is important to understand the pros and cons of using the SSIS package instead of using an Azure PaaS service such as **Data Factory**.

So far, we have covered **Synapse** pipelines and **Data Factory**, and now it's time to learn how to bring data to Azure Synapse using SQL Server Integration Services. Follow these steps to create your SSIS package in **Visual Studio**:

1. Launch **Visual Studio** and create a new **Integration Services project** in Visual Studio.

2. Enter the project name and provide a file location for saving SSIS packages.

3. Add **Data Flow Task** from the SSIS Toolbox to the canvas.

4. Go to the **Connection Managers** window and right-click to select **New OLE DB Connection...**:

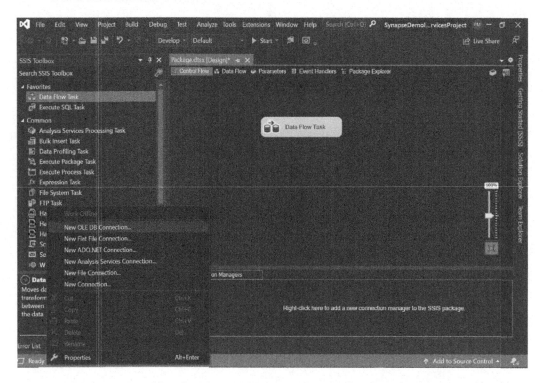

Figure 3.30 – Creating a new connection in Connection Managers of the integration services project

5. Click on **New** in the **Configure OLE DB Connection Manager** window.

6. Provide the server name of your source dataset and enter your credentials (**Username** and **Password**) to access the server.

7. Select or enter a database name in the respective field.

8. Click on **Test Connection** before clicking on **OK**:

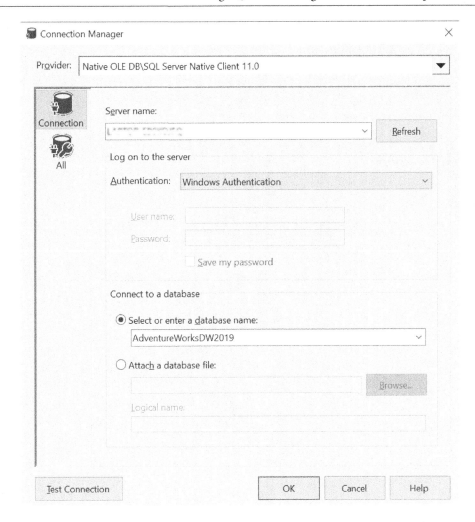

Figure 3.31 – Creating a connection for SQL Server using OLE DB Connection Manager

9. Similarly, now we will create a new connection for a **Synapse SQL pool**. Right-click on the **Connection Managers** window and select **New OLE DB Connection...** once again.

10. Click on **New** in the **Configure OLE DB Connection Manager** window.

11. Enter the server name of your **Synapse SQL pool**. You can find server information in the **Azure portal**.

Go to your Synapse workspace overview page in the Azure portal, copy the **SQL endpoint** field, and then paste it into the **Server name** field in **OLE DB Connection Manager** in the integration services project.

12. Enter your credentials to access the Synapse workspace and then click on **OK** after clicking on **Test Connection**:

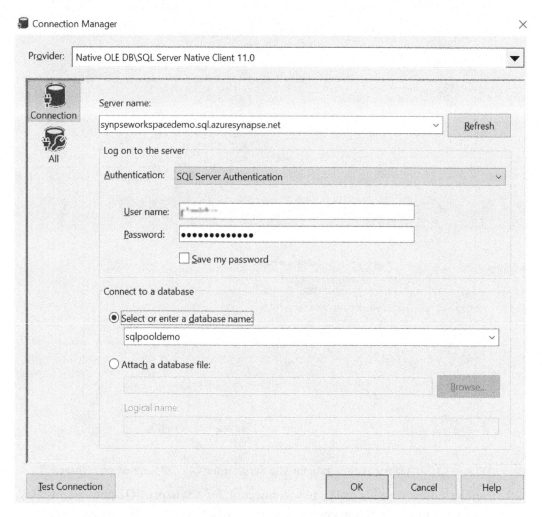

Figure 3.32 – Creating a connection for the Synapse SQL pool using OLE DB Connection Manager

13. Double-click on **Data Flow Task** on the canvas to go to the **Data flow** tab.

14. Drag **OLE DB Source** from the SSIS Toolbox to the canvas and double-click on it to open the **OLE DB Source Editor** window:

15. Select the OLE DB connection manager from the dropdown for your source and provide the name of the table or the view. In this example, we are trying to copy data from the *dbo.DimEmployee* table:

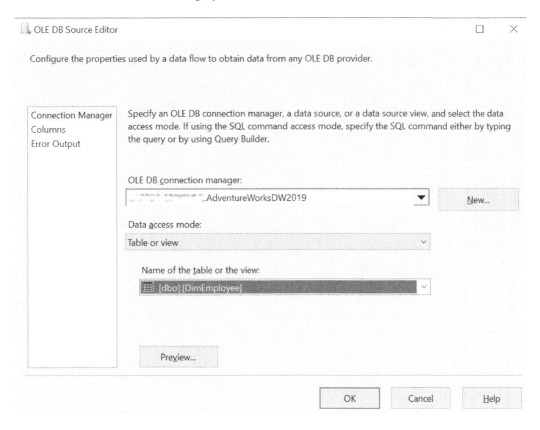

Figure 3.33 – OLE DB Source Editor to select the source table/view from the SQL server

16. Click on **Preview...** to validate the data and then click on **Columns** to check whether all the required columns are available in the source. Next, click on **OK** to save the changes:

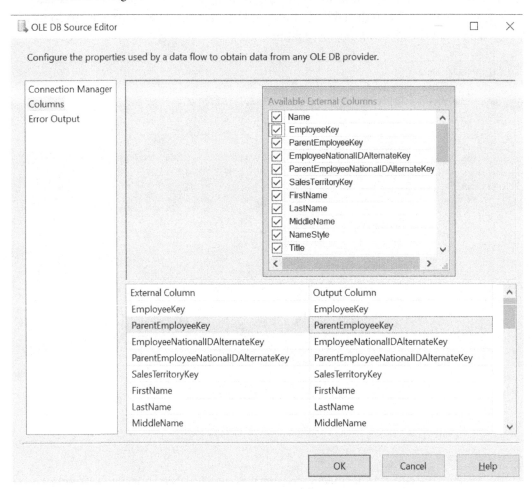

Figure 3.34 – A screenshot of OLE DB Source Editor displaying columns from the source table

17. Drag **OLE DB Destination** from the SSIS Toolbox to the canvas and join the precedence constraint from **OLE DB Source** to **OLE DB Destination**:

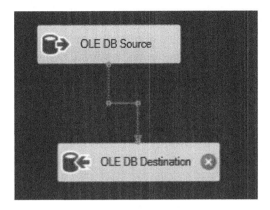

Figure 3.35 – Precedence constraint connecting the destination and source

18. Double-click on **OLE DB Destination** to open the **Editor** dialog box.

19. Select the appropriate OLE DB connection manager for the Synapse SLQ pool from the dropdown and select the target table name.

   In this example, I want to keep the identity and don't want to check the constraints. However, this will not be the case in most practical scenarios:

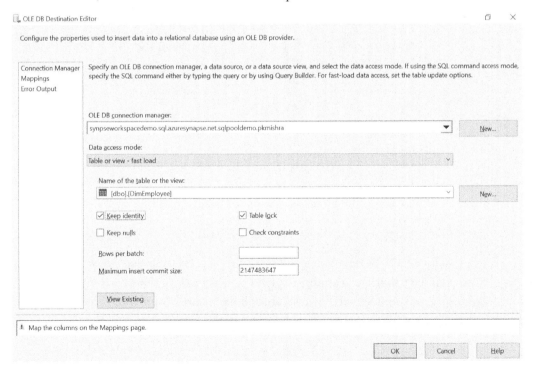

Figure 3.36 – OLE DB Destination Editor for selecting a target table from the Synapse SQL pool

20. Next, click on **Mappings** on the left-hand side of the dialog box to map the columns. You can change the column mapping by changing the column name from the **Input Column** drop-down list for that column. After defining the mappings, click on **OK** to save your changes and return to the canvas:

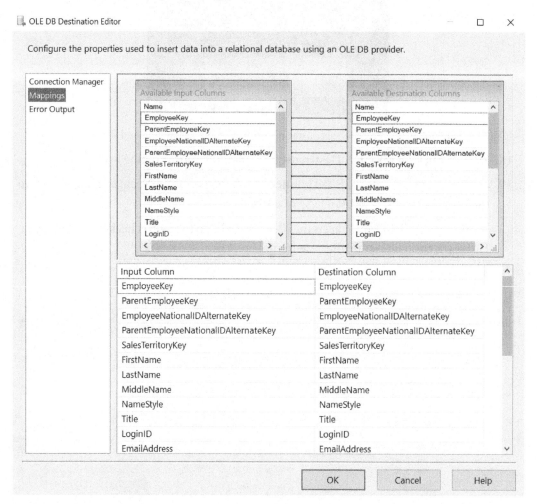

Figure 3.37 – Column Mappings page under OLE DB Destination Editor

Now, your SSIS package is almost ready to be executed. Before you initiate execution, make sure you have truncated all the records from your target table because we used the same table as the target in the previous example.

21. Run the following command in **Synapse Studio**, and make sure your SQL script notebook is connected to the correct database:

```
TRUNCATE TABLE dbo.DimEmployee
```

22. Go back to your SSIS package, right-click on **Package.dtsx** in **Solution Explorer**, and then click on **Execute Package**:

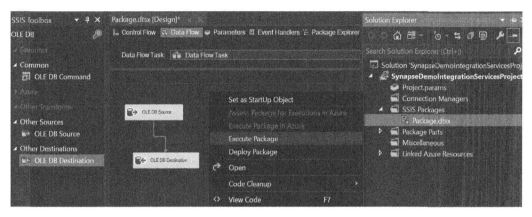

Figure 3.38 – A screenshot of an SSIS package with the Solution Explorer window displaying the Execute Package link

You can view the results in Synapse Studio once the package has completed execution by running the following query:

```
SELECT * FROM dbo.DimEmployee
```

So far, we have seen various tools that can be used for bringing the data from various sources to Azure Synapse. However, you can bring the data just by executing a COPY statement in Synapse SQL.

Using a COPY statement to import data

There are various ways in which to bring data from various sources to Azure Synapse SQL. However, it is recommended that you use a **COPY** statement if your data is residing in an Azure Storage account. The best part of following this technique is that you can copy the data just by running a single T-SQL statement. The syntax for the COPY statement is very simple, with a set of arguments to choose from. You can decide which argument you want to use with your COPY statement.

The following is the syntax that can be customized as per your business requirements to bring the data from an external source to the Azure Synapse SQL pool:

```
COPY INTO [schema.]table_name
[(Column_list)]
FROM '<external_location>' [,...n]
WITH
(
  [FILE_TYPE = {'CSV' | 'PARQUET' | 'ORC'} ]
  [,FILE_FORMAT = EXTERNAL FILE FORMAT OBJECT ]
  [,CREDENTIAL = (AZURE CREDENTIAL) ]
  [,ERRORFILE = '[http(s)://storageaccount/container]/errorfile_
directory[/]]'
  [,ERRORFILE_CREDENTIAL = (AZURE CREDENTIAL) ]
  [,MAXERRORS = max_errors ]
  [,COMPRESSION = { 'Gzip' | 'DefaultCodec'| 'Snappy'}]
  [,FIELDQUOTE = 'string_delimiter']
  [,FIELDTERMINATOR =  'field_terminator']
  [,ROWTERMINATOR = 'row_terminator']
  [,FIRSTROW = first_row]
  [,DATEFORMAT = 'date_format']
  [,ENCODING = {'UTF8'|'UTF16'}]
  [,IDENTITY_INSERT = {'ON' | 'OFF'}]
)
```

The simplest use of this statement would be copying data from public storage without defining any arguments.

Loading data from a public storage account

Run the following script to copy the data from an Azure Blob storage account to a dbo.Trip table in a Synapse SQL pool:

```
COPY INTO [dbo].[UserData] FROM 'https://gen2synapsedemo.blob.
core.windows.net/democsvfiles/*.csv'
WITH (
    FILE_TYPE = 'CSV'
 )
```

A public storage account can be accessed by anyone from anywhere if you are connected to the public internet, but if your storage account is private, then you need access keys to read the data from these storage accounts. We are going to learn about this in the following section.

Loading data from a private storage account using an SAS token

In order to access the data from a private storage account, we need to have a **Shared Access Signature** (**SAS**) token. Perform the following steps to generate an SAS token for your storage account:

1.   Go to your storage account on the Azure portal.

2.   Click on the **Shared access signature** link seen in the following screenshot:

Figure 3.39 – Generating an SAS for the storage account

3.   Select **Allowed services**, **Allowed resource types**, and **Allowed permissions** setting values. This selection will define the level of access to specific services on the storage account.

4. Select the start and expiry date/time for this key.

5. Leave the default values for the other fields and click on **Generate SAS and connection string** to generate the keys, and copy the SAS token somewhere because we are going to need it in this section; once you come out of this screen, you will not be able to see these keys anymore:

Figure 3.40 – Copying an SAS token for the storage account

6. Run the following SQL script, along with all the applicable options best suited for your business needs, to copy the data from Data Lake Gen2 to an Azure Synapse SQL pool:

```
COPY INTO TestTable (Col1 default 'myStringDefault' 1,
Col2 default 1 3)
FROM 'https://synapsedemoaccount.blob.core.windows.net/
myblobcontainer/folder1/'
WITH (
    FILE_TYPE = 'CSV',
    CREDENTIAL=(IDENTITY= 'Shared Access Signature',
SECRET='<Your_SAS_Token>'),
    FIELDQUOTE = '"',
    FIELDTERMINATOR=';',
    ROWTERMINATOR='0X0A',
```

```
    ENCODING = 'UTF8',
    DATEFORMAT = 'ymd',
    MAXERRORS = 10,
    ERRORFILE = '/errorsfolder',--path starting from the
storage container
    IDENTITY_INSERT = 'ON'
)
```

The code block mentions different properties. Let's try to understand these different properties in the following bullets:

- FILE_TYPE: This attribute specifies the external data format, and it supports three file types, namely, CSV, Parquet, or the **Optimizer Row Columnar (ORC)** format.

- CREDENTIAL: This attribute defines the authentication mechanism to access the external storage account.

- FIELDQUOTE: This attribute is only applicable to CSV files and defines the quote character (string delimiter) in the CSV files.

- FIELDTERMINATOR: Again, this is only applicable to CSV files. It specifies the field terminator being used in CSV files.

- ROWTERMINATOR: This attribute also only applies to CSV files and it specifies the row terminator that has been used in the CSV files.

- ENCODING: The default value for this attribute is UTF8, but you can change it to UTF16. This specifies the data encoding standard for the files.

- DATEFORMAT: This specifies the date format for the date column. Permitted values for this attribute are mdy, dmy, ymd, ydm, myd, and dym, where d stands for *date*, m stands for *month*, and y stands for *year*.

- MAXERRORS: This specifies the maximum number of rejected rows allowed during the load.

- ERRORFILE: This attribute is only applicable to CSV files and it is used to specify the directory where the rejected rows and corresponding error files need to be written.

- IDENTITY_INSERT: If you want to use identity values in the imported data files as an identity column, mark this attribute as ON, otherwise you need to specify the OFF value for this attribute.

You are free to use Azure Blob storage and Azure Data Lake Gen2 as well as an external source, but you need to be aware of the authentication mechanisms supported for different file types in both varieties of storage.

Using authentication mechanisms

There are primarily five types of authentication mechanisms that are supported by Azure Synapse Analytics:

- **Shared Access Signature**: An SAS is a URI that allows you to specify the permissions allowed for a storage account or the blob container. You can also specify the life span of this key.

- **Access Keys**: This is similar to a basic authentication method, using your storage account name and a key. Storage accounts come with a primary and secondary key. These keys can be regenerated as you wish.

- **Service Principal**: This is an identity explicitly created in a tenant's **Azure Active Directory** (**AD**). This identity can be applied to roles and access restrictions.

- **Managed Service Identity**: This is an identity that Azure creates for Azure services. The user does not have the overhead of generating or rotating keys in this case. If a service supports AD authentication, this identity can be used to authenticate.

- **Azure Active Directory**: A user within an Azure AD can authenticate themselves wherever AD authentication is supported.

Each storage type has its own authentication mechanisms. The following diagram describes the authentication mechanism supported by different types of files on Azure Blob storage and Azure Data Lake Gen2:

Storage	File Type	Shared Access Signature	Managed Service Identity	Service Principal	Access Keys	Azure Active Directory
Azure Blob Storage	CSV	•	•	•	•	•
	ORS	•			•	
	PARQUET	•			•	
Azure Data Lake Gen2	CSV	•	•	•		•
	ORS	•	•	•	•	•
	PARQUET	•	•	•	•	•

Figure 3.41 – Authentication mechanism supported by different types of files on different storage types

Now that we've covered authentication statements, let's recap the rest of the chapter.

Summary

In this chapter, we covered various ways to bring your data to Azure Synapse. We will be using these techniques further in upcoming chapters as per your requirements. You are the best person to decide which tool will be the best fit for your business, but it is important to have an understanding of all of these tools before you bet on any of these in particular.

In this chapter, we have covered data ingestion without any orchestration. However, in the next chapter you will learn how to orchestrate your data in Azure Synapse by using Synapse pipelines.

4
Using Synapse Pipelines to Orchestrate Your Data

Bringing data to Synapse is definitely a first big step, but it's not the final destination. You still need to cross many hurdles on the way before you start adding any flavor to your data. A Synapse pipeline comprises datasets and activities, but the main advantage is that you can reuse the same dataset with various pipelines. Synapse supports various data stores and provides feasibility to transform your data without writing any code. In this chapter, We will learn how to create Azure Synapse pipelines to orchestrate your data.

In this chapter, we will cover the following topics:

- Introducing Synapse pipelines
- Creating linked services
- Defining source and target datasets

- Using various activities in Synapse pipelines
- Scheduling Synapse pipelines
- Creating pipelines using samples

Technical requirements

Before you start orchestrating your data, certain prerequisites apply, as outlined here:

- You should have an Azure subscription, or access to any other subscription with contributor-level access.
- Create your Synapse workspace on this subscription. You can follow the instructions from *Chapter 1, Introduction to Azure Synapse*, to create your Synapse workspace.
- Create a **Structured Query Language (SQL)** pool and a Spark pool on Azure Synapse. This was covered in *Chapter 2, Considerations for Your Compute Environment*.
- You must have an **Azure Data Lake Storage Gen2** account with two containers, demozipfiles-ch04 and demozipfilestating-ch04, with read/write permissions.
- Download the sample zipped files from http://bit.ly/ch04-prerequisites and extract the ZIP files to get two zipped files, SampleUserData09262020.zip and SampleUserData09272020.zip.
- Upload these two zipped files to the demozipfiles-ch04 container in your Azure Data Lake Storage Gen2 account.
- Create a UserData table in your SQL pool, where your data is going to eventually land.

We will use the following **Transact-SQL (T-SQL)** code to create a UserData table in Synapse SQL:

```
CREATE TABLE UserData (
  UserID INT,
  Name VARCHAR(200),
  EmailID  VARCHAR(200),
  State  VARCHAR(50),
  City VARCHAR(50)
)
```

There are various steps to take before you can create a Synapse pipeline, and the first one is to create linked services for your source and target.

Let's understand what a linked service is and how can we create one in Azure Synapse.

Introducing Synapse pipelines

Synapse pipelines are used to perform **Extract, Transform, and Load** (**ETL**) operations on data. This service is similar to Azure Data Factory, but these pipelines can be created within Synapse Studio itself. In this section, we are going to learn how to create a pipeline for copying data from different sources to Azure Synapse Analytics. We will also see how we can use multiple activities within the same pipeline and create dependency endpoints to connect one activity with another activity in the pipeline.

The following screenshot shows a **Copy data** activity in a Synapse pipeline:

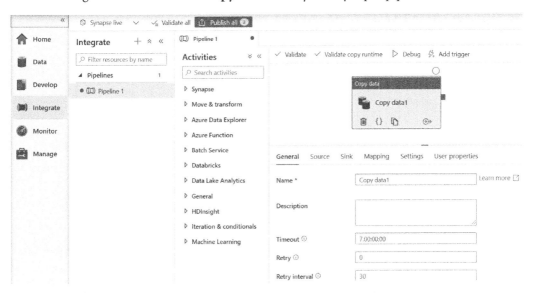

Figure 4.1 – A screenshot of a Synapse pipeline in Synapse Studio

These pipelines comprise various components, and we are going to learn about these components in brief in the following sections.

Integration runtime

An **Integration Runtime** (**IR**) is a compute infrastructure used by **Azure Data Factory** or **Synapse pipelines** to provide data movement, data flow, activity dispatch, and **SQL Server Integration Services** (**SSIS**) package execution capabilities across different network environments. There are two types of IR: **Self-Hosted** and **Azure**, as seen in the following screenshot:

Figure 4.2 – A screenshot of network environment options available to set up an IR

Let's begin with the self-hosted IR, which is used when you need to copy data from any on-premises environment.

Self-hosted IR

A self-hosted IR is used for running data flows, data movement, and pipeline activities in an on-premises or a private network. We need to install an IR on our on-premises environment, either manually or automatically. If we choose **Express setup**, keys will be automatically copied to the IR, and the IR is then ready to be used. However, if you choose the **Manual setup** option, you need to copy the key from the Azure portal to the IR once the installation is completed.

The following screenshot shows the primary and secondary keys required to complete the manual setup of an IR:

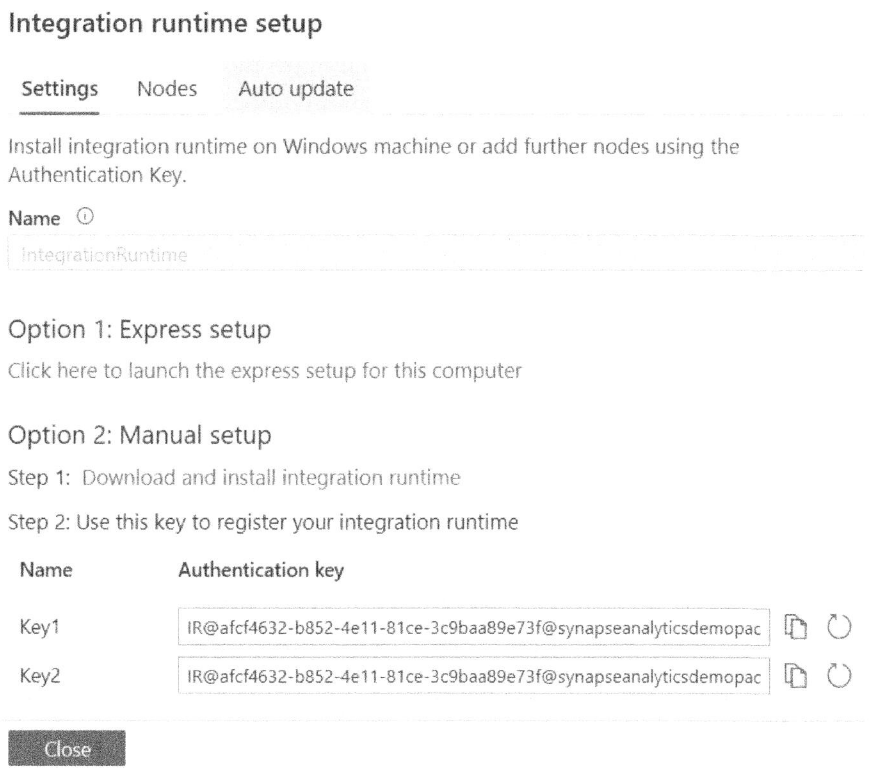

Integration runtime setup

Settings   Nodes   Auto update

Install integration runtime on Windows machine or add further nodes using the Authentication Key.

Name ⓘ

IntegrationRuntime

Option 1: Express setup

Click here to launch the express setup for this computer

Option 2: Manual setup

Step 1: Download and install integration runtime

Step 2: Use this key to register your integration runtime

Name	Authentication key		
Key1	IR@afcf4632-b852-4e11-81ce-3c9baa89e73f@synapseanalyticsdemopac		
Key2	IR@afcf4632-b852-4e11-81ce-3c9baa89e73f@synapseanalyticsdemopac		

Close

Figure 4.3 – Setting up a self-hosted IR on my computer

Now that we have learned how to install a self-hosted IR on our computer, let's try to learn about an Azure IR.

Azure IR

An Azure IR provides a fully managed, serverless compute in Azure and does not require infrastructure provisioning, software installation, patching, and so on. It is used for running data flows, data movement, and pipeline activities in a fully managed, serverless compute in Azure.

The following section provides a brief introduction to activities in a Synapse pipeline.

Activities

Activities are the most critical part of a Synapse pipeline, as they define actions that need to be performed on your data. You can perform a simple copy operation by using a **Copy data** activity on your data, however, you can also use a **Data flow** activity to perform various transformations on your data.

You are provided with options to perform operations by using Databricks notebooks, HDInsight activities, machine learning activities, and much more. You can also perform iterations and conditional operations by adding corresponding activities to your pipeline.

In the following section, we will learn more about using activities within a pipeline.

Pipelines

A Synapse pipeline can be created by using one or more activities, which can all be connected to each other by dependency endpoints. By default, you get a **Success** endpoint, but you can change this to **Failure**, **Completion**, or **Skipped** if required, as you can see in the following screenshot:

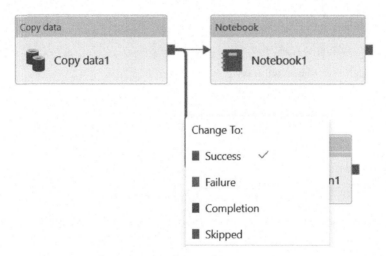

Figure 4.4 – Creating dependency endpoints for two activities in a Synapse pipeline

You can also loop through any activity by moving that activity inside an iteration activity such as the ForEach or Until activities. We will go through an example in the *Using various activities in Synapse pipelines* section, which will help you learn how to use iteration activities with other activities.

Pipelines are scheduled by triggers, and we will learn about these in the following section.

Triggers

Azure Synapse pipelines can be triggered manually (on-demand) as and when required. But practically, we need our pipelines to trigger automatically based on a certain event that has occurred, or based on a certain date/time specified for the trigger to occur. In the following sections, we are going to learn about different types of triggers supported by Synapse pipelines.

Schedule triggers

Schedule triggers are created when we want to run our pipeline by specifying a schedule (start time, recurrence, end date, and so on). This is the default trigger that gets created while setting up a new pipeline. As seen in the following screenshot, we need to provide the details for **Start date**, **Time zone**, and **Recurrence**, and you can also choose to provide a value for **End On** by checking the **Specify an end date** checkbox:

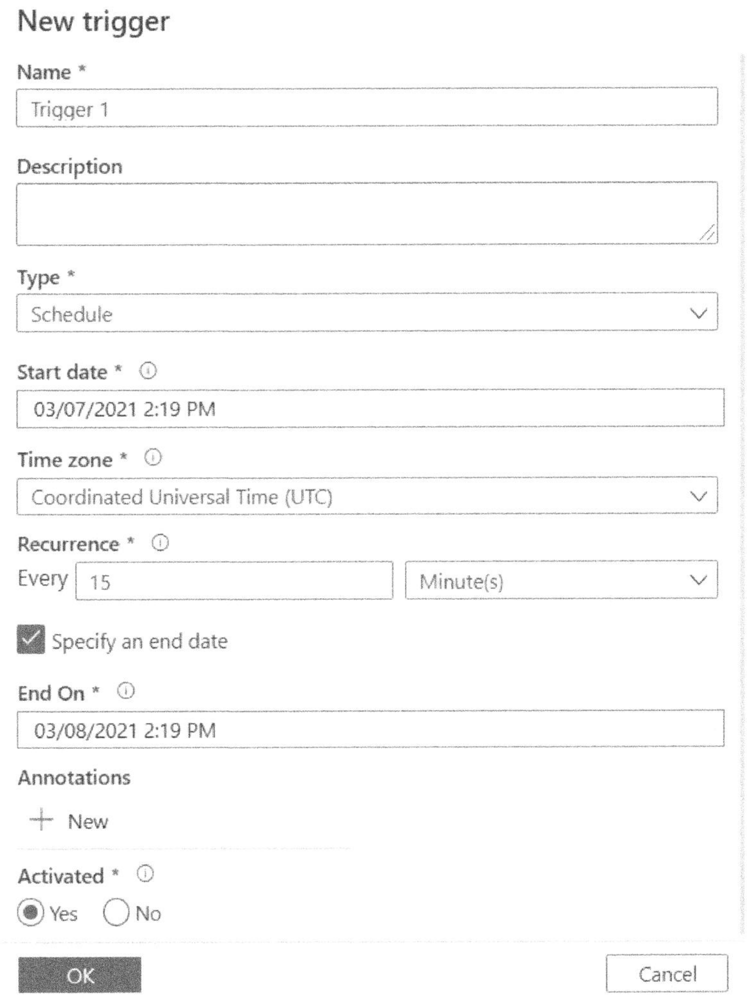

New trigger

Name *

Trigger 1

Description

Type *

Schedule

Start date * ⓘ

03/07/2021 2:19 PM

Time zone * ⓘ

Coordinated Universal Time (UTC)

Recurrence * ⓘ

Every 15   Minute(s)

☑ Specify an end date

End On * ⓘ

03/08/2021 2:19 PM

Annotations

+ New

Activated * ⓘ

⦿ Yes   ◯ No

OK   Cancel

Figure 4.5 – Creating a new schedule trigger for the pipeline

Although this is the most commonly used trigger for Synapse pipelines, we sometimes need to use a tumbling window trigger as well. The following section outlines further details about this particular type of trigger.

Tumbling window triggers

Unlike schedule triggers, tumbling window triggers have a one-to-one relationship with a pipeline. These triggers are fired at periodic time intervals from a specified start time, while retaining their state. Tumbling window triggers are non-overlapping and are triggered at contiguous time intervals. We can also set the dependency of one tumbling window trigger on another trigger.

The following screenshot displays the properties needed to create a tumbling window trigger:

New trigger

Type *

Tumbling window

Start Date (UTC) * ⓘ

03/07/2021 2:19 PM

Recurrence * ⓘ

Every | 15 | Minute(s)

☑ Specify an end date

End On (UTC) * ⓘ

03/08/2021 2:19 PM

◢ Advanced

Add dependencies

+ New | 🗑 Delete

	TRIGGER	OFFSET	WINDOW SIZE
		0.00:00:00	0.00:00:00

Delay ⓘ

00:00:00

Max concurrency * ⓘ

50

Retry policy: count ⓘ

0

OK   Cancel

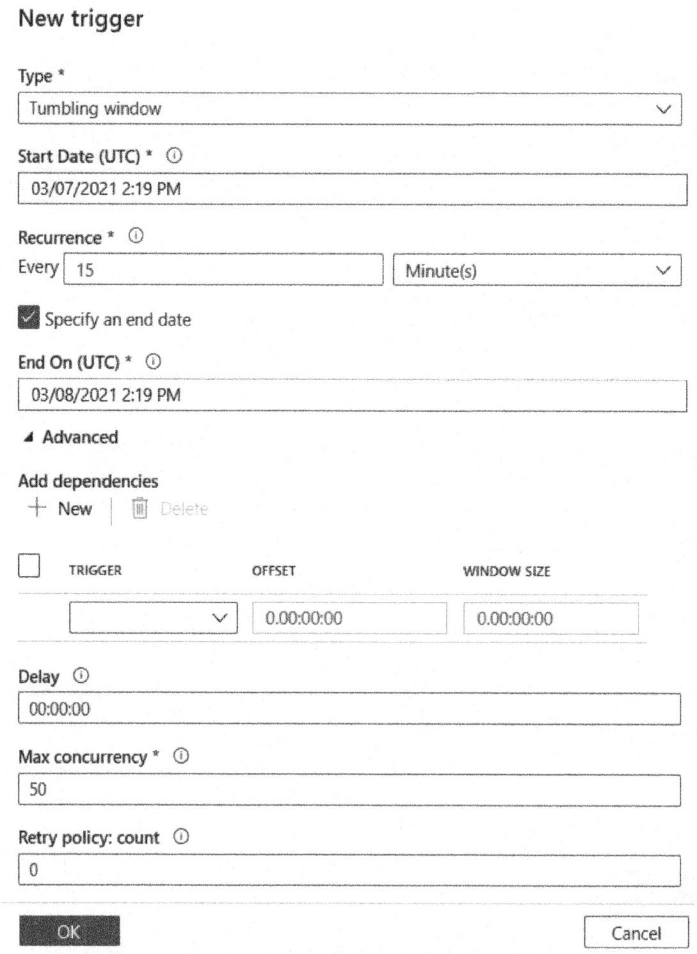

Figure 4.6 – Creating a tumbling window trigger on Synapse Studio

Schedule triggers can only be executed starting from the current time; however, tumbling window triggers can be scheduled for windows in the past.

In the following section, we are going to learn about one more type of trigger: a storage events trigger.

Storage events triggers

Sometimes, we need to trigger pipelines based on events happening in a storage account, such as the addition or deletion of files.

We need to provide details of the storage account and blob container in order to define this trigger type. You are also provided with the option of selecting an event, as seen in the following screenshot:

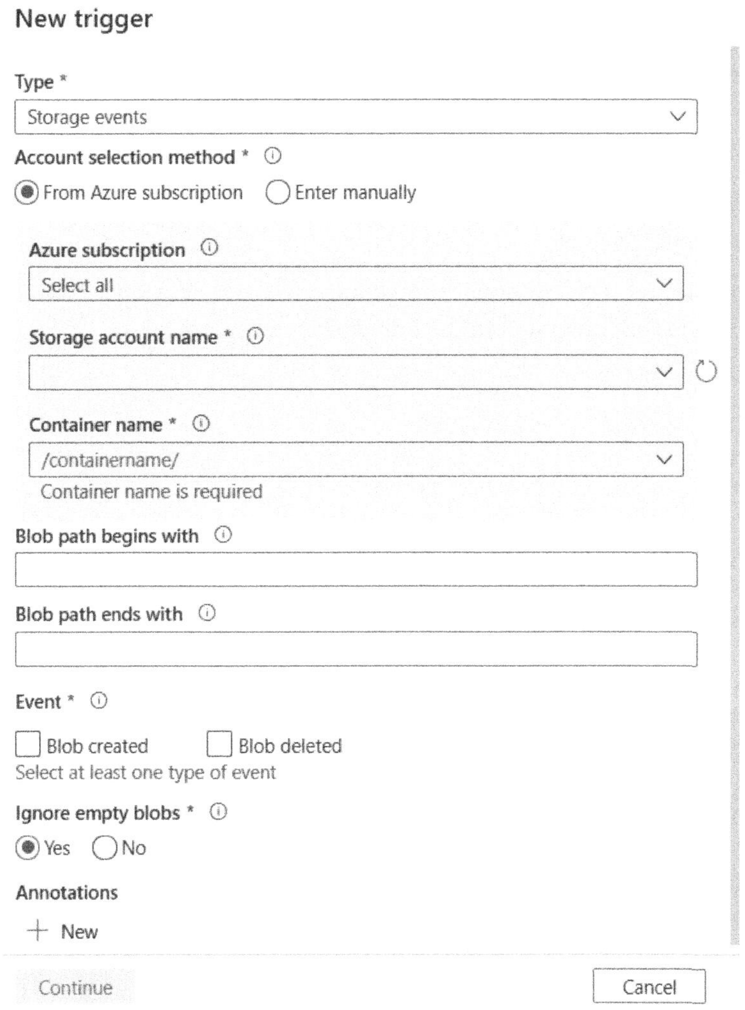

Figure 4.7 – Creating a storage events trigger on Synapse Studio

The following section outlines details about linked services, which are a vital component for Azure Synapse pipelines.

Creating linked services

Linked services define the connection information needed for a Synapse pipeline to connect to an external data source. These linked services are not specific to any pipeline, but you can use the same linked service for multiple pipelines at the same time if they share the same data source.

In this example, we are going to create a linked service for Azure SQL Database (which is our data source), with Synapse as our target.

Before we proceed with the steps to create the linked service for the source and target, make sure you have met all the technical requirements outlined at the start of this chapter. Then, proceed as follows:

1. Launch Synapse Studio by clicking on the **Synapse Studio** link on the **Synapse workspace**.

2. Click on **Linked services** under the **Manage** tab, and click on **+ New** to create a new linked service, as illustrated in the following screenshot:

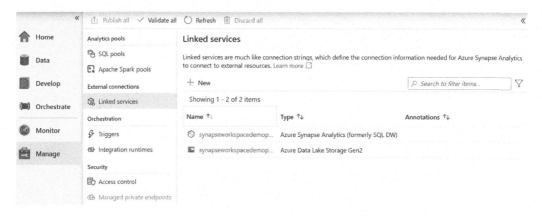

Figure 4.8 – Creating linked services in Azure Synapse

3. Select **Azure Data Lake Storage Gen2** from the list of available data sources and click on **Continue**, as illustrated in the following screenshot:

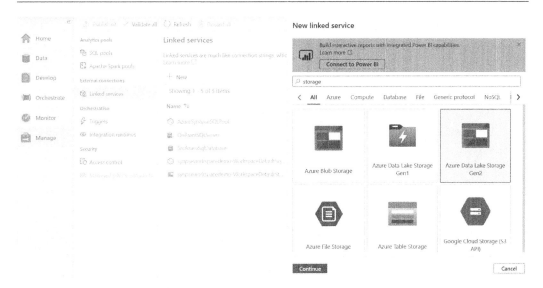

Figure 4.9 – Selecting Azure Data Lake Storage Gen2 to create a new linked service

4. Give a meaningful name to the linked service and add an appropriate **description**.

5. Select your **storage account name** from the dropdown if your storage account is in the same subscription; otherwise, you can click on the **Enter manually** radio button to provide the account details manually and then click on **Create**, as illustrated in the following screenshot:

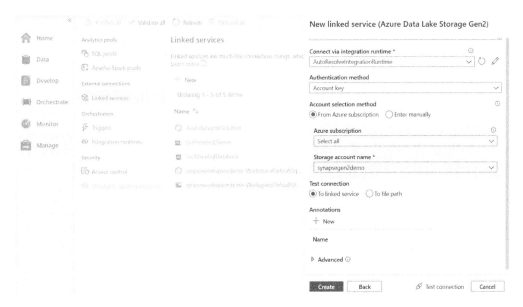

Figure 4.10 – Providing connection details for Azure SQL Database

6. After creating the linked service for the source, we will now create one for the target. Once again, click on the **+ New** link on the **Linked services** page in Synapse Studio.

7. Select **Azure Synapse Analytics** from the list of available data stores, and click on **Continue**.

8. Provide the SQL pool details of your Azure Synapse **server name**, **database name**, **username**, and **password**. Instead of filling in the values directly, we can also use variables, using **dynamic content**. Go to `https://docs.microsoft.com/en-us/azure/data-factory/parameterize-linked-services` to learn more about using parameters in Synapse pipelines. After filling in the details, click on **Create**, as illustrated in the following screenshot:

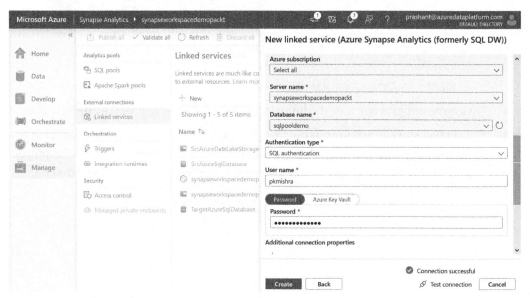

Figure 4.11 – Creating a linked service for Synapse Analytics

In this section, we have covered just a couple of data stores; however, Synapse supports various other ones. If you want to learn how to create a linked service for any data store, you can follow the steps mentioned at this link: `https://docs.microsoft.com/en-us/azure/data-factory/connector-overview`.

Now that you have created a linked service for your source and target, we will next create a pipeline, and we will try to learn how to perform several activities to transform the data.

Defining source and target datasets

Datasets are created in a pipeline in order to identify data stored in various data sources in different formats, such as tables, files, folders, documents, and so on. A dataset can be used by multiple activities or pipelines.

Before we start adding some transformations onto the data, we should have the required datasets in place. So, follow these instructions to create a dataset for the source:

1. Go to the **Data** tab in Synapse Studio and click on + on the **Data** canvas, as highlighted in the following screenshot:

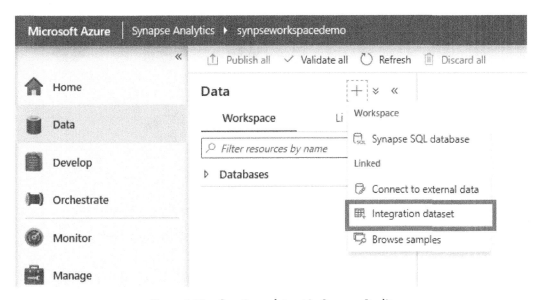

Figure 4.12 – Creating a dataset in Synapse Studio

2. Select **Integration dataset** from the dropdown, and select the required data store from the list of all available data stores appearing in the **Integration dataset** window. In this example, we are going to select **Azure Data Lake Storage Gen2** as our data store, and then click on **Continue**.

3. Select the **DelimitedText** format for your data from the list of all available options and click on **Continue**, as illustrated in the following screenshot:

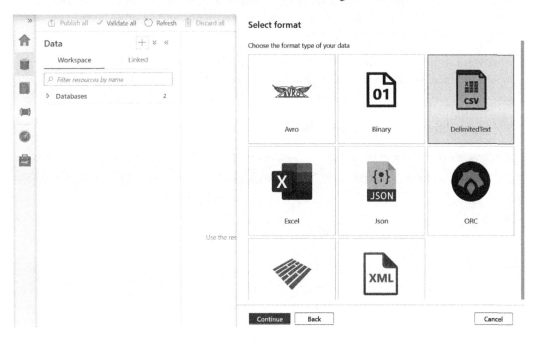

Figure 4.13 – Selecting the format for the dataset

4. Provide an appropriate name for your dataset and select the corresponding **linked service** from the dropdown.

5. Click on the small folder icon appearing right at the end of the **File path** field, select the correct directory in which the file is stored, and click on **OK**, as illustrated in the following screenshot:

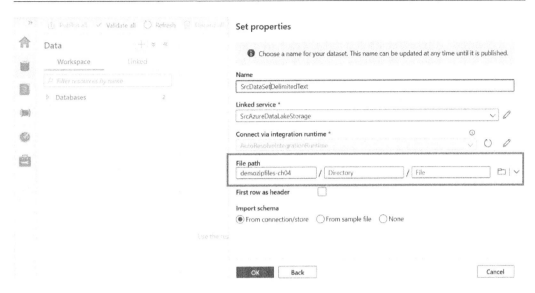

Figure 4.14 – Setting the properties for the source dataset

6. We are not yet done with the source dataset. Remember that our source files are in ZIP format, so let's define an appropriate **compression type** in the dataset properties. Select **ZipDeflate** from the drop-down list appearing from the **Compression type** field and don't forget to click on the **Publish all** link to save all your changes. The process is illustrated in the following screenshot:

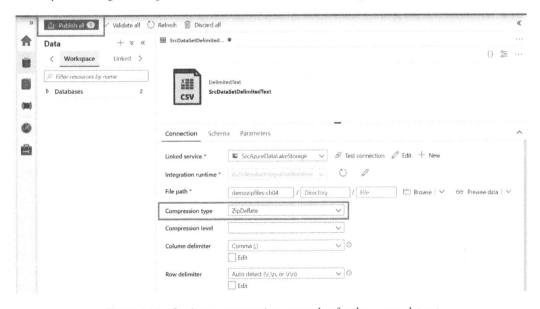

Figure 4.15 – Setting a compression type value for the source dataset

7. Follow *Steps 1* to *6* to create a staging dataset where all the unzipped files should be landing. This is illustrated in the following screenshot:

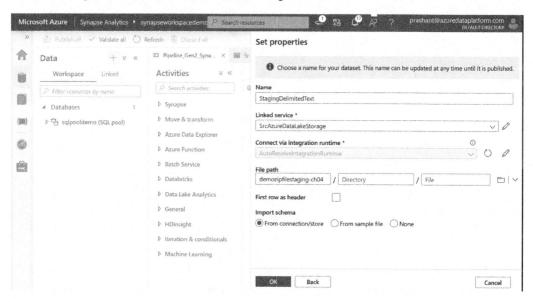

Figure 4.16 – Setting properties for the staging dataset

8. Now that we have already created a dataset for the source, we are going to create a dataset event for the target. Click on the + icon on the **Data** canvas and select **Integration dataset** once again from the drop-down list.

9. We are going to select **Azure Synapse Analytics** as our target, from the list of all available data stores.

10. Select a **linked service** from the dropdown that you already created for the Azure Synapse SQL pool.

11. Select a **table name** for where your data is supposed to land and click on **OK**. The process is illustrated in the following screenshot:

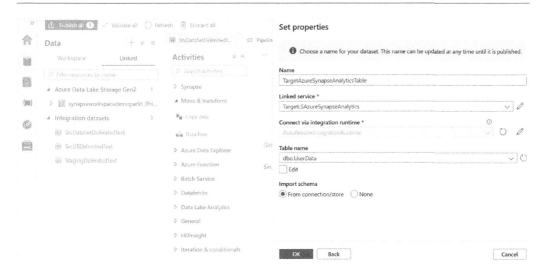

Figure 4.17 – Setting properties for the Azure Synapse SQL pool

After creating the datasets, it's time to create the pipeline and start adding transformations to your source dataset.

Using various activities in Synapse pipelines

Synapse pipelines give you the option to add various transformations; however, we will try to cover just a couple of transformations in this section. Proceed as follows:

1. Navigate to the **Integrate** tab on Synapse Studio and click on + to select **Pipeline** out of the other available options, as illustrated in the following screenshot:

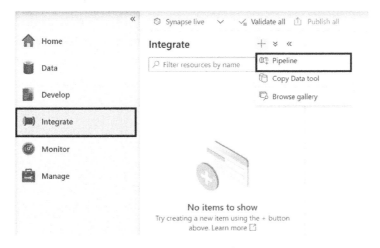

Figure 4.18 – Creating a Synapse pipeline in Synapse Studio

2. Fill in the **name** and **description** in the **Properties** window of the pipeline that you created in the preceding step and click on **Publish all** to save the changes.

3. Let's add some **activities** to the canvas. We are going to select the **Get Metadata** activity from the list of all available activities to begin with, as illustrated in the following screenshot:

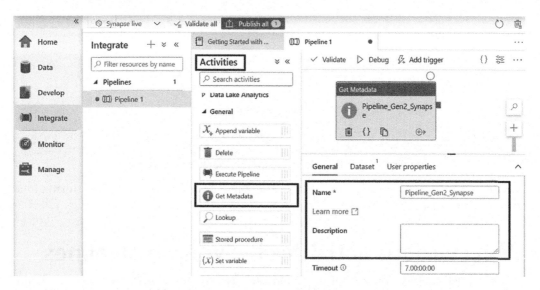

Figure 4.19 – Adding the Get Metadata activity to the Synapse pipeline canvas

4. Provide a **name** for this activity in the **General** tab. We are going to enter `GetMetadataForZipFiles` in the **Name** field so that it will be easy to identify the activity. We are going to use this name in the **ForEach** activity, so please make a note of this name.

5. Select the data source from the drop-down list and select **Child Items** in the **ARGUMENT** section of the dataset.

6. You can enter values for **Skip line count** and **Filter by last modified** if you require this information. However, I am leaving these fields blank as shown in the following screenshot.

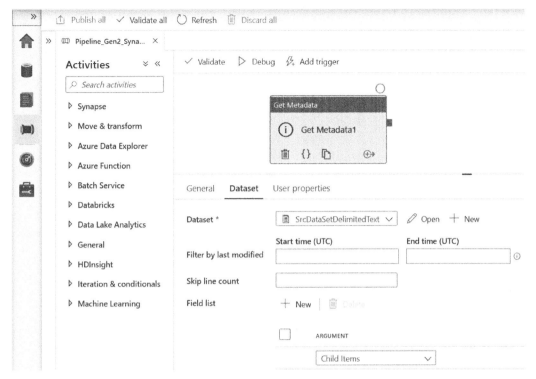

Figure 4.20 – A screenshot of the dataset property for the Get Metadata activity

7. Before we proceed further, click on the **Debug** button at this stage to validate that this activity is running successfully. You can view the status in the **Output** window, as highlighted in the following screenshot:

Figure 4.21 – Successful status of the pipeline having the Get Metadata activity

8. Next, we will iterate over all the files available in the source directory of the storage account. So, we are going to pull a **ForEach** activity to the canvas and connect it with the **Get Metadata** activity, as illustrated in the following screenshot:

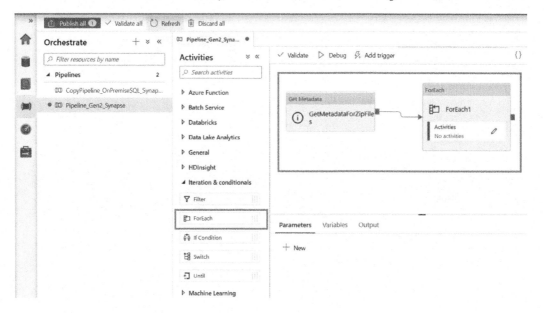

Figure 4.22 – Adding a ForEach activity to the canvas

9. Click on the **ForEach** activity on the canvas to set the properties. Provide an appropriate **name** on the **General** tab.

10. Go to the **Settings** tab and click on the **Items** field. Then, click on the **Add Dynamic Content** link, paste the following script, and click on **Finish**:

```
@activity('GetMetadataForZipFiles').output.childItems
```

In the following screenshot, we add dynamic content to the **Items** field of the **ForEach** activity:

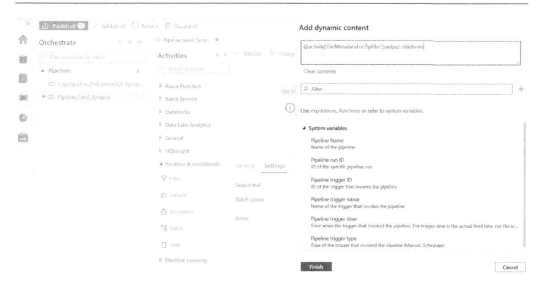

Figure 4.23 – Adding dynamic content to the Items field of the ForEach activity

11. Double-click on the **ForEach** activity on the canvas to add a **Copy data** activity within the **ForEach** activity.

12. Provide a name for the **Copy data** activity after you have added the **Copy data** activity to the **ForEach** activity, as illustrated in the following screenshot:

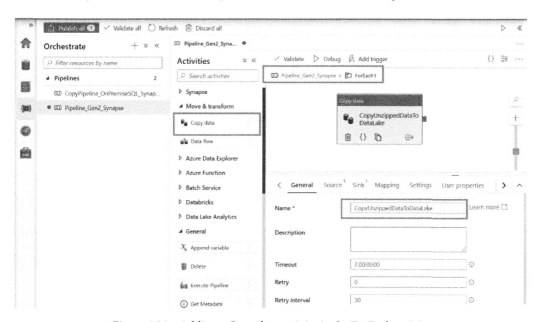

Figure 4.24 – Adding a Copy data activity in the ForEach activity

13. Go to the **Source** tab of the **Copy data** activity and select the linked service for **Azure Data Lake Storage Gen2**, where the ZIP files are residing.

14. Instead of providing the exact filename, we can use wildcards in the path to allow you to collect all files of a certain type within the specified directory. Select the **Wildcard file path** radio button for **File path type**, and click on the **Add dynamic content** link for **Wildcard file name** to paste the following script:

```
item().name
```

15. Make sure that the **Recursively** field is checked and that the **Preserve zip file name as folder** field is unchecked, as illustrated in the following screenshot:

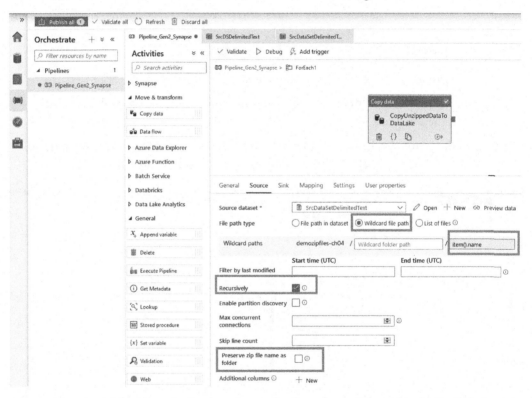

Figure 4.25 – Setting the properties for the source in the Copy data activity within the ForEach activity

16. Next, we are going to set the properties for **Sink**. Select the **StagingDelimitedText** sink dataset from the **Sink dataset** drop-down list.

17. Change the **Copy behavior** field to **Flatten hierarchy**, as seen in the following screenshot. This will enable us to copy all files residing within a different folder in the specified source directory to one specified folder within the `sink` directory:

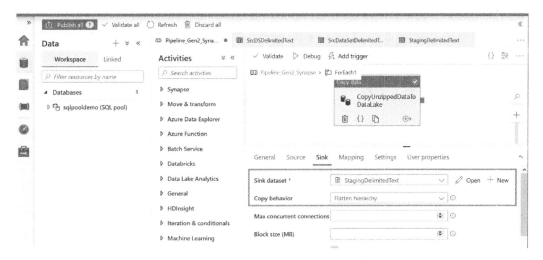

Figure 4.26 – Setting Sink properties for Copy activities in the ForEach activity

18. Click on **Debug** to run the pipeline—you can monitor the status in the **Output** window.

19. After validating that your pipeline is working as expected so far, come back to the main page where the **Get Metadata** and `ForEach` activities have been added, and add the `Copy` activity to the canvas.

20. Provide a name for the `CopyFromStagingBlobToSynapseSQL` Copy activity and join it with the `ForEach` activity.

21. This time, the source dataset for our `Copy` activity is going to be `StagingDelimitedText`, and `SinkSynapseSQL` will be our sink dataset.

22. Make sure to select the **Bulk Insert** copy method under the **Sink** properties. This method is used to import data in bulk from the data file.

23. Go to the **Mapping** section of the **Copy** activity and check that all the column mappings from source to sink are correct. You can make any necessary changes here if required; otherwise, we are good to go to publish our changes.

After completing your pipeline, we will next schedule the pipeline to run it at regular intervals.

Scheduling Synapse pipelines

Azure Synapse pipelines allow you to run your pipeline just once or trigger it manually whenever you need to run it. However, Synapse pipelines enable you to schedule the pipelines to run at regular intervals as well.

With Synapse pipelines, it's just a matter of a few clicks to schedule your pipeline. The following instructions will help you in scheduling your pipeline:

1. Go to the **Triggers** page under the **Monitor** tab in Synapse Studio and click on **+ New** at the top of the screen, as illustrated in the following screenshot:

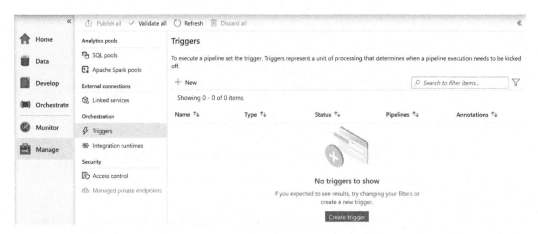

Figure 4.27 – A screenshot of the Triggers page in Synapse Studio

2. Provide a **name** and **description** for your trigger. It's better to keep your pipeline's line appended to the trigger's name so that in the case of any failure it will be easy to identify the corresponding pipeline. The fields are shown in the following screenshot:

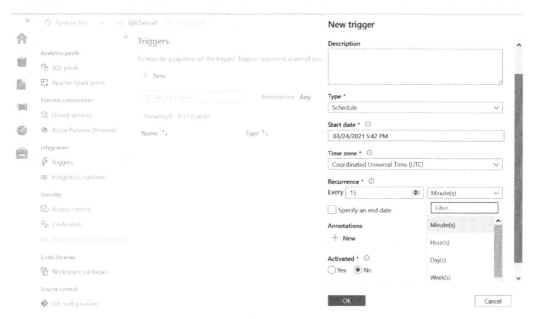

Figure 4.28 – Creating a trigger for the Pipeline_Gen2_Synapse pipeline

3. Select the **type of trigger** as per your business needs. In this example, we are going to select the **Schedule** radio button option from the list.

4. Provide a value for **Recurrence**. In our example, our pipeline must run once a day—hence, select **1** in the first field box and **Day(s)** in the second field box.

5. You have the flexibility to provide the start date as well, but we will stick to the default value because we want to enable this trigger as soon as it is created.

The properties are shown in the following screenshot:

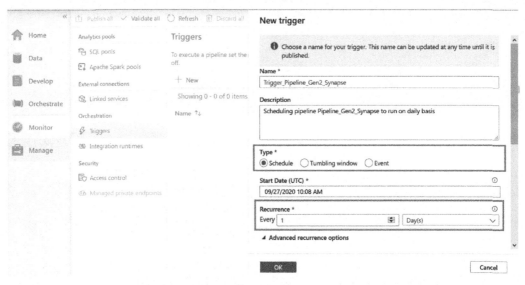

Figure 4.29 – Setting properties for the trigger

6. If you want to select a particular time of day to run your pipeline, then you need to provide the appropriate time under the **Advanced recurrence options** section.

7. Select the **On Date** radio button for the **End** section to provide a value for **End On (UTC)** if you want your trigger to stop after a certain time. However, we want our trigger to be active forever, so we will select the **No End** radio button.

8. Last but not least, select **Yes** for the **Activated** field—this will activate/deactivate the trigger after we do the publish operation. Next, click on **OK**, and you are all set. The process is illustrated in the following screenshot:

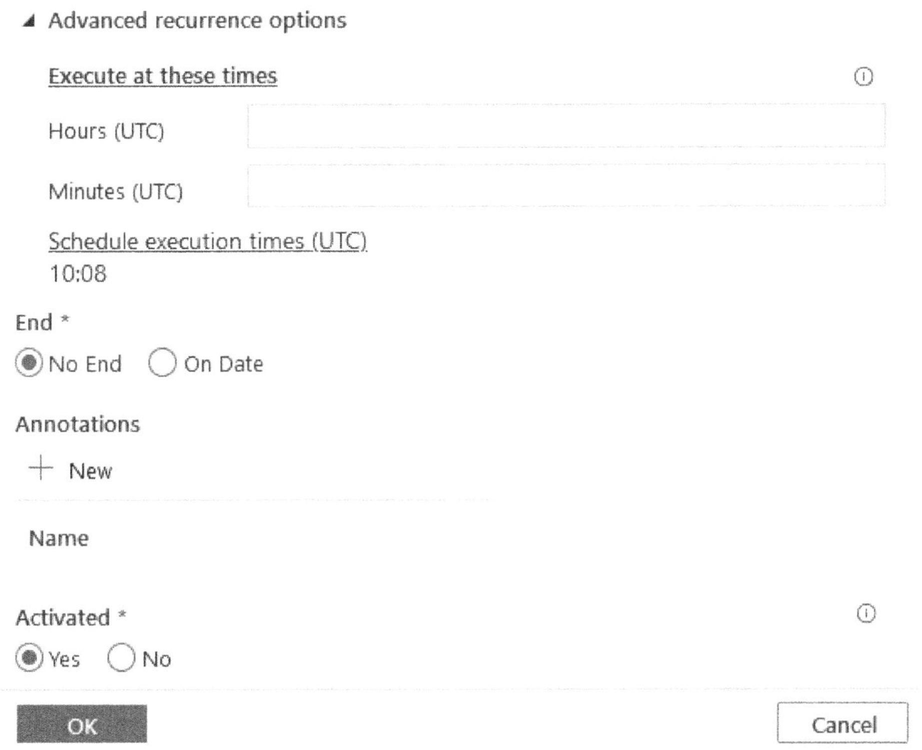

◢ Advanced recurrence options

Execute at these times   ⓘ

Hours (UTC)

Minutes (UTC)

Schedule execution times (UTC)
10:08

End *

⦿ No End   ◯ On Date

Annotations

╋ New

Name

Activated *   ⓘ

⦿ Yes   ◯ No

OK		Cancel

Figure 4.30 – A screenshot of the Trigger properties window with default values

In this section, we learned how to unzip multiple files, place these files in the blob containers dynamically, and then copy the data to the Synapse SQL pool; but in the real world, you may have more complex scenarios than this one. However, Synapse has made it quite easy for developers by providing sample scripts and notebooks within Synapse Studio itself.

Next, we are going to learn how to use these sample pipelines.

Creating pipelines using samples

Synapse has provided various sample pipelines that can help you in building your production-ready pipeline in just a few steps.

We will go through the following steps to create pipelines using samples provided by Synapse:

1. Go to the **Integrate** tab on the **Synapse Studio** screen.

2. Go to the sample center by clicking on **Browse samples**, as highlighted in the following screenshot:

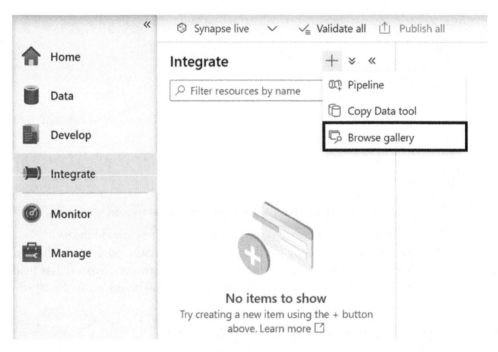

Figure 4.31 – A screenshot of the Browse samples link under the Integrate tab in Synapse Studio

3. You can see sample datasets, notebooks, and SQL scripts in the sample center. Let's try to use one of the sample notebooks. Go to the **Notebooks** section, select **Getting Started with Delta Lake**, and click on **Continue**. The following screenshot provides an overview of the **sample center**:

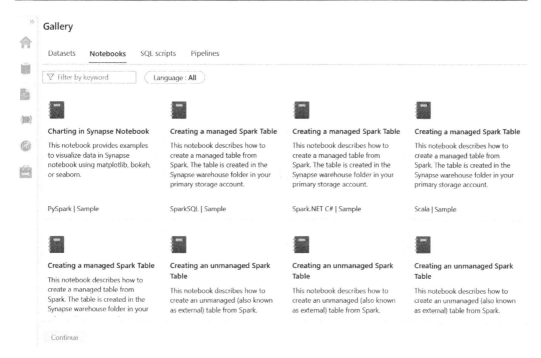

Figure 4.32 – A screenshot of the sample center in Synapse Studio

4. On the next screen, you can see a preview of the notebook that you selected. Click on **Next** after going through the **description** and **preview**.

5. If you do not have a **Spark pool** created already, you will see a pop-up window asking your permission to create a Spark pool of the required size to run this notebook. Click on **Create pool** after reviewing the size information, as illustrated in the following screenshot:

No Spark pools available

You'll need a Spark pool in order to run your notebook. We can create one for you now, or you can do so from the management hub at a later time.

Would you like to create a Spark pool?

Name: SampleSpark
Size: Small (4 vCPU / 32 GB) - 3 nodes

Create pool   Maybe later

Figure 4.33 – A screenshot of the pop-up window seeking permission to create a Spark pool

6. Your `SampleSpark` Spark pool will be available for your notebook in a couple of seconds, and then you can click on the **Run all** link above the notebook to run all the cells in the notebook, as illustrated in the following screenshot:

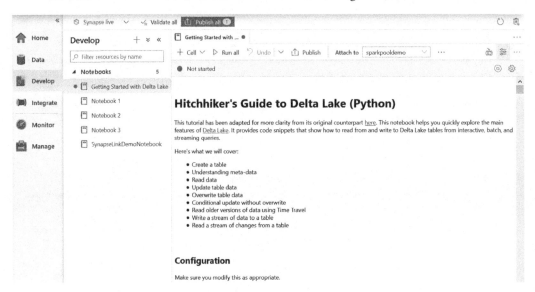

Figure 4.34 – A screenshot of the notebook attached to the SampleSpark Spark pool

7. Next, go to the **integrate** tab and create a new pipeline.

8. Provide a **name** for this pipeline in the **Properties** window and add the **Notebook** activity to the pipeline canvas, as illustrated in the following screenshot:

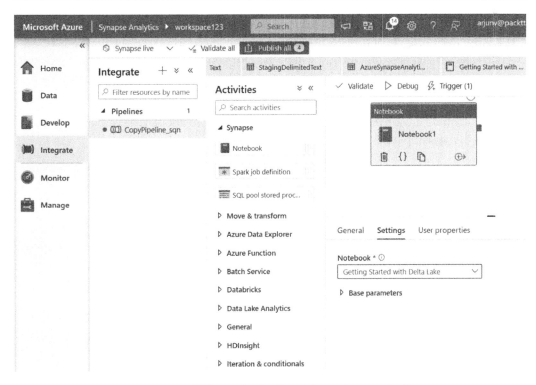

Figure 4.35 – Adding a Notebook activity to the new pipeline

9. Go to the **Settings** tab and select the correct notebook from the list of all available notebooks, as shown in *Figure 4.35*.

You are now all set to schedule this pipeline, so go ahead and start creating your pipelines. It's better to start with the sample pipelines provided in the sample gallery of Synapse Studio, if you have never worked on Azure Data Factory or Synapse pipelines before.

Summary

So far, we have learned how to create linked services, datasets, pipelines, and triggers. We learned how can we use multiple activities together in a pipeline. We got a fair understanding of variables and parameters in Synapse pipelines. Synapse has provided the option to use sample pipelines, but it's important to learn how to use these sample pipelines—therefore in this chapter, we also covered how we can start using these.

Synapse supports various data stores and various ways to transform your data, but we could only cover a couple of transformations in this chapter. However, now that you are comfortable with Synapse pipelines, it will be easy for you to add any activity to the pipeline as per your business requirements. You can go to `http://bit.ly/transform-data-on-synapse` if you want to learn more about any specific activity.

We will talk about a couple of other activities throughout the book that will give you more clarity on Synapse pipelines.

In the next chapter, we will talk about **Azure Synapse Link for Azure Cosmos DB**, which enables you to run near-real-time analytics over operational data in Azure Cosmos DB.

5
Using Synapse Link with Azure Cosmos DB

Azure Synapse Link is a new feature added to create a link between Azure Cosmos DB and Azure Synapse. It enables you to run near real-time analytics on data residing in the analytical store of your Cosmos DB account. The analytical store and transactional store are kept in sync in a Cosmos DB account. The transactional store in Cosmos DB is optimized for transactional reads and writes whereas the analytical store is optimized for analytical queries. Synapse Link creates an integration between Cosmos DB and Synapse Analytics. In this chapter, we are going to learn how to enable an analytical store in Cosmos DB and how we can query data directly from this analytical store with Azure Synapse Spark.

We are going to cover the following topics in this chapter, which will help you learn about the concept of Synapse Link and how it can fulfill your business needs:

- Enabling the analytical store in Cosmos DB
- Data storage
- Querying the Cosmos DB analytical store

Technical requirements

Before you start orchestrating your data, there are certain prerequisites that you should meet:

- You should have your Azure subscription or access to any other subscription with contributor-level access.

- Create your Synapse workspace on this subscription. You can follow the instructions from *Chapter 1*, *Introduction to Azure Synapse*, to create your Synapse workspace.

- Create a SQL pool and Spark pool on Azure Synapse. This has been covered in *Chapter 2*, *Consideration for Your Compute Environments*.

- Create your Azure Cosmos DB account and three containers: **Products**, **RetailSales**, and **StoreDemoGraphics**. You can go through the following link to create your Cosmos DB account: `https://docs.microsoft.com/en-us/azure/cosmos-db/create-cosmosdb-resources-portal`.

- Go to the link `https://github.com/PacktPublishing/Limitless-Analytics-with-Azure-Synapse` to download `Chapter 05 - RetailData.zip`, and extract and save all the files.

- Prior knowledge of Python and Spark will be required to follow the examples provided in this chapter.

Once you have met all the prerequisites, you can start leveraging Synapse Link, however, you need to enable the analytical store in Cosmos DB to use Synapse Link.

Enabling the analytical store in Cosmos DB

You can enable Synapse Link on Cosmos DB directly from the Azure portal:

1. Log in to the Azure portal at `https://porta.azure.com`.
2. Go to your Cosmos DB account and click on **Data Explorer**.

3. Click on the **Enable** link while creating a new container:

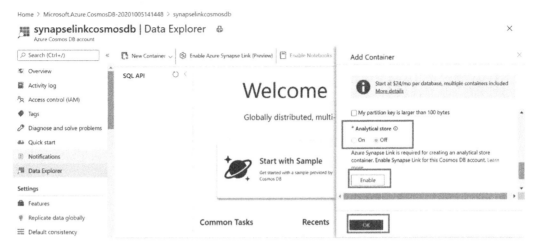

Figure 5.1 – Enabling Azure Synapse Link on a Cosmos DB account

4. You can click on the **Features** tab to verify whether **Azure Synapse Link** is enabled or not. You have the option to enable it from there as well if it is not enabled yet:

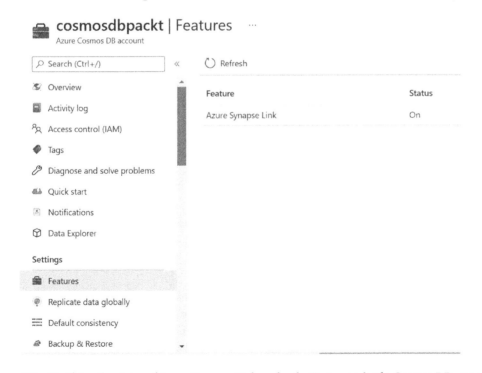

Figure 5.2 – Verifying the status of Azure Synapse Link under the Features tab of a Cosmos DB account

> **Important note**
> The analytical store can only be enabled for new containers.

5. After you enable the analytical store, it creates a container with the **Analytical Storage Time to Live** property associated with the container. The default value is -1, which means infinite retention, however, we can change this value to any number of days and as many days as we want the data to live in the storage account. This is an analytical store that retains all the historical versions of records. You can change this value at any point under the **Settings** tab of your container:

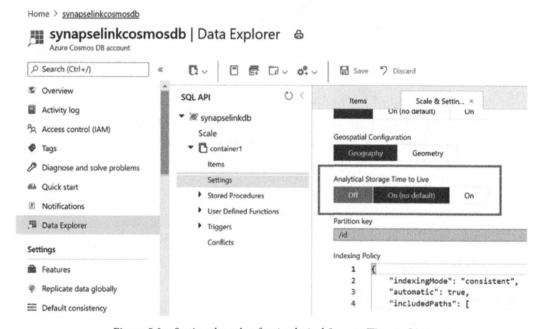

Figure 5.3 – Setting the value for Analytical Storage Time to Live

Cosmos DB supports two types of storage internally: transactional storage and analytical storage. The following section will cover this topic in more detail.

Data storage

A Cosmos DB analytical store is fully isolated from transactional workloads. The operational data in a Cosmos DB container is internally stored in row-based transactional stores in order to allow fast transactional reads and writes.

It is not recommended to run complex queries on your transactional workload – it may cause bad performance for your application running these queries. Ideally, you should add an analytical data layer on top of Cosmos DB transactional data if you want to perform complex operations on the data. The major caveat for this architecture is an ETL operation for data sync between transactional and analytical data stores. This additional step may lead to increased **Total Cost of Operation** (**TCO**) and overhead of maintaining the data in sync always.

With this new feature of Synapse Link, Cosmos DB gives you the flexibility to enable an analytical store within your Cosmos DB account without performing an ETL operation. Both the data layers are kept in sync within the Cosmos DB container and Synapse Link allows you to access the analytical store directly from Synapse to perform complex queries.

The following diagram shows how Synapse Link integrates a Cosmos DB storage account and Synapse Analytics together. This is called **Hybrid Transactional/Analytical Processing** (**HTAP**) architecture, and this is used for optimizing your business processes. This also eliminates ETL processes and lets you run near real-time BI, analytics, and ML pipelines over operational data.

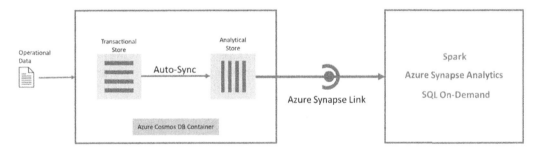

Figure 5.4 – Synapse Link integration with Cosmos DB and Synapse Analytics

Next, we will try to understand how the transactional store is different from the analytical store and how the data is kept in sync in both data stores of the Cosmos DB account.

Transactional store

The transactional store is a schema-agnostic, indexed row-based data store in the Cosmos DB container that holds the operational data. The row store format is designed to allow fast transactional reads and writes in order-of-milliseconds response times.

When you enable the analytical store to automatically update the schema according to the operational data, you cannot have more than 200 properties at any nesting level in the schema, with a maximum nesting depth of 5.

Property names are case insensitive and must be kept unique.

Analytical store

Column store format is suitable for large-scale analytical queries to be performed in an optimized manner, resulting in improving the latency of such queries. The analytical store is actually a column store in the Cosmos DB container that is designed to deal with complex queries running on a large dataset. The column store in the Cosmos DB container is fully isolated from the transactional store; you can run large-scale analytics queries without any impact on your transactional workloads. Any changes to operational data (insert/update/delete) will be automatically synced to the analytical store.

> **Important note**
> The automatic backup and restore option is not supported in the analytical store of a Cosmos DB account, however, Cosmos DB will continue taking backups of your data in the transactional store.

So, now it is important to understand how Cosmos DB represents schema for operational data in tabular format. There are two types of schema representation in the analytical store of Cosmos DB with certain trade-offs. Let's have a look at both modes.

Well-defined schema representation

When the analytical store is enabled on the **Azure Cosmos DB SQL (core) API**, a well-defined schema representation is the default schema representation in the analytical store. Cosmos DB supports five different types of API: Core(SQL), MongoDB API, Cassandra, Azure Table, and Gremlin (graph), however, Synapse Link is applicable only for the **Core(SQL) API** and **Azure Cosmos DB API** for MongoDB as of now. You can refer to the link https://docs.microsoft.com/en-us/learn/modules/choose-api-for-cosmos-db/ to learn about all these APIs in detail. In this chapter, we are going to use the Core(SQL) API. It creates simple tabular representations of operational data. However, there are certain properties that need to be kept in mind, as listed here:

- A property must have the same data type across multiple items. In the case of different types, the analytical store will consider the data type of the first occurring item in the lifetime of the container.

- An array must contain a single repeated type. If an array contains values of mixed data types, it cannot represent a well-defined schema.

Sometimes you do not want to drop any items even if these items have different data types than all other items. Then, the **full fidelity schema representation** should be used instead of the **well-defined schema representation**.

Full fidelity schema representation

When the analytical store is enabled on the **Azure Cosmos DB MongoDB API**, the full fidelity schema representation is the default schema representation in the analytical store. The main advantage of this schema representation is that no items are dropped from the analytical store even if a property has different data types across the container or if the array contains mixed types.

The leaf property names are suffixed with data types to be stored as distinct columns in the analytical store so that they can be queried without ambiguity.

In the following example, two distinct columns will be created for the same property, `address.object.streetNo.int32` and `address.object.streetNo.string`:

```
address: {
  streetNo: 1234,
  streetName: "23rd St.",
  },
address: {
  streetNo: "1342",
  streetName: "20th St.",
  },
```

Now that we have learned different storage options provided by a Cosmos DB account, it's time to learn how to read data from a Cosmos DB analytical store from Azure Synapse.

Querying the Cosmos DB analytical store

With Azure Synapse, you get the option to choose between Spark or SQL as your compute environment. You can query a Cosmos DB analytical store using Spark and SQL Serverless, however, this feature is not available with SQL provisioned as of now.

Let's learn how to query data in the analytical store of a Cosmos DB container.

Querying with Azure Synapse Spark

Azure Synapse Spark allows you to analyze data in your Synapse Link enabled Azure Cosmos DB containers. You can query an analytical store from Spark in two possible ways:

- Loading data to a Spark DataFrame
- Creating a Spark table

A Spark DataFrame leverages the cached metadata through the lifetime of the Spark session, so any change in the source data will not be reflected here until you start a new Spark session. The metadata of the analytical store is reloaded on every query execution against the Spark table.

You can ingest data to the analytical store of a Cosmos DB container using Azure Synapse Spark, however, it's important to understand that data gets ingested to the transactional store of the Cosmos DB container and later the auto-sync operation updates the analytical store.

Let's try to learn the step-by-step process to query Cosmos DB data with Azure Synapse Spark.

Loading data to a Spark DataFrame

In order to query your data stored in your Cosmos DB account, first, we need to load that data to a Spark DataFrame in Azure Synapse. You can use any supported language to perform this operation, however, in this example, we are going to use the Python language.

The following **Python** syntax can be used for loading Cosmos DB data to a **Spark DataFrame** without impacting the transactional store:

```
df = spark.read.format("cosmos.olap")\
    .option("spark.synapse.linkedService", "<enter linked
service name>")\
    .option("spark.cosmos.container", "<enter container
name>")\
    .load()
```

> **Important note**
> To select a preferred list of regions in a multi-region Azure Cosmos DB account, add `.option("spark.cosmos.preferredRegions",` `"<Region1>,<Region2>")`.

You can ingest the data from your DataFrame to your Cosmos DB account using the following **Python** syntax:

```
# Write a Spark DataFrame into an Azure Cosmos DB container
# To select a preferred list of regions in a multi-region Azure
Cosmos DB account, add .option("spark.cosmos.preferredRegions",
"<Region1>,<Region2>")
```

```
DataFrameName.write.format("cosmos.oltp")\
    .option("spark.synapse.linkedService", "<enter linked
service name>")\
    .option("spark.cosmos.container", "<enter container
name>")\
    .option("spark.cosmos.write.upsertEnabled", "true")\
    .mode('append')\
    .save()
```

Let's try to ingest `RetailData` from our primary storage account of Azure Synapse to a Cosmos DB container using a Spark DataFrame. Create a `demosynapselink-ch05` folder within the root directory of your storage account in Synapse Studio. Upload to this folder the CSV files that are placed within the folder with the same name as this repository:

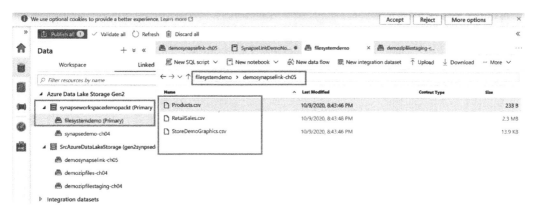

Figure 5.5 – A screenshot of sample files in the demosynapselink-ch05 blob container

You can go through the following instructions to create linked services for a Cosmos DB account and query data using Spark SQL in Synapse Studio:

1. Log in to the Azure portal at `https://portal.azure.com` and go to your Cosmos DB account.

2. Click on **Data Explorer** and create a new database, **SynapseLinkDemoDB**.

3. Create three analytical store-enabled containers: **StoreDemoGraphics**. We are going to use **id** as our partition key for all three containers:

Figure 5.6 – Creating containers in a Cosmos DB account

4. Now that we have the required containers in place, it's time to create a linked service for this Cosmos DB account in the **Azure Synapse** workspace. Go to your Azure Synapse workspace and navigate to **Synapse Studio**.

5. Click on **Linked Services** under the **Manage** tab to create a new linked service.

6. Click on the **+New** link and search for **Azure Cosmos DB(SQL API)** from the list of all available data stores, select that, and click on **Continue**.

7. Provide an appropriate name and description for the linked service.

8. Select your Azure subscription, Azure Cosmos DB account name, and the database name that you created in *Step 2*. Click on **Create** after providing all the details.

> **Important note**
>
> Even if you have selected the correct Azure subscription and Azure Cosmos DB account name, you may get a firewall error if you have not whitelisted your IP on the firewall settings of your Cosmos DB account.

The following screenshot shows the process of creating linked services for a Cosmos DB account:

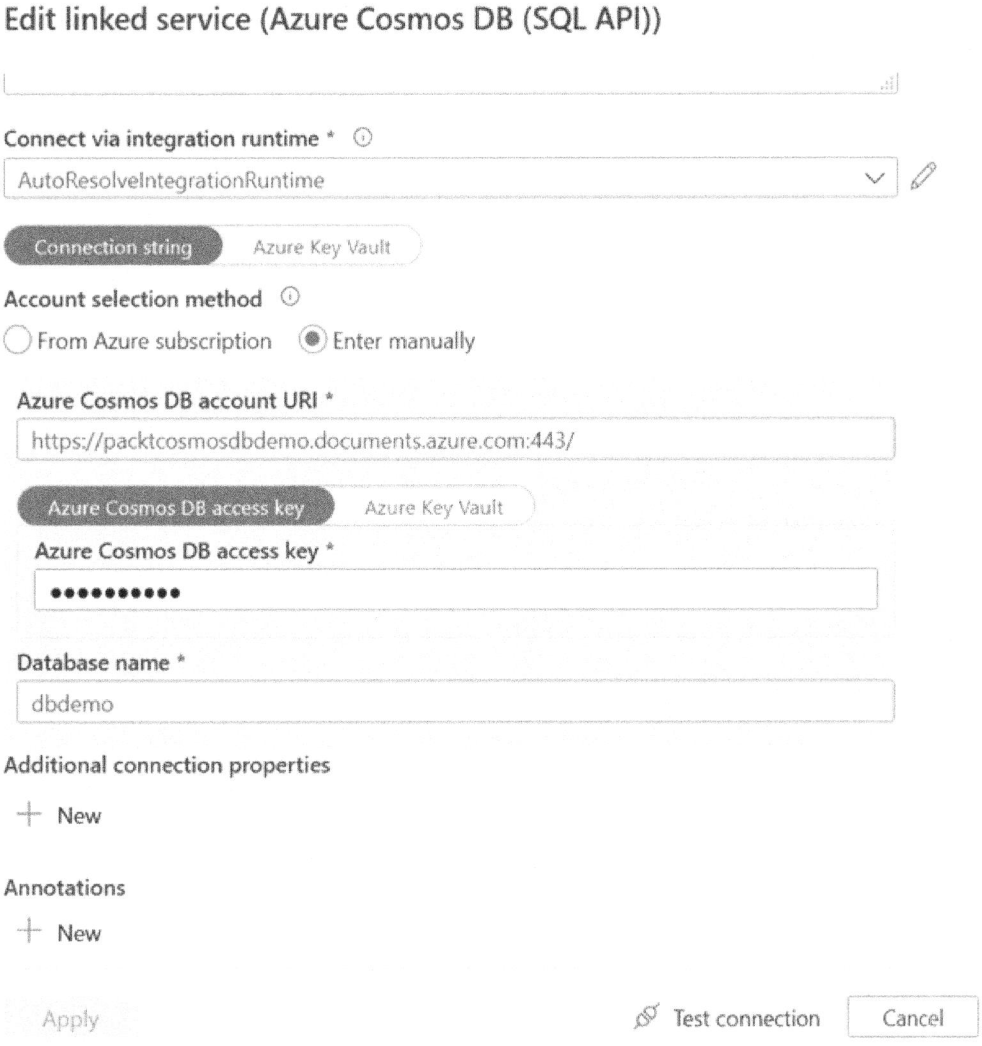

Edit linked service (Azure Cosmos DB (SQL API))

Connect via integration runtime * ⓘ

AutoResolveIntegrationRuntime ⌄ ✎

(**Connection string**   Azure Key Vault)

Account selection method ⓘ

◯ From Azure subscription   ⦿ Enter manually

Azure Cosmos DB account URI *

https://packtcosmosdbdemo.documents.azure.com:443/

(**Azure Cosmos DB access key**   Azure Key Vault)

Azure Cosmos DB access key *

••••••••••

Database name *

dbdemo

Additional connection properties

+ New

Annotations

+ New

Apply   𝒮 Test connection | Cancel |

Figure 5.7 – Creating a linked service for a Cosmos DB account

9. Before we proceed further, let's check whether we can locate our CSV files in Azure Synapse. Go to the **Linked** tab under the **Data** section of Synapse Studio and click on your storage account where you uploaded the CSV files. If you can see your files here, it means we are good to proceed further now:

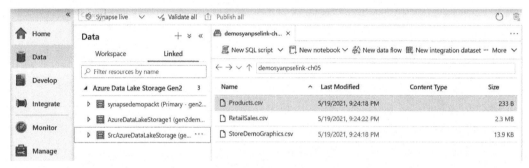

Figure 5.8 – A screenshot of sample files in the Data tab of Synapse Studio

10. Go to the **Develop** section and click on + to create a new notebook and give it an appropriate name, such as **SynapseLinkDemoNotebook**. Make sure to click on **Publish** after any changes.

11. Paste the following code in your notebook and run the cell:

```
dfStoreDemoGraphics = (spark
                .read
                .csv("/demosynapselink-ch05/
StoreDemoGraphics.csv", header=True, inferSchema='true')
                )
```

12. After the preceding code runs successfully, paste the following and last piece of the code in your notebook in the same cell and run the cell:

```
dfStoreDemoGraphics.write\
            .format("cosmos.oltp")\
            .option("spark.synapse.linkedService",
"RetailSalesDemoDB")\
            .option("spark.cosmos.container",
"StoreDemoGraphics")\
            .option("spark.cosmos.write.upsertEnabled",
"true")\
            .mode('append')\
            .save()
```

You can ingest data from the other two files as well using the same logic. You can download the notebook from this link: https://github.com/PacktPublishing/ Limitless-Analytics-with-Azure-Synapse/blob/master/Chapter%20 05%20-%20SampleNotebook.zip.

Now that we have learned enough about Spark DataFrames, it is worth learning about Spark tables as well.

Creating a Spark table

Azure Synapse gives you the feasibility to create Spark tables using the data stored in a Cosmos DB account. You need your linked service name and Cosmos DB container name to create a Spark table in Synapse.

You can create a Spark table in Synapse Studio using the following syntax:

```sql
%%sql
create table sample_table using cosmos.olap options (
    spark.synapse.linkedService '<enter linked service name>',
    spark.cosmos.container '<enter container name>',
    spark.cosmos.autoSchemaMerge '<true/false>'
)
```

If you want to keep the schema updated with the schema changes of the underlying Cosmos DB container, set the spark.cosmos.autoSchemaMerge property to true in the preceding syntax.

After creating the Spark table using the data stored in the Cosmos DB account, next we are going to learn how to implement business logic on top of this data within Azure Synapse.

Querying with Azure Synapse SQL Serverless

In this section, we'll see how Synapse SQL Serverless allows you to analyze the data in a Cosmos DB container if Synapse Link is enabled, just as you can analyze the same data in Synapse Spark. You can query data from an analytical store using familiar T-SQL syntax.

> **Important note**
> As of now, we cannot access a Cosmos DB analytical store with a Synapse provisioned SQL pool.

SQL Serverless uses `OPENROWSET` syntax to analyze the data in the analytical store of a Cosmos DB container, as you can see in the following code block:

```
OPENROWSET (
        'CosmosDB',
        '<Azure Cosmos DB connection string>',
        <Container name>
    )   [ < with clause > ]
```

> **Important note**
> The Cosmos DB container name is specified without quotes in the
> `OPENROWSET` syntax. It's better to keep the name wrapped within the []
> (square brackets) in the `OPENROWSET` syntax to avoid any errors.

In most cases, you are going to deal with nested objects and arrays. With `OPENROWSET`, you can still read these values by using **SQL JSON** functions:

```
SELECT
    title = JSON_VALUE(metadata, '$.title'),
    authors = JSON_QUERY(metadata, '$.authors'),
    first_author_name = JSON_VALUE(metadata, '$.authors[0].
first')
FROM
    OPENROWSET (
        'CosmosDB',
        'account=MyCosmosDbAccount;database=covid;region=westus2;
key=C0Sm0sDbKey==',
        Cord19
    WITH ( metadata varchar(MAX) ) AS docs;
```

As an alternative option, you can also specify the paths to nested values in the objects when using the `WITH` clause. Also, you can apply the `OPENJSON` function on the nested array to flatten the nested structure:

```
SELECT
    *
FROM
    OPENROWSET (
```

```
        'CosmosDB',          'account=MyCosmosDbAccount;
database=covid;region=westus2;key=C0Sm0sDbKey==',
        Cord19
    ) WITH ( title varchar(1000) '$.metadata.title',
            authors varchar(max) '$.metadata.authors' ) AS
docs
        CROSS APPLY OPENJSON ( authors )
                WITH (
                        first varchar(50),
                        last varchar(50),
                        affiliation nvarchar(max) as json
                ) AS a
```

The following screenshot displays the output of the preceding code block:

title	authors	first	last	affiliation
Supplementary Information An eco-epidemi...	[{"first":"Julien","last":"Mé lade","suffix":"","affiliatio n":{"laboratory":"Centre de Recher...	Julien	Mélade	{"laboratory":"Centre de Recher...
Supplementary Information An eco-epidemi...	[{"first":"Nicolas","last":"4 #","suffix":"","affiliation":{ "laboratory":"","institutio n":"U...	Nicolas	4#	{"laboratory":"","institution":"U...
Supplementary Information An eco-epidemi...	[{"first":"Beza","last":"Ra mazindrazana","suffix":"", "affiliation":{"laboratory": "Centre de Recher...	Beza	Ramazindrazana	{"laboratory":"Centre de Recher...
Supplementary Information An eco-epidemi...	[{"first":"Olivier","last":"Fl ores","suffix":"","affiliatio n":{"laboratory":"UMR C53 CIRAD, ...	Olivier	Flores	

Figure 5.9 – Result set of the preceding query displaying the values for title, authors, first, last, and affiliation

We saw a very simple example of how to query data stored in a Cosmos DB account. However, you can go through the following link if you want to learn more about interacting with Cosmos DB in Azure Synapse: https://docs.microsoft. com/en-us/azure/synapse-analytics/synapse-link/how-to-query- analytical-store-spark?branch=release-build-synapse.

Summary

In this chapter, we covered Azure Synapse Link, which is a new feature added to Azure Synapse, and we learned a step-by-step process to query data directly from an Azure Cosmos DB account. This feature dispenses with the need for ETL processes to bring data from a Cosmos DB account to Synapse. Now, we know that we can write queries directly on Cosmos DB data by creating corresponding linked services. We also saw how the transactional store syncs the data in the analytical store through auto-sync, and we learned about modes of schema representation in the analytical store. We used the Python language in this chapter; however, you are free to use any supported language that you are comfortable with.

There are many possible use cases of Azure Synapse Link. You can find a couple of these use cases mentioned in Microsoft Docs: `https://docs.microsoft.com/en-us/azure/cosmos-db/synapse-link-use-cases`.

In the next chapter, we are going to get some good coding experience on Azure Synapse SQL. We will learn how T-SQL can be used with Azure Synapse and its limitations.

Section 3: Azure Synapse for Data Scientists and Business Analysts

The objective of this section is to introduce you to the various ways of querying or reading data on Azure Synapse.

This section comprises the following chapters:

- *Chapter 6, Working with T-SQL in Azure Synapse*

- *Chapter 7, Working with R, Python, Scala, .NET, and Spark SQL in Azure Synapse*

- *Chapter 8, Integrating a Power BI Workspace with Azure Synapse*

- *Chapter 9, Perform Real-Time Analytics on Streaming Data*

- *Chapter 10, Generate Powerful Insights on Azure Synapse Using Azure Machine Learning*

6
Working with T-SQL in Azure Synapse

Azure Synapse **Structured Query Language** (**SQL**) enables you to query your data using the **Transact-SQL** (**T-SQL**) language, which means you do not need to learn any new languages if you already have prior experience working with SQL. As we now know, Azure Synapse SQL supports two types of consumption models, dedicated and serverless, and you will notice some differences in the supported features of both models. In this chapter, we are going to cover T-SQL language elements that are supported in Synapse SQL pools. We will also learn how we can create stored procedures and views in Synapse SQL pools. As with SQL Server and Azure SQL, we will learn which system views are supported in a Synapse SQL pool.

This chapter will help you get familiar with the features supported in Azure Synapse SQL. We will learn how to use T-SQL queries on unstructured data as well.

We are going to cover the following topics in this chapter, which will help you learn supported features of T-SQL in Azure Synapse SQL:

- Supporting T-SQL language elements in a Synapse SQL pool
- Creating stored procedures and views in Synapse SQL
- Optimizing transactions in Synapse SQL
- Supporting system views in a Synapse SQL pool
- Using T-SQL queries on semi-structured and unstructured data

Technical requirements

Before you start orchestrating your data, here are certain prerequisites that you should meet:

- You should have an Azure subscription, or access to any other subscription with contributor-level access.
- Create your Synapse workspace on this subscription. You can follow the instructions from *Chapter 1*, *Introduction to Azure Synapse*, to create your Synapse workspace.
- Create a SQL pool on Azure Synapse. This has been covered in *Chapter 2*, *Considerations For Your Compute Environment*.
- Download the script from the following link: `http://bit.ly/T-SQL-samples`.

Once you have met all the prerequisites, you can start transforming your business logic into code by using T-SQL. In the following section, we will learn about some of the supported features by using some sample queries.

Supporting T-SQL language elements in a Synapse SQL pool

The `SELECT` statement in **T-SQL** retrieves rows from a database and enables the selection of columns and rows from one or multiple tables in Azure Synapse SQL. You can use the `SELECT` statement with `WHERE`, `GROUP BY`, `HAVING`, and `ORDER BY` clauses in dedicated and serverless SQL pools. The syntax for the `SELECT` statement in Synapse SQL is similar to that found in Azure SQL Database or SQL Server.

The following code snippet provides an example of using a SELECT statement:

```
SELECT OrderDateKey, SUM(SalesAmount) AS TotalSales
FROM FactInternetSales
GROUP BY OrderDateKey
HAVING OrderDateKey > 20010000
ORDER BY OrderDateKey;
```

We can also create **Common Table Expressions** (**CTEs**) in Synapse SQL pools. We will learn about these in the following section.

CTEs

A CTE is a temporary result set that is used to simplify complex joins and subqueries. CTEs can also be used to query hierarchical data such as an organization chart. We can even create CTEs in Azure Synapse SQL pools for similar operations.

The following code block defines a CTE that will create a temporary dataset called CTE with first_name and last_name columns derived from a UserData table. The SELECT query against this temporary dataset will fetch all the records:

```
WITH CTE(id, first_name, last_name)
AS
(SELECT
U.[id]
,[first_name]
,[last_name]
 FROM [dbo].[UserData] U
)
 SELECT * FROM CTE;
```

Likewise, there are various other T-SQL language elements that are not only supported in SQL Server or Azure SQL but also in Synapse SQL pools. We will learn about these in the following sections.

SELECT – OVER clause

An OVER clause is used with some window functions that we will cover in this section. It is used to determine the partitioning and ordering of a set of rows before the associated window function is applied. The associated window function is applied on this set of rows to compute a value as per the business demand. A few of the most commonly used calculations are moving averages, cumulative aggregates, and running totals, among others.

Ranking functions

Ranking functions are used to assign a rank to each row in a partition or set of rows and return an aggregated value for each partitioning row. Ranking functions are also known as window functions.

We can use RANK, DENSE_RANK, ROW_NUMBER, and NTILE ranking functions in **Azure Synapse SQL**. These are outlined as follows:

- The RANK function returns 1 plus the number of ranks that come before the row in question, and it provides the same numeric values for ties.

- ROW_NUMBER is used to get the temporary unique sequential number of a row within a partition of a result set. It assigns rank one for the first row and increments the value by 1 for each row; even if a row has similar values, it will still get assigned a unique number.

- DENSE_RANK is similar to the RANK function, with a minor difference: it assigns the same rank for duplicate or similar values.

- The NTILE function is used to divide records into a specified number of groups, and each group will be assigned a rank as per the specified condition. We need to specify the number of groups as a parameter value to the NTILE function—for example, NTILE(2).

Let's run the following example to understand different ranking functions and where we should use them. In the following code block, we are using PARTITION BY only with the ROW_NUMBER() function; however, feel free to use it with other functions as well, as per your business need:

```
SELECT p.FirstName, p.LastName
    , ROW_NUMBER() OVER(PARTITION BY PostalCode ORDER BY
SalesYTD DESC) AS "Row Number"
    ,RANK() OVER (ORDER BY a.PostalCode) AS Rank
    ,DENSE_RANK() OVER (ORDER BY a.PostalCode) AS "Dense Rank"
    ,NTILE(4) OVER (ORDER BY a.PostalCode) AS Quartile
```

```
     ,s.SalesYTD
     ,a.PostalCode
FROM Sales.SalesPerson AS s
    INNER JOIN Person.Person AS p
        ON s.BusinessEntityID = p.BusinessEntityID
    INNER JOIN Person.Address AS a
        ON a.AddressID = p.BusinessEntityID
WHERE TerritoryID IS NOT NULL AND SalesYTD <> 0;
```

You can see the output of this code block in the following screenshot:

```
 1   SELECT p.FirstName, p.LastName
 2       , ROW_NUMBER() OVER(PARTITION BY PostalCode ORDER BY SalesYTD DESC) AS "Row Number"
 3       ,RANK() OVER (ORDER BY a.PostalCode) AS Rank
 4       ,DENSE_RANK() OVER (ORDER BY a.PostalCode) AS "Dense Rank"
 5       ,NTILE(4) OVER (ORDER BY a.PostalCode) AS Quartile
 6       ,s.SalesYTD
 7       ,a.PostalCode
 8   FROM Sales.SalesPerson AS s
 9       INNER JOIN Person.Person AS p
10           ON s.BusinessEntityID = p.BusinessEntityID
11       INNER JOIN Person.Address AS a
```

Results   Messages

	FirstName	LastName	Row Number	Rank	Dense Rank	Quartile	SalesYTD	PostalCode
1	Linda	Mitchell	1	1	1	1	4251368.5497	98027
2	Michael	Blythe	2	1	1	1	3763178.1787	98027
3	Jillian	Carson	3	1	1	1	3189418.3662	98027
4	Tsvi	Reiter	4	1	1	1	2315185.6110	98027
5	Garrett	Vargas	5	1	1	2	1453719.4653	98027
6	Pamela	Ansman-Wolfe	6	1	1	2	1352577.1325	98027
7	Jae	Pak	1	7	2	2	4116871.2277	98055
8	Ranjit	Varkey Chudukatil	2	7	2	2	3121616.3202	98055

Figure 6.1 – A SQL query and the corresponding output in a Synapse notebook

The preceding code block uses all the ranking functions, which will help you understand all the different functions. As well as these functions, we can also use aggregate functions in Azure Synapse SQL pools. We will learn about these aggregate functions in the next section.

Aggregate functions

Aggregate functions are used to perform a calculation on a set of values such that it returns a single aggregated value. Aggregate functions can be used as expressions in the select list of a SELECT statement or with a HAVING clause.

T-SQL provides various aggregate functions, such as MIN, MAX, SUM, COUNT, AVG, and many more. We will try to learn a few of them here, as follows:

- MIN: Returns the minimum value in an expression. It ignores any NULL values and can even be used for character data columns, where MIN will return the lowest in the sort sequence.

- MAX: Returns the maximum value in an expression. It ignores any NULL values and can even be used for character data columns, where MAX will return the highest in the sort sequence.

- SUM: Can be used with numeric columns only. It returns a sum of all the values, or only the distinct values. It ignores all NULL values.

- COUNT: Can be used with numeric columns only. It returns a count of all the values, or only the distinct values. It ignores all NULL values.

- COUNT_BIG: This function operates like the COUNT function; the only difference is the data type of the value returned. In the case of the COUNT function, this is INT, whereas for the COUNT_BIG function, it is BIGINT.

- APPROX_COUNT_DISTINCT: This function is used to return the approximate number of unique non-null values in a group.

- AVG: AVG can only be used with numeric columns. It is used to calculate the average value of a given expression in a defined group, ignoring all NULL values.

- STDEV: Statistical standard deviation of all values in a given expression within a defined group can be calculated using the STDEV function.

- STDEVP: In STDEVP, *P* stands for *population*. This function is similar to STDEV, but unlike STDEV, STDEVP is used when a group of numbers being evaluated is the whole population, not only a partial sampling of the whole population.

Most of these functions can even be used with an OVER clause to get the aggregated value for each group in the returned row set, as illustrated in the following code block:

```
SELECT DISTINCT Name
        , MIN(Rate) OVER (PARTITION BY edh.DepartmentID) AS
MinSalary
```

```
        , MAX(Rate) OVER (PARTITION BY edh.DepartmentID) AS
MaxSalary
        , AVG(Rate) OVER (PARTITION BY edh.DepartmentID) AS
AvgSalary
        ,COUNT(edh.BusinessEntityID) OVER (PARTITION BY edh.
DepartmentID) AS EmployeesPerDept
FROM HumanResources.EmployeePayHistory AS eph
JOIN HumanResources.EmployeeDepartmentHistory AS edh
    ON eph.BusinessEntityID = edh.BusinessEntityID
JOIN HumanResources.Department AS d
 ON d.DepartmentID = edh.DepartmentID
WHERE edh.EndDate IS NULL
ORDER BY Name;
```

The preceding code block uses all aggregate functions mentioned in this section. You can go to the following link if you want to learn more about these functions: `https://docs.microsoft.com/en-us/sql/t-sql/functions/aggregate-functions-transact-sql`.

Now that we have learned about ranking functions and aggregate functions, let's understand in our next section how analytic functions can be used in Azure Synapse.

Analytic functions

Analytic functions are used in various different ways to perform calculations on the data stored in a Synapse SQL pool. We can use these functions to get top-N results or to perform aggregate operations within a group. These functions can return multiple rows for each group.

Azure Synapse SQL supports the following analytic functions:

- `CUME_DIST`: This function can be used when you want to know the relative position of a specific value within a group of values.
- `FIRST_VALUE`: We can use this function to get the first value in an ordered set of values.
- `LAG`: Using the `LAG` function, you can access a row at a given physical offset that comes before the current row.
- `LAST_VALUE`: Similar to `FIRST_VALUE`, we can use the `LAST_VALUE` function to get the last value in an ordered set of values.
- `LEAD`: Using the `LEAD` function, you can access a row at a given physical offset that comes after the current row.

To learn about many other analytic functions, go to the following link: `https://docs.microsoft.com/en-us/sql/t-sql/functions/analytic-functions-transact-sql?view=sql-server-ver15`.

Sometimes, we need to construct a SQL statement dynamically. This is also known as dynamic SQL, which we will learn about in the next section.

Using dynamic SQL in Synapse SQL

Although in most situations static SQL statements work well, there could be certain situations when we need to use **dynamic SQL** statements. Dynamic SQL is a programming technique applied to frame SQL statements at runtime.

You can use `sp_executesql` to run dynamic SQL scripts, as follows:

```
DECLARE @sql_fragment NVARCHAR(1000)='SELECT * from dbo.
Employee'
EXECUTE sp_executesql @sql_fragment
```

A SQL pool does not support blob data types that include both `VARCHAR(MAX)` and `NVARCHAR(MAX)`. Because of this limitation, you may have difficulty in building a large dynamic SQL string; however, you can break the code into chunks and concatenate all the chunks together with an `EXEC` statement, as follows:

```
DECLARE @sql_fragment1 VARCHAR(8000)=' SELECT name '
,       @sql_fragment2 VARCHAR(8000)=' FROM sys.system_views '
,       @sql_fragment3 VARCHAR(8000)=' WHERE name like
''%table%''';

EXEC( @sql_fragment1 + @sql_fragment2 + @sql_fragment3);
```

The preceding code block has three different SQL statements that are assigned to three different variables: `sql_fragment1`, `sql_fragment2`, and `sql_fragment3`. In the end, all the SQL statements are concatenated by using the + sign, and then the consolidated SQL statement is executed by using an `EXEC` statement.

Dynamic SQL statements can be used in situations where you need to run similar SQL statements multiple times with minor changes in the statement.

In the next section, we will learn about `GROUP BY` options in Synapse SQL. If you are already familiar with T-SQL language elements in SQL Server, you can skip the next section, but it's worth spending a few minutes on it to brush up your knowledge.

Learning GROUP BY options in Synapse SQL

A GROUP BY clause is used with a SELECT statement to arrange identical data into groups.

A GROUP BY clause can be used when we need to use aggregate functions such as SUM, AVG, and so on to fetch the aggregated value of a grouped set of records. GROUP BY can also be used with CUBE, ROLLUP, and GROUPING SETS.

However, GROUP BY is not supported with CUBE in an Azure Synapse SQL pool. We will learn about the workarounds further on in this section. For now, we will proceed as follows:

1. Let's begin with simple usage of a GROUP BY clause. First, we will run a script to create a sample table to use. You can find this script here: http://bit.ly/T-SQL-samples.

2. Now that we have a sample table created in our SQL pool, we will run the following script to understand basic usage of GROUP BY:

```
SELECT
    Department,
    Category,
    SUM(Salary) as Salary
FROM EmployeeSalary
GROUP BY Department, Category
```

You can see the output of this query in the following screenshot:

Results   Messages

	Department	Category	Salary
1	IT	A	8000.0000
2	Sales	A	7000.0000
3	IT	B	8000.0000
4	Sales	B	5000.0000
5	IT	C	3000.0000
6	Sales	C	6000.0000

Figure 6.2 – Result set in a Synapse notebook

3. Next, we will use `GROUP BY` with a `HAVING` clause to filter the data, as follows:

```
SELECT
    Department,
    Category,
    SUM(Salary) as Salary
FROM EmployeeSalary
GROUP BY Department, Category
HAVING SUM(salary) = 8000
```

You should get the total salary categorized by department and category in the result set, as seen in the following screenshot:

	Department	Category	Salary
1	IT	A	8000.0000
2	IT	B	8000.0000

Figure 6.3 – The result set of a SQL query in a Synapse notebook

4. If you want to calculate the aggregated value on individual groups and the cumulative aggregated value together, `GROUP BY ROLLUP` can be used with a `SELECT` statement, as illustrated in the following code snippet:

```
SELECT
    Department,
    Category,
    SUM(Salary) as Salary
FROM EmpSalary
GROUP BY ROLLUP(Department, Category)
```

You can see the result in the following screenshot, which first displays the salary for each department and category under **GroupingID** 0, followed by the aggregated salary for each category, and finally, the total salary:

	Department	Category	Salary	GroupingID
1	IT	A	8000.00	0
2	Sales	A	7000.00	0
3	IT	B	5000.00	0
4	Sales	B	4000.00	0
5	IT	C	3000.00	0
6	Sales	C	2000.00	0
7	NULL	A	15000.00	1
8	NULL	B	9000.00	1
9	NULL	C	5000.00	1
10	NULL	NULL	29000.00	3

Figure 6.4 – Result set for the preceding query on SQL Server Management Studio (SSMS)

> **Important note**
>
> As we know, we can use a GROUP BY CUBE clause as well to achieve similar results in SQL, but Synapse SQL does not support GROUP BY CUBE.

Using T-SQL loops in Synapse SQL

Azure Synapse SQL allows you to use a WHILE loop to execute statements repeatedly, as long as the specified condition is True. The following code block will help you understand the WHILE loop in Synapse SQL:

```
DECLARE @i INT=1
WHILE(@i<5)
            BEGIN
                    SELECT @i
                    /*Your logic goes here*/
                    SET @i+=1
            END
```

We can control WHILE loops by inserting a BREAK keyword inside the loop. Let's look at the following example to understand this better:

```
WHILE (SELECT AVG(SalesAmount) FROM dbo.FactInternetSales) <
$2000
BEGIN
    UPDATE dbo.FactInternetSales
        SET SalesAmount = SalesAmount * 2
    SELECT MAX(SalesAmount) FROM dbo.FactInternetSales
```

```
    IF (SELECT MAX(SalesAmount) FROM dbo.FactInternetSales) >
$5000
        BREAK
    END
```

In the preceding code block, we are using a `WHILE` statement to create a loop and a `BREAK` statement to come out of the loop. We can write any business logic within the loop as per the business demand, but it would be better to avoid looping unless this is required for better performance.

In this section, we have learned about all the T-SQL language elements that are supported in Azure Synapse. In the next section, we are going to learn how to use these language elements to create stored procedures and views in Synapse SQL.

Creating stored procedures and views in Synapse SQL

You can create stored procedures and views in a Synapse SQL pool using SSMS, Azure Data Studio, or Synapse Studio. In this section, we are going to learn the syntax for creating stored procedures and views. We will learn more about the usage and limitations of stored procedures and views further on in this section.

Stored procedures

A stored procedure is prepared SQL code that can be saved and reused. One important thing to keep in mind is that stored procedures are not precompiled in a Synapse SQL pool. When stored procedures are executed, SQL statements are parsed, translated, and optimized at runtime. As with SQL Server, you can pass parameters to stored procedures in a SQL pool as well.

The following code block provides a simple example of how to create stored procedures in a SQL pool:

```
CREATE PROCEDURE Usp_samplestoredprocedure (@MinPriceCondition
MONEY,
                                    @MaxPriceCondition MONEY)
AS
    BEGIN
        WHILE (SELECT Avg(salesamount)
```

```
                FROM     dbo.factinternetsales) < @MinPriceCondition
        BEGIN
            UPDATE dbo.factinternetsales
            SET     salesamount = salesamount * 2

            SELECT Max(salesamount)
            FROM     dbo.factinternetsales

            IF (SELECT Max(salesamount)
                FROM     dbo.factinternetsales) > @
MaxPriceCondition
                BREAK
        END
    END
```

When you execute the preceding code your stored procedure will be created, and now you are ready to execute the stored procedure, as follows:

```
EXEC Usp_samplestoredprocedure
    @MinPriceCondition=$2000,
    @MaxPriceCondition=$5000
```

You can consume the result set of a stored procedure with an INSERT statement in a SQL pool. You can use the following code snippet as reference:

```
Create Table #temp
(
[Department] varchar(100),
[Category] char(1),
salary Money
)
GO
Create PROCEDURE SP_ResultSet
as
SELECT
    Department,
    Category,
    SUM(Salary) as Salary
```

```
FROM EmployeeSalary
GROUP BY Department, Category
HAVING SUM(salary) = 8000
GO
Insert into #temp EXEC SP_ResultSet
GO
Select * from #temp
```

You can see the records stored in the #temp table in the following screenshot:

	Department	Category	salary
1	IT	A	8000.0000
2	IT	B	8000.0000

Figure 6.5 – Records available in the #temp table

Stored procedures can be called from other stored procedures, and these are called nested stored procedures. We can create nested stored procedures for up to 32 levels. As with SQL Server, you can create a nested stored procedure in a SQL pool as well. We will try to learn more about nested stored procedures in the following section.

Nested stored procedures

There could be various levels of nested stored procedures. However, a SQL pool supports a maximum of eight nesting levels, whereas SQL Server supports a maximum of eight nesting levels.

The following code block provides an example of how a stored procedure consists of a simple SELECT statement:

```
CREATE PROCEDURE usp_NestingProcDemo1
AS
SELECT 'This is NestingProcDemo1'
```

Next, we will create another procedure that we will call a preceding procedure. This can be considered as nesting level 1:

```
CREATE PROCEDURE Usp_nestingprocdemo2
AS
    BEGIN
```

```
        SELECT 'Calling from usp_NestingProcDemo2'
        EXEC Usp_nestingprocdemo1
    END
GO
EXEC Usp_nestingprocdemo2
```

> **Important note**
>
> SQL pools do not currently support @@NESTLEVEL.

The following screenshot shows the usage of a nested stored procedure within a main stored procedure. You can execute the same query on either SSMS or Azure Data Studio:

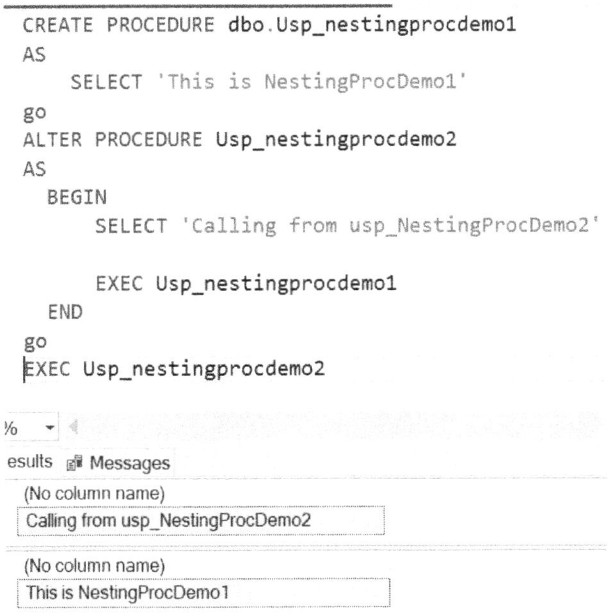

```
CREATE PROCEDURE dbo.Usp_nestingprocdemo1
AS
    SELECT 'This is NestingProcDemo1'
go
ALTER PROCEDURE Usp_nestingprocdemo2
AS
  BEGIN
      SELECT 'Calling from usp_NestingProcDemo2'

      EXEC Usp_nestingprocdemo1
  END
go
EXEC Usp_nestingprocdemo2
```

```
% ▾ ◄
esults  Messages
(No column name)
Calling from usp_NestingProcDemo2

(No column name)
This is NestingProcDemo1
```

Figure 6.6 – A stored procedures and its result set

Although a SQL pool allows you to create and use stored procedures, it restricts you from using certain aspects of T-SQL stored procedures, such as the following:

- Temporary stored procedures
- Numbered stored procedures
- Extended stored procedures

- **Common Language Runtime (CLR)** stored procedures
- Encryption options
- Replication options
- Table-valued parameters
- Read-only parameters
- Default parameters
- Execution contexts
- Return statements

Now that we have learned about creating stored procedures in a SQL pool, it's time to learn about user-defined views.

Views

Views create a virtual table consisting of a set of named columns and rows of data. Synapse SQL allows you to CREATE, ALTER, and DROP your views, as illustrated in the following code snippet:

```
CREATE VIEW dbo.SampleViewWithEncryption
AS
SELECT
    Department,
    Category,
    SUM(Salary) as Salary
FROM EmpSalary
GROUP BY ROLLUP(Department, Category)
```

Synapse serverless SQL allows you to create views in the same way you created views earlier in this section. If you have an **external data source**, you can use the OPENROWSET function DATA_SOURCE and its relative file path, as illustrated in the following code snippet:

```
DROP VIEW IF EXISTS populationView;
GO

CREATE VIEW populationView AS
SELECT *
FROM OPENROWSET(
```

```
        BULK 'csv/population/population.csv',
        DATA_SOURCE = 'SqlOnDemandDemo',
        FORMAT = 'CSV',
        FIELDTERMINATOR =',',
        ROWTERMINATOR = '\n'
    )
WITH (
    [country_code] VARCHAR (5) COLLATE Latin1_General_BIN2,
    [country_name] VARCHAR (100) COLLATE Latin1_General_BIN2,
    [year] smallint,
    [population] bigint
) AS [r];
```

The preceding code block will create a view, populationView, by using the OPENROWSET function to read data from the Population.csv file. Once the view is created, we can query the data directly without worrying about copying the data to any relational table.

So, now that we have learned how to create stored procedures and views in Synapse SQL, let's learn how to handle transactions in Synapse SQL.

Optimizing transactions in Synapse SQL

In simple words, a group of data modification operations is called a transaction. If all operations are successful, we can call it a successful transaction. In a successful transaction, all the modifications are committed and become a permanent part of the database; otherwise, all the data modifications will be erased.

In this section, we are going to learn how to manage transactions in Synapse SQL pools. In the case of any failure, you will need to roll back all the changes made during the execution of stored procedures in order to maintain consistency in your data. You can handle any sort of exceptions in stored procedures using a TRY-CATCH block, as illustrated in the following code snippet:

```
SET NOCOUNT ON;
DECLARE @xact_state smallint = 0;
BEGIN TRAN
    BEGIN TRY
        DECLARE @i INT;
                    SET @i=@i+1
```

```
        --SET @i='ABC'-- If you uncomment this statement,
you will encounter exception
        END TRY
    BEGIN CATCH
        SET @xact_state = XACT_STATE();
        IF @@TRANCOUNT > 0
        BEGIN
            ROLLBACK TRAN;
            PRINT 'ROLLBACK';
        END
        SELECT    ERROR_NUMBER()    AS ErrNumber
        ,         ERROR_SEVERITY()  AS ErrSeverity
        ,         ERROR_STATE()     AS ErrState
        ,         ERROR_PROCEDURE() AS ErrProcedure
        ,         ERROR_MESSAGE()   AS ErrMessage
        ;
    END CATCH;

IF @@TRANCOUNT >0
BEGIN
    PRINT 'COMMIT';
    COMMIT TRAN;
END
SELECT @xact_state AS TransactionState;
```

In the preceding code block, if you uncomment SET @i='ABC' you will encounter an error message, and the TransactionStatus value will be -2. You can use a XACT_STATE() function to know the status of a transaction; in the case of a successful transaction its value will be 0, and in the case of any failure, its value will be -2.

The following screenshot displays the use of a TRY-CATCH block in a transaction being executed on **SSMS**:

```
SET NOCOUNT ON;
DECLARE @xact_state smallint = 0;

BEGIN TRAN
    BEGIN TRY
        DECLARE @i INT;

        SET @i=@i+1
        SET @i='ABC' -- If you uncomment this statement, you will encounter exception

    END TRY
    BEGIN CATCH
        SET @xact_state = XACT_STATE();
```

% ▼ ◀

esults ▦ Messages

ErrNumber	ErrSeverity	ErrState	ErrProcedure	ErrMessage
245	16	1	NULL	Conversion failed when converting the varchar va...

TransactionState

-2

Figure 6.7 – Code and exception with TransactionState value

A SQL pool implements **Atomic, Consistent, Isolated, and Durable** (ACID) transactions with read uncommitted as the default isolation. Run the following command to check if your SQL pool has a read committed snapshot isolation level:

```
SELECT name, is_read_committed_snapshot_on
FROM sys.databases
WHERE name = DB_NAME();
```

You can change it to a read committed snapshot isolation by running the following script when connected to the master database:

```
ALTER DATABASE SQLPoolDemo
SET READ_COMMITTED_SNAPSHOT ON
```

> **Important note**
>
> A SQL pool does not support distributed transactions, nested transactions, named transactions, marked transactions, or save points. You cannot have **Data Definition Language** (DDL) such as CREATE TABLE inside a user-defined transaction.

It is important to implement transactions efficiently in your code; otherwise, you may lose all modified data in the case of any issue during transactions. In this section, we learned how we can use a TRY-CATCH block to handle exceptions during any transaction.

In the next section, we are going to learn what system views are and how these views can be leveraged to monitor your workload.

Supporting system views in a Synapse SQL pool

System views are built-in views in SQL that are used to monitor the health of a SQL pool and diagnose problems associated with the performance of a SQL pool.

Synapse SQL supports various system views, and we will be covering a few of these in this section, as follows:

- sys.pdw_column_distribution_properties: Holds distribution information for columns.

- sys.pdw_distributions: Holds information about the distributions on the appliance. It lists one row per appliance distribution.

- sys.pdw_index_mappings: Maps the logical indexes to the physical name used on compute nodes, as reflected by a unique combination of the object_id of the table holding the index and the index_id of a particular index within that table.

- sys.pdw_loader_backup_run_details: Contains information about ongoing and completed backup and restore operations in Azure Synapse Analytics (SQL Data Warehouse).

- sys.pdw_loader_backup_runs: This is similar to sys.pdw_loader_backup_run_details. However, comparatively, it gives more detailed information.

- sys.pdw_materialized_view_column_distribution_properties: This view displays distribution information for columns in a materialized view.

- sys.pdw_materialized_view_distribution_properties: This view displays distribution information materialized views.

- sys.pdw_materialized_view_mappings: Displays the physical names for the materialized view and the corresponding object_id.

- sys.pdw_nodes_column_store_dictionaries: This view contains a row for each dictionary used in columnstore indexes.

- `sys.pdw_nodes_column_store_row_groups`: Provides information about clustered columnstore indexes on a per-segment basis. It has a column for the total number of rows physically stored and a column for the number of rows marked as deleted.

- `sys.pdw_nodes_column_store_segments`: This view contains a row for each column in a columnstore index.

- `sys.pdw_nodes_columns`: This view shows columns for user-defined tables and views.

- `sys.pdw_nodes_indexes`: This view returns indexes for Azure Synapse Analytics.

- `sys.pdw_nodes_partitions`: Contains each partition of all the tables and most types of indexes in an Azure Synapse Analytics (SQL Data Warehouse) database.

- `sys.pdw_nodes_pdw_physical_databases`: Returns information about each physical database on a compute node.

- `sys.pdw_nodes_tables`: Contains records for each table object on which the principal has some permission.

- `sys.pdw_permanent_table_mappings`: This returns a physical name for the table corresponding to each `object_id`.

- `sys.pdw_replicated_table_cache_state`: This view is used to return the state of the cache associated with a replicated table.

- `sys.pdw_table_distribution_properties`: This is one of the most important views if you are using distributions in your table. It holds distribution information for tables.

- `sys.pdw_table_mappings`: This view associates user tables with internal object names by `object_id`.

- `sys.workload_management_workload_classifier_details`: Returns information about each classifier and can be joined with `sys.workload_management_workload_classifiers`.

- `sys.workload_management_workload_classifiers`: Returns details for workload classifiers.

- `sys.workload_management_workload_groups`: Returns details for workload groups.

There are many other dynamic management views that you should know about if you are working on Azure Synapse SQL. You can go to the following link to learn about all the dynamic management views supported by Synapse SQL: https://docs.microsoft.com/en-us/azure/synapse-analytics/sql-data-warehouse/sql-data-warehouse-reference-tsql-system-views.

So far in this chapter, we have learned how to use T-SQL on structured data, but in the next section, we are going to learn how we can use T-SQL queries on semi-structured and unstructured data.

Using T-SQL queries on semi-structured and unstructured data

Azure Synapse SQL on-demand allows you to query data in your data lake. The OPENROWSET function is used in SQL on-demand to query an external data source. We will learn how to use this function for reading different types of files.

Reading Parquet files

Parquet is an open source file format that is designed for efficient, as well as performant, flat columnar storage of data. Synapse provides a feature to read Parquet files directly, using the OPENROWSET function.

The easiest way to read a Parquet file's content is to provide the file **Uniform Resource Locator** (**URL**) to the OPENROWSET function and specify the Parquet format, as illustrated in the following code snippet:

```
select top 10 *
from openrowset(
    bulk 'https://pandemicdatalake.blob.core.windows.net/
public/curated/covid-19/ecdc_cases/latest/ecdc_cases.parquet',
    format = 'parquet') as rows
```

You can explicitly specify the columns that you want to read from the files, using a WITH clause. This is illustrated in the following code snippet:

```
select top 10 *
from openrowset(
        bulk 'latest/ecdc_cases.parquet',
        data_source = 'covid',
```

```
        format = 'parquet'
    ) with ( date_rep date, cases int, geo_id varchar(6) ) as
rows
```

Ideally, you do not need to use a WITH clause with OPENROWSET when reading Parquet files, as column names and data types are automatically read from Parquet files.

We can use the OPENROWSET function to read **JavaScript Object Notation (JSON)** files as well, and we are going to learn more about this in the following section.

Reading JSON documents

The OPENROWSET function can be used to read JSON documents as well. The best possible way to learn how to read JSON documents in Azure Synapse SQL is to go to the sample SQL script that has been made available to end users via Synapse Studio. We will go through the following steps to get the sample SQL script that uses the OPENROWSET function to read JSON files:

1. Log in to the Azure portal at https://portal.azure.com.

2. Go to your Synapse workspace and launch Synapse Studio.

3. Go to the **Develop** tab on Synapse Studio and navigate to **Browse samples** by clicking on the + icon, as highlighted in the following screenshot:

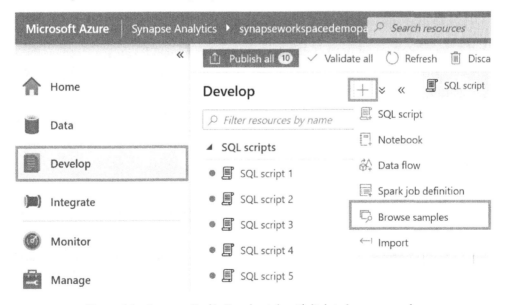

Figure 6.8 – Synapse Studio Develop tab with link to browse samples

4.   Select **Query JSON files** under the **SQL scripts** tab and click on **Continue**, as illustrated in the following screenshot:

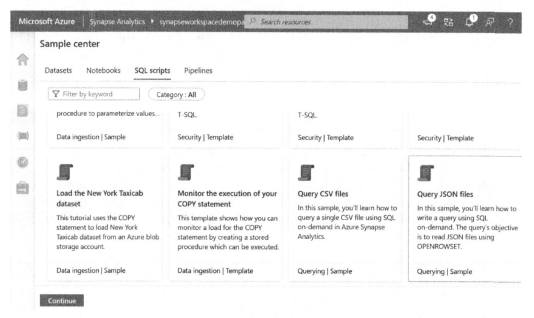

Figure 6.9 – Sample scripts in Synapse Studio

5.   On the next screen, you can see all the details about the script you selected. Click on **Open script** after reviewing the **Description** tab.

The JSON document in the following sample query includes an array of objects. The query returns each object as a separate row in the result set:

```
SELECT TOP 10 *
FROM OPENROWSET(
        BULK 'https://pandemicdatalake.blob.core.windows.
net/public/curated/covid-19/ecdc_cases/latest/ecdc_cases.
jsonl',
        FORMAT = 'csv',
        FIELDTERMINATOR ='0x0b',
        FIELDQUOTE = '0x0b'
    ) with (doc nvarchar(max)) as rows
```

The following screenshot shows the result from the preceding query:

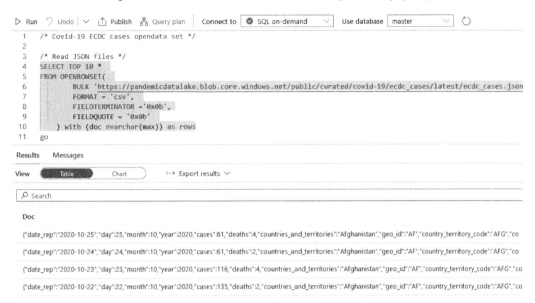

Figure 6.10 – Query retrieving JSON documents in Synapse SQL on-demand using OPENROWSET

You can use `JSON_QUERY` to retrieve objects and arrays, and `JSON_VALUE` to retrieve scalar values from a JSON document.

The following screenshot shows the usage of `JSON_VALUE` to retrieve the scalar values' title and publisher:

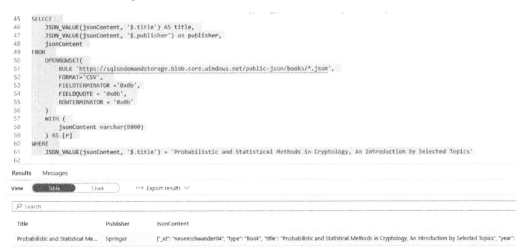

Figure 6.11 – Query result displaying the usage of JSON_VALUE to retrieve scalar values

The following script is an example of using JSON_QUERY to retrieve authors, which is an array, from a book with the title *Probabilistic and Statistical Methods in Cryptology, An Introduction by Selected Topics*:

```
SELECT
      JSON_QUERY(jsonContent, '$.authors') AS authors,
      jsonContent
FROM
      OPENROWSET(
            BULK 'https://sqlondemandstorage.blob.core.
windows.net/public-json/books/*.json',
            FORMAT='CSV',
            FIELDTERMINATOR ='0x0b',
            FIELDQUOTE = '0x0b',
            ROWTERMINATOR = '0x0b'
      )
      WITH (
            jsonContent varchar(8000)
      ) AS [r]
WHERE
      JSON_VALUE(jsonContent, '$.title') = 'Probabilistic
and Statistical Methods in Cryptology, An Introduction
by Selected Topics'
```

The following screenshot displays the result set produced by running the preceding query. The code block shown here retrieves the author for a particular book:

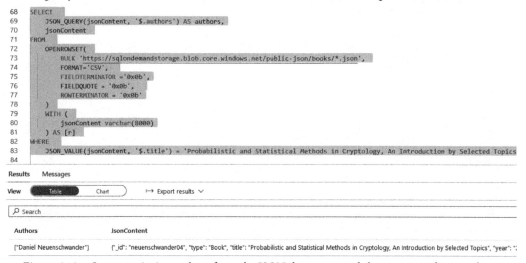

Figure 6.12 – Query retrieving authors from the JSON document and the corresponding result set

In this section, we learned various ways to retrieve different attributes from a JSON file. In the next section, we are going to learn about external tables in detail.

External tables

An external table points to data located in Hadoop, Azure Storage blob, or Azure Data Lake Storage. With Synapse SQL, you can use external tables to read and write data to a SQL pool or SQL on-demand (preview).

Similar to the preceding example, we can use a sample SQL script to learn how to use external tables to read data from a data lake.

The following screenshot displays the sample SQL scripts available in Synapse Studio:

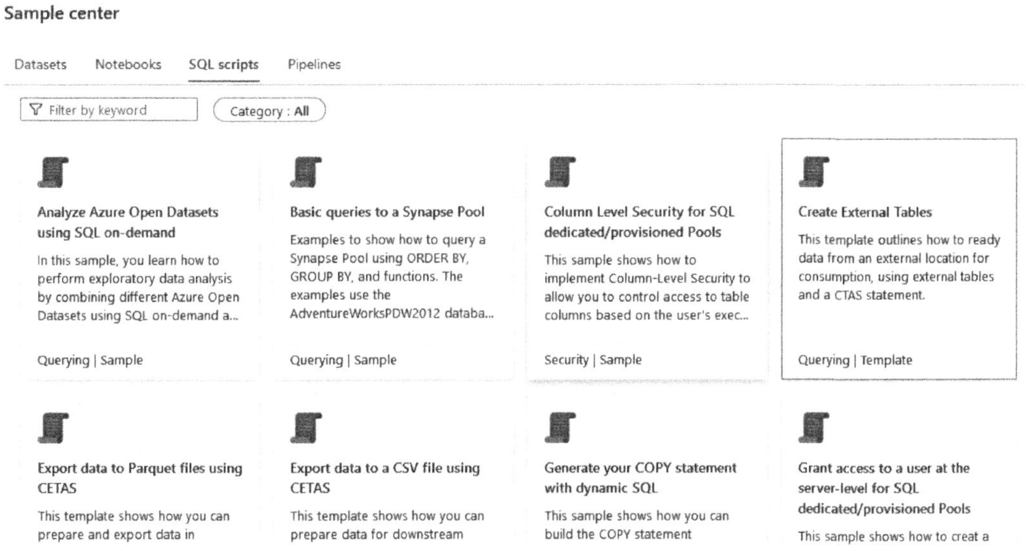

Figure 6.13 – Sample SQL scripts in Synapse Studio

We will go through the following steps to get a sample SQL script that uses external tables:

1. Go to the **Develop** tab in Synapse Studio and navigate to **Browse samples** by clicking on the + icon.

2. Search for **Create External Tables** from the list of all sample **SQL scripts**, and click on **Continue**.

3. On the next screen, you can see a **Description** about the script, and you get an option to select a SQL pool or create a new one. Let's select a SQL pool and a database, as illustrated in the following screenshot:

Figure 6.14 – Description for Create External Tables sample script

4. Click on **Open Script** to get scripts to read an external table.

5. The following code block consists of a script to create a scoped credential database:

```
CREATE DATABASE SCOPED CREDENTIAL MyCredential
WITH
    IDENTITY = 'SHARED ACCESS SIGNATURE',
    SECRET = '<your_SAS_token>' ;
```

6. Next, we can see a script to create an **external data source**, as follows:

```
CREATE EXTERNAL DATA SOURCE MyDataSource
WITH (
    TYPE = HADOOP,
    LOCATION = 'abfss://<container>@<storage_account>.
dfs.core.windows.net',
    CREDENTIAL = MyCredential
)
```

7. The following code block consists of a script to create an **external file format**:

```
CREATE EXTERNAL FILE FORMAT MyTextFileFormat
WITH
(
     FORMAT_TYPE = DELIMITEDTEXT,
     FORMAT_OPTIONS (
          FIELD_TERMINATOR = ',',
          STRING_DELIMITER = '"',
          USE_TYPE_DEFAULT = False)
)
```

8. Next, we will create an **external table**, as follows:

```
CREATE EXTERNAL TABLE [dbo].[MyExtTable] (
     [f1] int NOT NULL,
     [f2] char NOT NULL,
     [f3] int NOT NULL
)
WITH (LOCATION='<my_file_location>',
     DATA_SOURCE = MyDataSource,
     FILE_FORMAT = MyTextFileFormat
);
```

9. Next, we have a script to create a local table using an external table, as shown in the following code snippet:

```
CREATE TABLE MyLocalCopy
WITH (DISTRIBUTION = ROUND_ROBIN)
AS SELECT * FROM
[dbo].[MyExtTable];
```

You can modify the value for different parameters used in the preceding examples as per your business need. We will be covering a couple of scenarios in the upcoming chapter, which should make you feel more comfortable using Synapse SQL.

Summary

This chapter was primarily focused on Synapse SQL. We learned different T-SQL language elements that are supported in Synapse SQL, as well as their limitations. We learned how we can use T-SQL statements with structured, semi-structured, or unstructured data. In this chapter, we also covered how to manage transactions efficiently to avoid any transaction failures. We also learned that we could create stored procedures and views in Synapse SQL in a similar way to how we do this in SQL Server. Synapse SQL provides a few additional features to read data directly from a data lake.

We saw some of the system views supported in Synapse SQL. We also learned how to use sample scripts to build our logic as per the business need.

The next chapter will be more focused on Synapse Spark, where we will learn how to write code in different languages in Synapse Spark without worrying about infrastructure management. We will also learn how to use notebooks in Synapse Studio.

7
Working with R, Python, Scala, .NET, and Spark SQL in Azure Synapse

Azure Synapse gives you the freedom to query data on your terms, by using either serverless on-demand or provisioned resources—at scale. You can query data directly in the Synapse notebook using PySpark, Spark (Scala), Spark SQL, or .NET for Apache Spark (C#).

Azure Synapse Studio notebooks support four languages. You can set the primary language in a notebook, as seen in the following screenshot; however, you can use multiple languages in the same notebook by using the correct language magic command at the beginning of a cell:

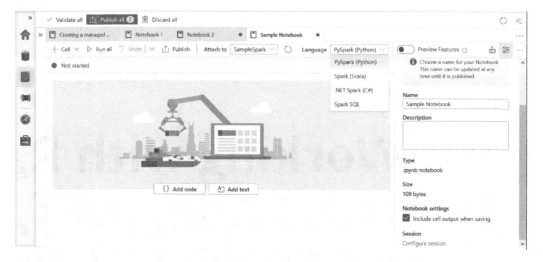

Figure 7.1 – A screenshot of a Synapse notebook highlighting various supported languages

In this chapter, we are going to pick a couple of examples from the sample gallery provided within the Synapse workspace, to understand how to use different languages in a Synapse notebook. This chapter outlines the use of sample data and scripts to understand how to use a Synapse notebook to perform various operations on the data. If you are new to Azure Synapse Analytics, this chapter is specifically for you. You are going to learn how the sample scripts can be used against the sample data within Synapse Studio. You will also learn how we can read the data from Azure Data Lake Storage Gen2 accounts or how to save the data back to the data lake in different formats.

In this chapter, we will cover the following topics:

- Using Azure Open Datasets
- Using sample scripts

Technical requirements

Before you start orchestrating your data, here are certain prerequisites that you should meet:

- You should have your Azure subscription, or access to any other subscription, with contributor-level access.

- Create your Synapse workspace on this subscription. You can follow the instructions from *Chapter 1, Introduction to Azure Synapse,* to create your Synapse workspace.

- Create a Spark pool and a SQL pool on Azure Synapse. This has been covered in *Chapter 2, Consideration for Your Compute Environment.*

Using Azure Open Datasets

This chapter helps you learn how you can use Azure Open Datasets to start exploring various features offered by Azure Synapse Analytics. We will also learn how we can read the data from these open datasets using Synapse notebooks. Microsoft provides a variety of datasets on Azure that can be accessed directly from Synapse. Synapse provides an option to add a dataset from the gallery of Azure Open Datasets. You just need to follow a couple of steps to bring the data to your Synapse account from the gallery of sample datasets:

1. Log in to the Azure portal at `https://portal.azure.com`.

2. Go to your Synapse workspace on the Azure portal and launch Synapse Studio.

3. Click on the **Data** tab in Synapse Studio and click on + to browse through the sample gallery:

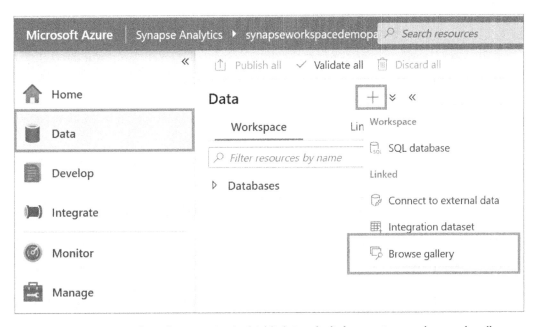

Figure 7.2 – A screenshot of Synapse Studio highlighting the link to navigate to the sample gallery

4. You can see various samples from Azure Open Datasets. We are going to select the dataset for **Bing COVID-19 Data** in this chapter:

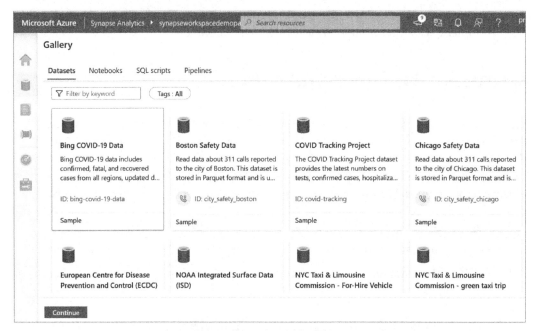

Figure 7.3 – A screenshot of the gallery in Synapse Studio

5. Click on **Continue** to go through the description and then click on **Add dataset**.

It will take couple of seconds for it to get added to your linked Azure Blob storage section:

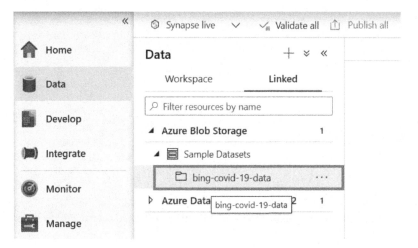

Figure 7.4 – A screenshot of the bing-covid-19-data dataset in your Synapse workspace

6. Click on **…** next to **bing-covid-19-data** and then click on **New notebook | Load to DataFrame**, as highlighted in the following screenshot:

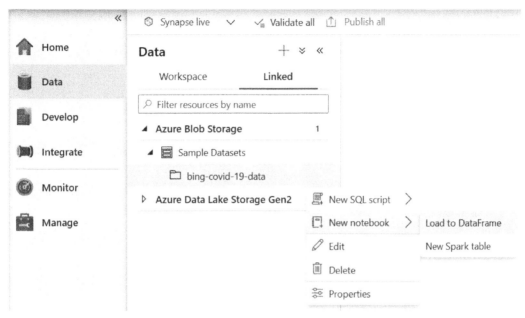

Figure 7.5 – Creating a new notebook to query the bing-covid-19-data dataset

7. On the next screen, you need to select your Synapse pool to run the script. So, let's select your Synapse pool from the drop-down list.

8. The default selected language is **PySpark (Python)**. However, you can change it to any language that you are comfortable with. In this example, we will continue with **PySpark (Python)**.

9. You can see a Python script that reads data from `bing-covid-19-data`. Run the cell to see the output:

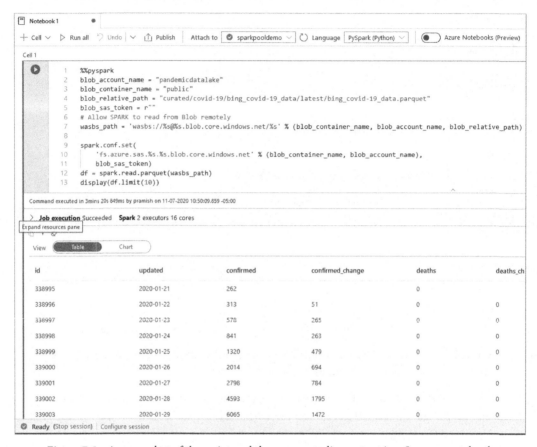

Figure 7.6 – A screenshot of the script and the corresponding output in a Synapse notebook

As we observed in this example, we are trying to access `bing-covid-19-data` from a blob storage that has been made publicly accessible to anyone. However, you can also read the data from a private storage account.

If you want to query your files stored in Azure Blob storage or Azure Data Lake Gen2, you need to connect to the external data source on Synapse:

1. Go to the **Data** tab on **Synapse Studio,** click on the + icon as highlighted in the following screenshot, and then click on the **Connect to external data** tab:

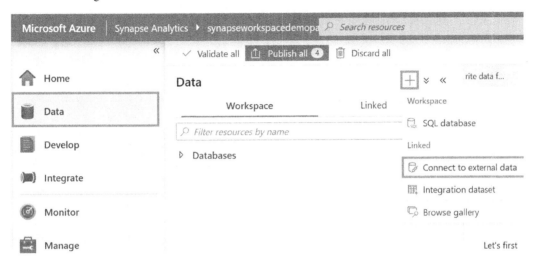

Figure 7.7 – A screenshot highlighting the link to connect to external data

2. Select the data store of your choosing. In this example, let's select **Azure Data Lake Storage Gen2** and then click on **Continue**.

3. Provide an appropriate name for the linked service.

4. Select an **Azure subscription** and **Storage account name** option from the corresponding dropdowns and then click on **Create**:

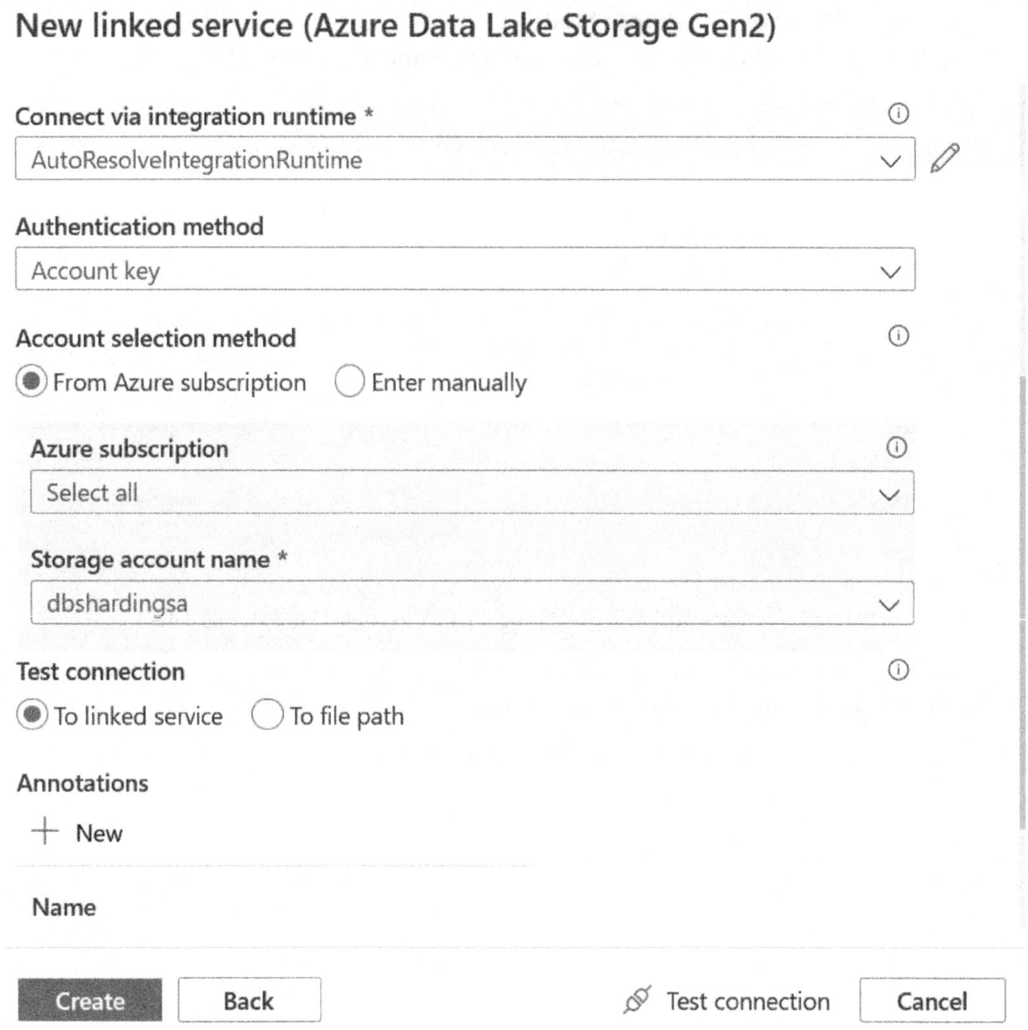

New linked service (Azure Data Lake Storage Gen2)

Connect via integration runtime *   ⓘ

| AutoResolveIntegrationRuntime | ∨ | 🖉 |

Authentication method

| Account key | ∨ |

Account selection method   ⓘ

◉ From Azure subscription   ◯ Enter manually

Azure subscription   ⓘ

| Select all | ∨ |

Storage account name *

| dbshardingsa | ∨ |

Test connection   ⓘ

◉ To linked service   ◯ To file path

Annotations

+ New

Name

| Create | Back | | 🖉 Test connection | Cancel |

Figure 7.8 – Creating a linked service for Azure Data Lake Storage Gen2

> **Important note**
> You can click on the **Enter manually** radio button to enter account details manually.

5. Click on **Linked services** under the **Manage** hub in Synapse Studio to view your newly created linked service:

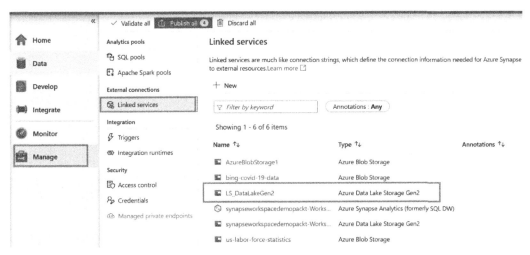

Figure 7.9 – A screenshot of the Linked services tab that highlights the newly created linked service

In the next section, we are going to learn how to use different languages in a Synapse notebook to perform various operations on the dataset.

Using sample scripts

Similar to sample data, Synapse provides a gallery of sample scripts. If you are new to Synapse Spark, this could definitely be a great place to start. We are going to pick a couple of scripts from the gallery to get ourselves acquainted with the different languages supported by Synapse.

Before we can start reading the data from Azure Data Lake Gen2, we need to get a **Shared Access Signature** (**SAS**) key for our blob storage. These keys will be used in our notebooks to access the corresponding blob storages. We can do so by performing the following steps:

1. Go to your Azure Blob storage account on the Azure portal.

2. Click on **Shared access signature**, check the **Container** box under **Allowed resource types**, and then click on **Generate SAS and connection string**:

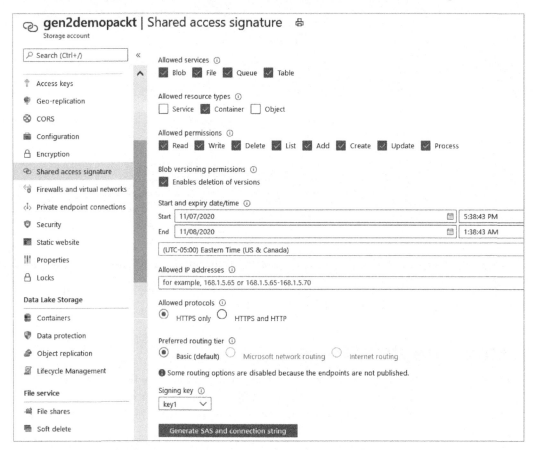

Figure 7.10 – Generating an SAS for the Azure Blob storage account

In the sections that follow, we will learn about the different languages supported in a Synapse notebook to read data from Azure Data Lake Gen2.

PySpark (Python)

We will create a new notebook to start from scratch. In order to create our new notebook, we need to go through the following steps:

1. Log in to the Azure portal (`https://portal.azure.com`).

2. Navigate to your Synapse workspace and launch Synapse Studio.

3. Go to the **Develop** hub in Synapse Studio.

4. Click on + and select **Notebook** to create your blank notebook, as seen in the following screenshot:

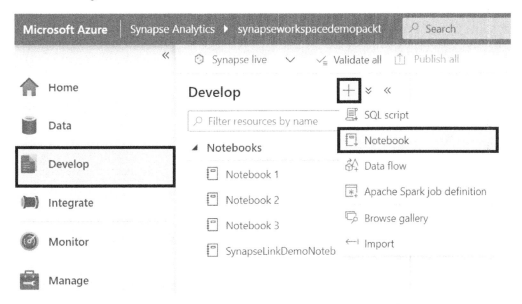

Figure 7.11 – Creating a blank notebook in Synapse Studio

You can choose the default language for the notebook from the drop-down list; however, you can use the Synapse Spark **magic commands** to switch to any other language in any particular cell. For this example, we will select **Scala** as the default language for our notebook. Click on the { } **Add code** link to add a new cell to the notebook:

Figure 7.12 – A screenshot of the notebook on Synapse Studio

In the following section, we will learn how we can read data from an Azure Data Lake Storage Gen2 account using the Python (PySpark) language.

Reading data from Azure Data Lake Storage Gen2 using Python

We will start with the basic task of reading data from Azure Data Lake Storage Gen2. We will select Python as the default language for this notebook. However, if your default language is Scala or any other language, use the `%%pyspark` magic command to start writing code in Python:

```
%%pyspark
blob_account_name = "testblobaccount"
blob_container_name = "testcontainer"
from pyspark.sql import SparkSession
#Creating Spark Session
sc = SparkSession.builder.getOrCreate()
token_library = sc._jvm.com.microsoft.azure.synapse.
tokenlibrary.TokenLibrary
blob_sas_token = token_library.
getConnectionString("AzureBlobStorage1")
#Reading data from blob and loading it to Spark DataFrame
spark.conf.set(
    'fs.azure.sas.%s.%s.blob.core.windows.net' % (blob_
container_name, blob_account_name),
    blob_sas_token)
df = spark.read.load('wasbs://testcontainer@testblobaccount.
blob.core.windows.net/austria.csv', format='csv'
## If header exists uncomment line below
, header=True
)
display(df.limit(10))
```

Next, we will save the DataFrame in **Resilient Distributed Dataset (RDD)** format. RDD is a collection of elements partitioned across the nodes of the cluster that can be operated on in parallel.

You can run the following code snippet to save your data in RDD form in your Spark pool:

```
austin_RDD = df.rdd
type(austin_RDD )
```

Once your data is saved in the RDD form in Spark, you have the option to save the data in any format as per your business requirements. In the following code snippet, first we will define the target path and where we want to store the data in text format. You can also create variables to define the file path instead of hardcoding the value in the code:

```
adls_path='wasbs://mycontainer@mystorageaccount.blob.core.
windows.net/'
text_path = adls_path + 'austintext.txt'
austin_RDD.saveAsTextFile(text_path)
df.write.csv('wasbs://mycontainer@mystorageaccount.blob.core.
windows.net/austria_csv.csv', mode = 'overwrite', header =
  'true')
```

You can also save your RDD in different formats. The following code block can be used to save RDD in Parquet, JSON, or CSV files:

```
parquet_path = adls_path + 'austin_parquet.parquet'
json_path = adls_path + 'austin_json.json'
csv_path = adls_path + 'austin_csv.csv'
```

So now, your data is residing in a file saved on your Data Lake Gen2 storage account. You can read this data for further explorations or data visualizations. Instead of creating a DataFrame, you can also choose to create a managed Spark table in Azure Synapse Analytics, and we are going to learn how to do that in the following section.

Creating a managed Spark table

There are primarily two types of Spark tables – external and managed. In this section, we will learn how to create a managed Spark table. A Spark SQL table for which Spark manages both the data and the metadata is known as a Spark managed table.

The following code block will create a Spark table in a Synapse workspace:

```
spark.sql("CREATE TABLE cities  (name STRING, population INT)
USING PARQUET")
```

The following script can be used to ingest the records in this table:

```
spark.sql("INSERT INTO cities VALUES (\'Seattle\', 730400),
(\'San Francisco\', 881549), (\'Beijing\', 21540000),
(\'Bangalore\', 10540000)")
```

We can validate the records by running the `display` command, as highlighted in the following screenshot:

name	population
Bangalore	10540000
Beijing	21540000
San Francisco	881549
Seattle	730400

Figure 7.13 – A screenshot that shows the running of the Python script and the result in Synapse Studio

In the following sections, we will use a couple of scripts similar to the Python script to learn how to use Scala in Synapse Studio.

Spark (Scala)

We will select Scala as the default language for this notebook. Similar to the Python script, we can use Scala to read data from Azure Data Lake Storage Gen2.

Reading data from Azure Data Lake Storage Gen2 using Scala

Data stored in an Azure Data Lake Storage Gen2 account can also be read using Scala, similar to a Python application. In this case, too, we require a storage account name, a blob container name, and a blob relative path, along with an SAS key to access the data. We are going to use the same SAS key that we generated in the *Using sample scripts* section.

Modify the corresponding values in the following code block to read data from your storage account:

```
// set blob storage account connection for open dataset
val hol_blob_account_name = "mystorageaccount"
val hol_blob_container_name = "myblobcontainer"
val hol_blob_relative_path = ""
```

```
val hol_blob_sas_token = "?sv=2019-12-
12&ss=bfqt&srt=c&sp=rwdlacupx&se=2020-11-15T07:13:44Z&st=2020-
11-14T23:13:44Z&spr=https&sig=%2FvxxFUcgAGc36SyUy%2BCKZzkVoh
YCuDHT4q8H%2BW36N1o%3D"
```

```
val hol_wasbs_path = f"wasbs://$hol_blob_container_name@$hol_
blob_account_name.blob.core.windows.net/$hol_blob_relative_
path"
spark.conf.set(f"fs.azure.sas.$hol_blob_container_name.$hol_
blob_account_name.blob.core.windows.net",hol_blob_sas_token)
```

Now, after setting the blob storage account connection, we will load the sample data into a Spark DataFrame using the Scala language:

```
val hol_df = spark.read.parquet(hol_wasbs_path)
hol_df.show(5, truncate = false)
```

The following screenshot displays the records saved in the DataFrame:

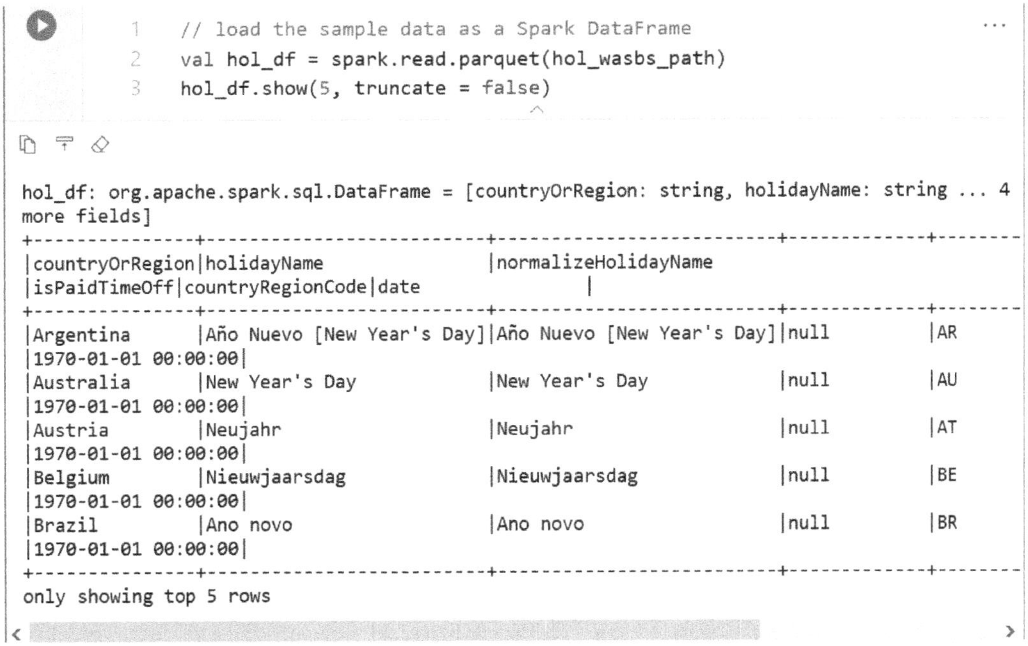

Figure 7.14 – A screenshot of the Scala code and its result set

You need to provide values for the storage account name, container name, and relative path in the following code snippet to retrieve the path of your Azure Data Lake Storage Gen2 account where you would like to save your files:

```
// set your storage account connection

val account_name = "" // replace with your blob name
val container_name = "" //replace with your container name
val relative_path = "" //replace with your relative folder path

val adls_path = f"abfss://$container_name@$account_name.dfs.
core.windows.net/$relative_path"
```

You can use the following script to save the DataFrame in different formats:

```
import org.apache.spark.sql.SaveMode
// set the path for the output file
val parquet_path = adls_path + "holiday.parquet"
val json_path = adls_path + "holiday.json"
val csv_path = adls_path + "holiday.csv"

hol_df.write.mode(SaveMode.Overwrite).parquet(parquet_path)
hol_df.write.mode(SaveMode.Overwrite).json(json_path)
hol_df.write.mode(SaveMode.Overwrite).option("header", "true").
csv(csv_path)
```

In the following section, we will learn how to create a DataFrame or Spark table using the C# language in Azure Synapse Analytics.

.NET Spark (C#)

Synapse supports C# with Spark. This change makes work for developers who are already comfortable with the language easier.

Creating Spark DataFrames using the CreateDataFrame API

In this example, we will be creating **Spark DataFrames** by using the CreateDataFrame API. It accepts the data in the form of Row objects and returns a DataFrame object.

The following code block will create a DataFrame with Name and Age attributes:

```
List<StructField>()
{
    new StructField("Name", new StringType()),
    new StructField("Age", new IntegerType())
});


// Calling CreateDataFrame with the data and schema
DataFrame df = spark.CreateDataFrame(data, schema);


// Displaying the returned dataframe
df.Show();
```

The following screenshot displays the records stored in the DataFrame:

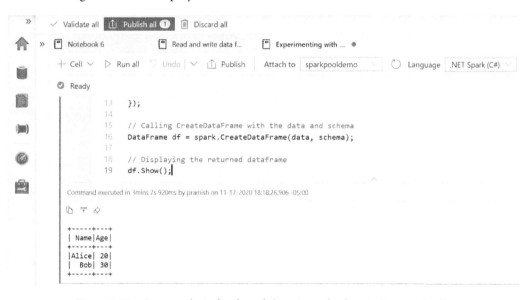

Figure 7.15 – A screenshot of code and the returned values in Synapse Studio

You can even create functions in a Synapse notebook. The following function can be used to convert the `Time` column from `StringType` to `TimestampType`:

```
public DataFrame CastColumn(DataFrame df_, string colName,
string t)
{
    df_ = df_.WithColumn("NewCol__", df_[colName].Cast(t));
    df_ = df_.Drop(colName);
    df_ = df_.WithColumnRenamed("NewCol__", colName);
    return df_;
}
```

Now we have learned how we can use PySpark and Scala to read or write data to an Azure Data Lake Storage Gen2 account. The following section outlines the use of Spark SQL in the Synapse workspace.

Spark SQL

The Spark SQL syntax is similar to T-SQL; hence, you will not have difficulty in using this as your primary language. However, keep in mind that Spark SQL does not support all the features available in T-SQL. Spark SQL has another added advantage that we will learn about gradually throughout this book.

In this section, we will select **Spark SQL** as the default language for our notebook.

Creating a managed Spark table using Spark SQL

The following script will create a managed table from Spark. The table is created in the Synapse warehouse folder in your primary storage account. The table will be synchronized and available in Synapse SQL pools:

```
CREATE TABLE cities
   (name STRING, population INT)
   USING PARQUET
```

You can go to your primary storage account to validate whether the table is created after running the preceding Spark SQL code, which can be seen in the following screenshot:

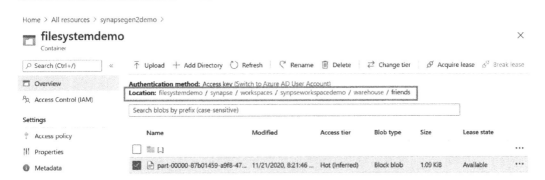

Figure 7.16 – A screenshot of the primary storage account that shows the data available under the highlighted path

After creating the table, let's insert some records in it:

```
INSERT INTO cities VALUES ('Seattle', 730400),
('San Francisco', 881549), ('Beijing', 21540000),
('Bangalore', 10540000)
```

When you run any script in Spark SQL, you can see the Spark job running in the output window. Once the job is complete, the **Status** field will be updated to **Succeeded**:

Figure 7.17 – A screenshot of the INSERT script and the job execution status

Next, you can perform the SELECT operation on this table to validate whether the data has been inserted correctly:

Figure 7.18 – A screenshot displaying the records in the cities table

Similar to the managed Spark table, you can also create an unmanaged Spark table in Synapse, which we will be looking at in the next section.

Creating an unmanaged Spark table

An unmanaged Spark table is also known as an external table. You can create external tables from Spark by using Spark SQL. We need to provide a value for the LOCATION parameter, which defines the path where the Spark table must be created:

```
CREATE TABLE cities
   (name STRING, population INT)
   USING PARQUET
   LOCATION '/datalake/cities'
   OPTIONS ('compression'='snappy')
```

Just as we can ingest data in an external table, in the same way, we can ingest the records in the managed table:

```
INSERT INTO cities VALUES ('Seattle', 730400),
('San Francisco', 881549), ('Beijing', 21540000),
('Bangalore', 10540000)
```

You can also validate whether the file is present in the specified location. Go to the **Linked** section of the **Data** tab in Synapse Studio and click on your primary storage account:

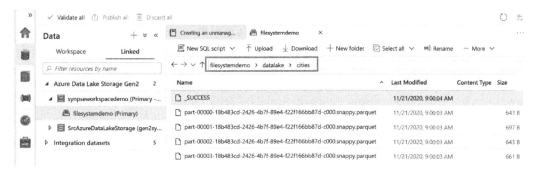

Figure 7.19 – A screenshot of files created under the specified path: filesystemdemo/datalake/cities

In the following screenshot, we can view the data on a Synapse notebook as well:

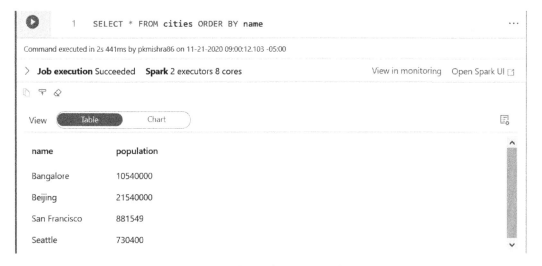

Figure 7.20 – A screenshot of records present in the cities external table

In this chapter, we looked at just a couple of examples, but it is recommended to go through all the sample scripts provided in the gallery of Synapse Studio. Make sure that you delete your Spark pool and SQL pool after practicing all the sample scripts.

Summary

In this chapter, we learned how to use different languages in a Synapse notebook to query data. Magic commands allow you to easily switch to any different language within the same notebook. We covered how to use Azure Open Datasets within a Synapse workspace. We also learned that a DataFrame or Spark table can be created using all the supported languages in Azure Synapse Analytics. In this chapter, we learned how to read data from Azure Data Lake Storage Gen2 accounts, how to create Spark DataFrames, and how to create Spark tables using PySpark, Scala, or .NET languages. We also covered how we can write data back to an Azure Data Lake Storage Gen2 account. Although we only covered Azure Data Lake Storage Gen2, we can use a similar approach for accessing data on blob containers.

So far, we have learned about using a Spark pool and SQL pool, and using different languages against these pools. However, our next area of focus will be the reporting tool.

In the next chapter, we will learn how to connect Synapse data to Power BI and create powerful reports.

8

Integrating a Power BI Workspace with Azure Synapse

In previous chapters, we learned about the concepts of SQL pool, Spark pool, and SQL on-demand. We learned how to query our data in a Synapse notebook by using different languages. Now, in this chapter, we are going to learn how we can add more value to this data by integrating our Synapse workspace with Power BI. Azure Synapse gives you the flexibility to bring Synapse data to your Power BI desktop as well. In this chapter, we will learn how to use different endpoints to connect to the Power BI desktop. We are also going to learn how to integrate the Power BI workspace with the Synapse workspace. This chapter also outlines the steps for modifying Power BI reports directly in Synapse Studio and publishing it back to the Power BI workspace. The topics covered in this chapter will give you a fair understanding of integrating Power BI with Azure Synapse.

In this chapter, we will cover the following topics:

- Connecting to a Power BI workspace
- Creating your own dashboard on Azure Synapse
- Connecting Azure Synapse data to Power BI Desktop

Technical requirements

Before you start orchestrating your data, there are certain prerequisites that you should meet, including the following:

- You should have your Azure subscription, or access to any other subscription, with contributor-level access.

- Create your Synapse workspace on this subscription. You can follow the instructions from *Chapter 1*, *Introduction to Azure Synapse*, to create your Synapse workspace.

- Create a Spark pool and SQL pool on Azure Synapse. This has been covered in *Chapter 2*, *Consideration for Your Compute Environments*.

- You should have access to the Power BI workspace and a basic knowledge of Power BI Desktop and the Power BI service.

- Download the financial sample file (shared by Microsoft) from the following location (`https://go.microsoft.com/fwlink/?LinkID=521962`) and save it on your local machine.

Connecting to a Power BI workspace

Azure Synapse gives you the flexibility to connect to your Power BI workspace, which means you need to have your own Power BI workspace, or you must access the Power BI workspace to utilize this feature. Once you are connected to the Power BI workspace, you can view and modify your reports directly from the Synapse workspace. In this section, we are going to learn about working with Power BI reports within Synapse Studio.

We will perform the following steps to connect our Synapse workspace to the Power BI workspace:

1. Go to your Synapse workspace and click on the **Open Synapse Studio** link, as highlighted in the following screenshot:

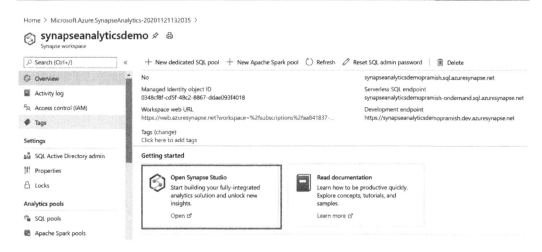

Figure 8.1 – A screenshot of the Azure Synapse workspace highlighting the link to Open Synapse Studio

2. In Synapse Studio, click on the **Visualize** tab on the **Home** page, as shown in *Figure 8.2*, or go to the **Manage** tab in Synapse Studio and then go to the **Linked Services** section to add a new linked service:

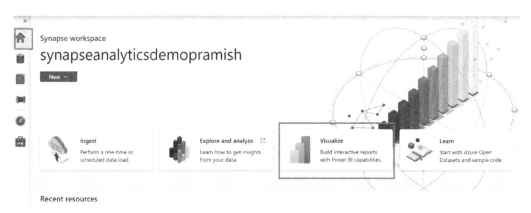

Figure 8.2 – A screenshot of Synapse Studio highlighting the Visualize link

3. Provide an appropriate name and description for the Power BI workspace. This name can be different to the actual Power BI workspace name.

4. Select **Tenant** and **Workspace name** from the drop-down lists and then click on **Create**:

Connect to Power BI

ⓘ Choose a name for your linked service. This name cannot be updated later.

Connect a Power BI workspace to create reports and datasets from data in your workspace.
Learn more ⬓

Name *

```
PowerBIWorkspace1
```

Description

Tenant

Workspace name *

☐ Edit

Annotations

+ New

▷ Advanced ⓘ

Create   Cancel

Figure 8.3 – Connecting a Power BI workspace to Azure Synapse

5. Click on the **Develop** tab to verify whether you can see your Power BI workspace under the **Power BI** section. You should be able to see **Power BI datasets** and **Power BI reports** associated with your Power BI workspace:

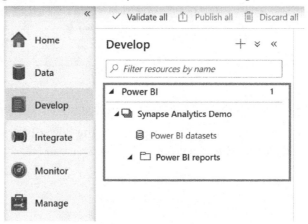

Figure 8.4 – A screenshot of a Power BI workspace within Synapse Studio

Now that we have connected our Synapse workspace to the Power BI workspace, it's time to create some valuable reports to visualize our data.

Creating your own dashboard on Azure Synapse

Before we can start creating our Power BI reports, we need to create our datasets to visualize the data through Power BI reports. So, we will divide this section into two subsections. First, we will learn how to create a new Power BI dataset in Azure Synapse and then we will learn how to create a Power BI report.

Creating new Power BI datasets

We need to add a Power BI dataset from a data source and publish it to Power BI to build reports in Azure Synapse Studio. We can add the dataset directly to the Power BI service or we can add a dataset to the Power BI Desktop version and then publish it to the Power BI service.

The following section comprises the steps for adding data from a sample Excel file from a local machine as a new dataset to the Power BI service.

Adding a dataset to the Power BI service

In order to add a new dataset to the Power BI service, sign in to https://powerbi. com and click on your workspace:

1. Click on **+ New**, which is on top of the screen and select **Dataset** from the list of all available options:

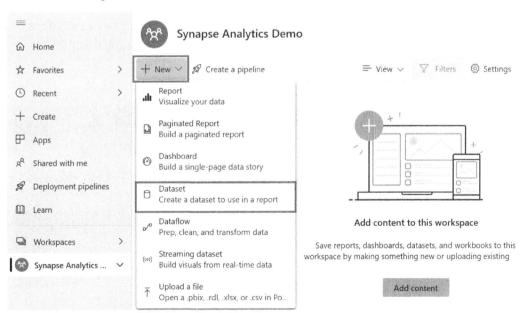

Figure 8.5 – A screenshot highlighting the link to create a new dataset in the Power BI workspace

2. There are various ways in which to create your dataset, as highlighted in the following screenshot, but we are going to select **Files** for our example. Therefore, click on the **Get** tab, which is under the **Files** tab:

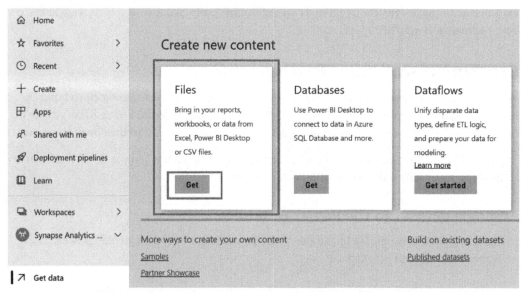

Figure 8.6 – Tab for creating datasets from files

3. Click on **Local File** and select the `Financial Sample.xlsx` file from your local machine. You need to have downloaded the `Financial Sample.xlsx` file as mentioned in the *Technical requirements* section before performing this step:

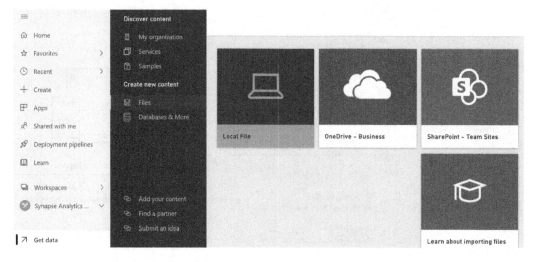

Figure 8.7 – A screenshot of the Power BI workspace where we are trying to get data from a local file

4. Select the `Financial Sample.xlsx` file from your local machine.

5. You can decide how you want to use the data in Power BI. You can choose to import the Excel data to Power BI or you can import the Excel file into Power BI to view and interact with it, just as you would in Excel Online. Next, let's click on the **Import** tab to bring data into Power BI, as seen in the following screenshot:

Figure 8.8 – Tab for importing the data into Power BI

6. Now, we will go back to Synapse Studio and refresh **Power BI datasets** to validate whether we are able to see the dataset that we created in Power BI:

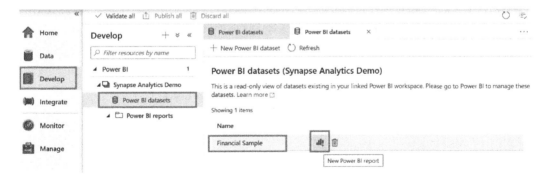

Figure 8.9 – A screenshot of a Power BI dataset in Synapse Studio

You can click on the Power BI icon next to your dataset to create a new Power BI report for the selected dataset.

Adding a dataset to your Power BI desktop

Similar to Power BI online, we can add the dataset to the Power BI desktop. We need to have Power BI installed on our local machine to begin with. You can download the Power BI Desktop executable file from the following link: `https://www.microsoft.com/en-us/download/details.aspx?id=58494`:

1. Open your Power BI desktop application on your local machine.

2. Click on the **Get data** icon at the top of the screen, as highlighted in the following screenshot:

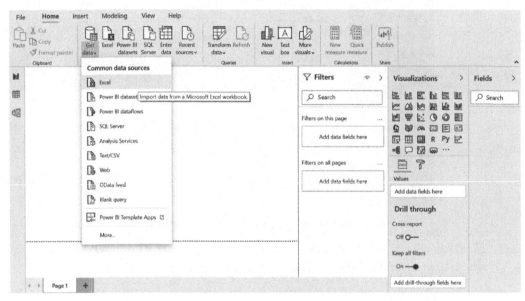

Figure 8.10 – Adding a new dataset to Power BI Desktop

3. Click on **Excel** and then select the `Financial Sample.xlsx` file that you downloaded earlier in the *Technical requirements* section.

4. Select **financials** on the next screen and then click on **Load**:

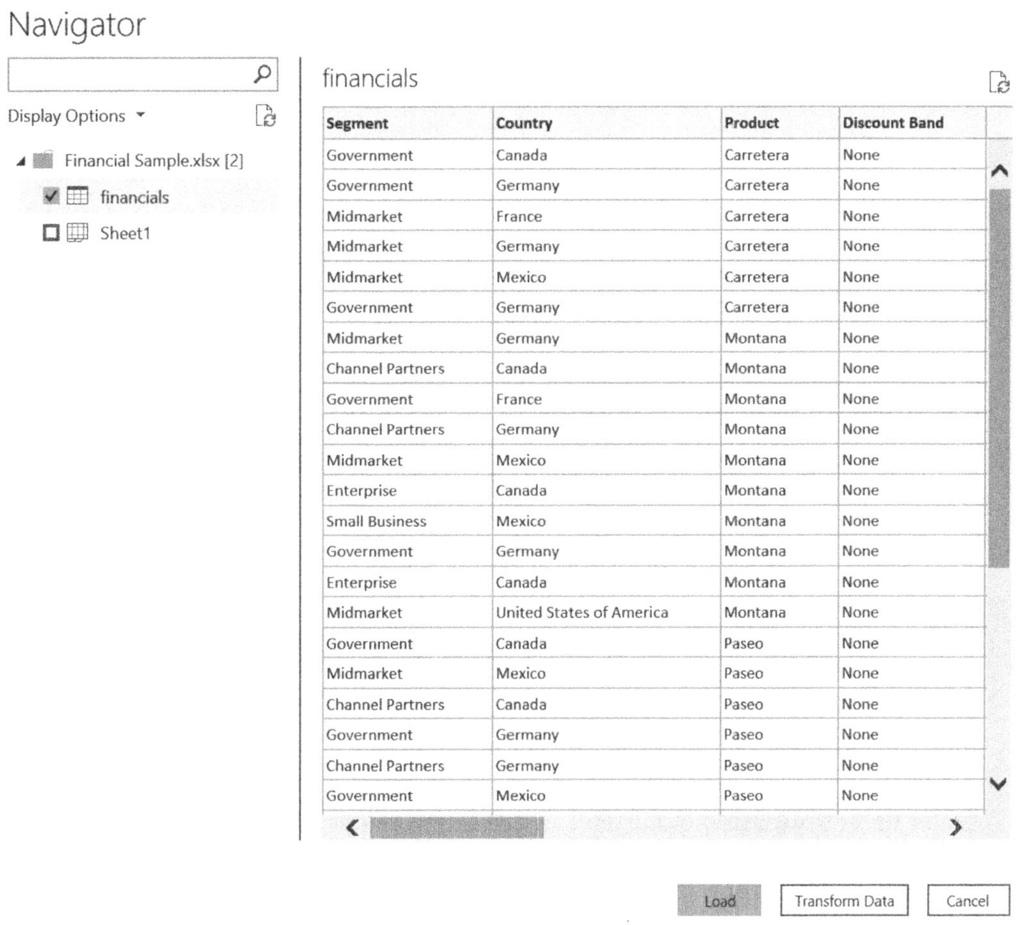

Navigator

Segment	Country	Product	Discount Band
Government	Canada	Carretera	None
Government	Germany	Carretera	None
Midmarket	France	Carretera	None
Midmarket	Germany	Carretera	None
Midmarket	Mexico	Carretera	None
Government	Germany	Carretera	None
Midmarket	Germany	Montana	None
Channel Partners	Canada	Montana	None
Government	France	Montana	None
Channel Partners	Germany	Montana	None
Midmarket	Mexico	Montana	None
Enterprise	Canada	Montana	None
Small Business	Mexico	Montana	None
Government	Germany	Montana	None
Enterprise	Canada	Montana	None
Midmarket	United States of America	Montana	None
Government	Canada	Paseo	None
Midmarket	Mexico	Paseo	None
Channel Partners	Canada	Paseo	None
Government	Germany	Paseo	None
Channel Partners	Germany	Paseo	None
Government	Mexico	Paseo	None

Navigator sidebar:
Display Options ▾

▲ Financial Sample.xlsx [2]
  ☑ financials
  ☐ Sheet1

financials

Load | Transform Data | Cancel

Figure 8.11 – A screenshot of data available in the financials sheet

5. Now that your dataset has been added to Power BI Desktop, it's time to publish your Power BI file to the Power BI service. Click on the **Publish** icon, which is on the top of the screen.

6. Provide a username to sign in to your account where you have created your Power BI workspace:

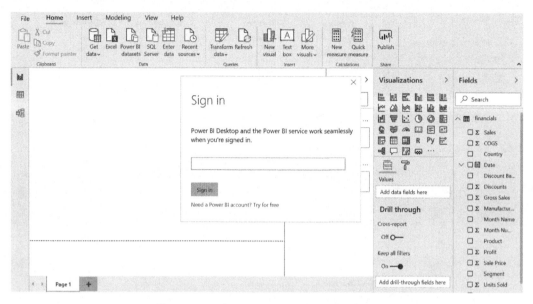

Figure 8.12 – Signing in to Power BI Desktop

7. Select the destination where you want to publish your Power BI report and click on **Select**. It may take a couple of seconds based on your data volume. Then, you will be able to see a **Success!** notification, as seen in the following screenshot:

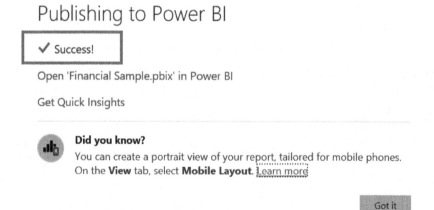

Figure 8.13 – A screenshot of the notification tells us that the Power BI file created on the Power BI Desktop has been successfully published to the Power BI service of Azure synapse

8. Now that the Power BI report has been published, we can validate it in Synapse
    Studio. Click on the **Develop** tab in Synapse Studio and refresh the Power BI
    datasets to view the newly added dataset.

Now that we have our reports published on the Power BI workspace, it's time to start
adding charts to these reports for visualization in Synapse Studio.

Creating Power BI reports

We can create Power BI reports either on the Power BI service, Power BI Desktop, or
directly on Synapse. If you create a report on Power BI Desktop, you need to publish the
file to your workspace and you will be able to see all the changes automatically in Synapse
Studio. As we have already published our Power BI Desktop file, we will see a new report
appearing under the **Power BI Reports** section.

Click on **Power BI experience** under the **Develop** hub of Synapse Studio and you will get
a blank report, as seen in the following screenshot:

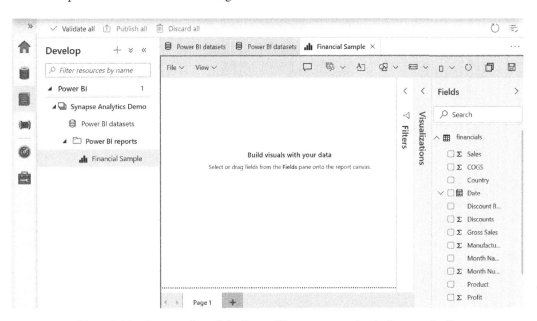

Figure 8.14 – A screenshot of the Power BI report appearing in Synapse Studio

However, if you create any report in Synapse Studio, it will automatically be reflected in your Power BI workspace. In this section, we are going to learn how to create reports in Synapse Studio:

1. Click on the **Financial Sample** report under the Power BI reports section under the **Develop** tab of Synapse Studio. You will see a blank report appear on your screen. Let's start creating new reports here.

2. Click on the **Visualizations** tab in the Power BI window and then click on the stacked bar chart.

3. Next, add **Sales** to the **Values** field and **Country** to the **Axis** field.

4. After adding the report to Power BI, click on the **Save** icon in the top-right corner to save all the changes:

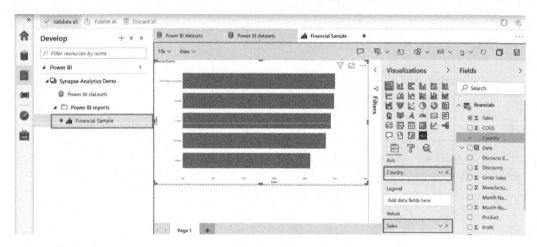

Figure 8.15 – A screenshot of the Power BI report created in Synapse Studio

5. Now, let's go to the Power BI service to validate whether you can see these charts added to the report published in the Power BI workspace:

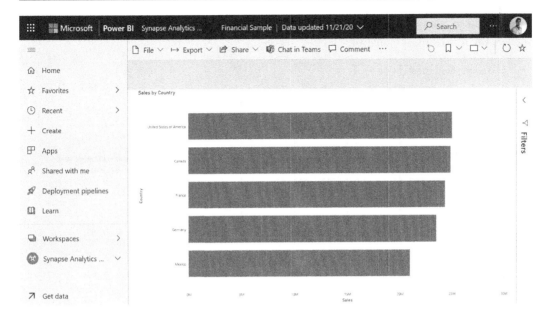

Figure 8.16 – A screenshot of the Sales by Country chart on the Power BI service

Now we know how to bring Power BI data and reports to Azure Synapse, but we still need to know how to connect Azure Synapse data to Power BI Desktop. When you publish this Power BI desktop to your Power BI workspace, you will be able to generate Power BI reports directly in Synapse Studio, and this time the data source will also be Synapse.

So far, we have learned how to create Power BI visualizations in Synapse Studio using the data from various data sources, but in the following section, we are going to learn how to bring data from Synapse SQL pools to Power BI Desktop.

Connecting Azure Synapse data to Power BI Desktop

Before we proceed further on this topic, it is important to understand what the different end points in the Synapse workspace are. When you go to your Synapse workspace within the Azure portal, you can see all the details pertaining to the workspace in the **Overview** section of the Synapse workspace.

In this section, we will learn about all the endpoints related to the Synapse workspace, as seen in the following screenshot:

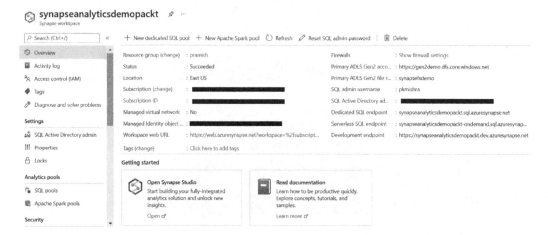

Figure 8.17 – A screenshot of the Synapse workspace in the Azure portal highlighting different endpoints

To ensure that you are able to navigate the workspace without limitations and that functionality is not limited, ensure that the following URLs are accessible on port 80 and 443, respectively.

> **Important note**
>
> In the event that you try and connect to your SQL pool or SQL on-demand database in your Synapse workspace after creating it, you could experience a network error or AJAX error. This prevents you from accessing the database objects, executing scripts, or viewing objects within the Synapse workspace. To mitigate these issues, allow access to the services on ports 443 and 1433, which would grant access to the web endpoint of the database services.

Go through the following bullets to understand the significance of all the endpoints in Azure Synapse Analytics. These are generic URLs where you just need to replace the * icon with your Synapse workspace name:

- `https://web.azuresynapse.net`: This will redirect you to your Azure Synapse workspace and you need to select **Azure Active Directory**, **Subscription**, and **Workspace name** to access your workspace:

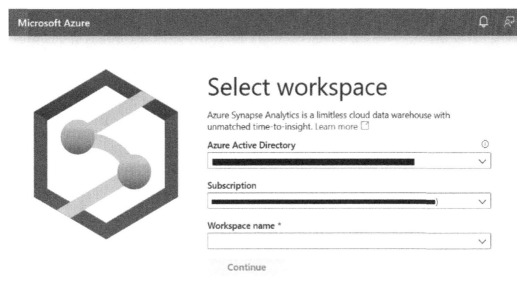

Select workspace

Azure Synapse Analytics is a limitless cloud data warehouse with unmatched time-to-insight. Learn more ⃞

Azure Active Directory   ⓘ

Subscription

Workspace name *

Continue

Figure 8.18 – Providing the details to access your Azure Synapse workspace

- `https://*.dev.azuresynapse.net`: This is a development endpoint, and you can ascertain the URL for this endpoint in the **Overview** section of your Synapse workspace within the Azure portal, as highlighted in *Figure 8.17*.

- `https://*.database.windows.net`: This endpoint can be used to access the provisioned SQL pool from any application; you just need to provide your Synapse workspace name in place of *.

- `https://*-ondemand.database.windows.net`: This endpoint is similar to the preceding endpoint. However, this endpoint will connect to a serverless SQL pool in Azure Synapse. Make sure you replace * with your Azure Synapse workspace name.

- `https://*.sql.azuresynapse.net`: This endpoint can also be used to access the provisioned SQL pool from any application. This is also known as a dedicated SQL endpoint and you can find the endpoint available in your Synapse workspace within the Azure portal, as highlighted in *Figure 8.17*.

- `https://*-ondemand.sql.azuresynapse.net`: This endpoint can also be used to access a serverless SQL pool in Azure Synapse. This is also known as a serverless SQL endpoint, and you can find the endpoint available in your Synapse workspace within the Azure portal, as highlighted in *Figure 8.17*.

Now that we understand all the endpoints, we will be able to connect to these endpoints using Power BI. The following section outlines how to use a dedicated SQL endpoint with Power BI Desktop.

Connecting to a Synapse-dedicated SQL pool

Data stored in the dedicated SQL pools of Synapse Analytics can be used to create visualizations using Power BI. A dedicated SQL pool in Azure Synapse is nothing other than an Azure SQL Data warehouse and reports play a critical role in analyzing data stored in data warehouses. You can follow the same steps that you would do for connecting Power BI to Azure SQL DW:

1. Open the Power BI Desktop application and select **Get data**.

2. Select **Azure Synapse Analytics (SQL DW)** from the list of all data sources available:

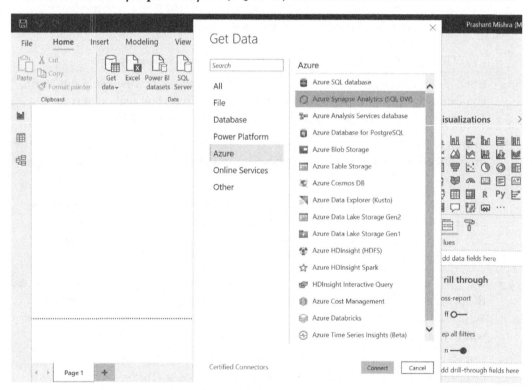

Figure 8.19 – A screenshot of available data sources in Power BI Desktop

3. Type the dedicated SQL endpoint in the **Server** field and then type the database name. Select the **Import** option and then select **OK**:

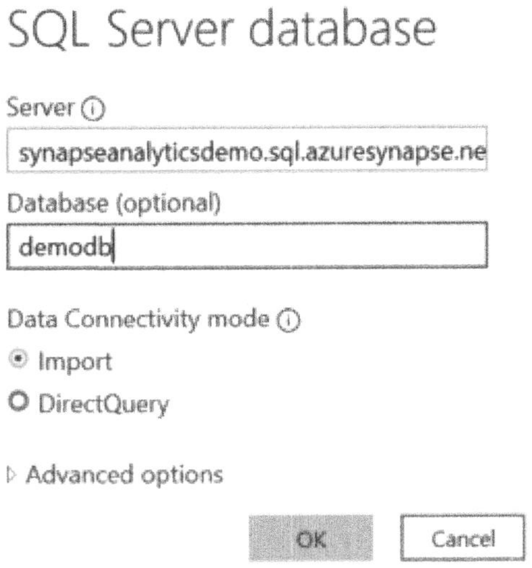

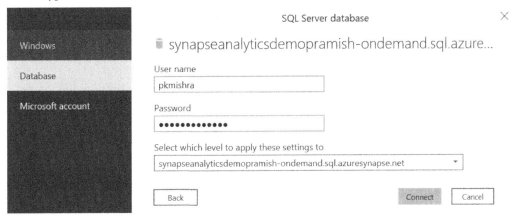

Figure 8.20 – Connecting Azure Synapse Analytics (SQL DW) data to Power BI Desktop

4. Select the preferred authentication method. In this example, we will select **Database**. Type **User name** and **Password** for the authentication and click on **Connect**:

Figure 8.21 – Providing authentication details for connecting a serverless SQL pool to Power BI

5. Select your view, and then click on **Load**.

In the following section, we will learn that we can perform data visualizations on the data residing in a serverless SQL pool as well.

Connecting to a Synapse serverless SQL pool

Similar to a dedicated SQL pool, we can use a serverless SQL endpoint to connect serverless SQL pool data to Power BI desktop. Before we proceed further, we will try to create a view in a serverless SQL pool by using the same example as provided in the Microsoft documentation.

Follow these steps to create a view on a serverless SQL pool and then bring in the data from this view to Power BI Desktop to create visualizations:

1. Open any SQL query tool, **SQL Server Management Studio** (**SSMS**), or Azure Data Studio and connect it to a serverless SQL pool using the serverless SQL endpoint.

2. Open a new query window and run the following code against the master database:

```
-- Drop database if it exists
DROP DATABASE IF EXISTS Demo
GO
-- Create new database
CREATE DATABASE [Demo];
GO
```

3. After creating the database, run the following script against the **Demo** database in **SSMS** to create a view, usPopulationView, on a serverless SQL pool:

```
-- There is no credential in data source. We are using
public storage account which doesn't need a secret.
CREATE EXTERNAL DATA SOURCE AzureOpenData
WITH ( LOCATION = 'https://azureopendatastorage.blob.
core.windows.net/')
GO
DROP VIEW IF EXISTS usPopulationView;
GO

CREATE VIEW usPopulationView AS
SELECT
    *
FROM
    OPENROWSET(
```

```
        BULK 'censusdatacontainer/release/us_population_
county/year=20*/*.parquet',
        DATA_SOURCE = 'AzureOpenData',
        FORMAT='PARQUET'
    ) AS uspv;
```

4. Let's validate `Records` by running a `SELECT` statement on `usPopulationView` in **SSMS**:

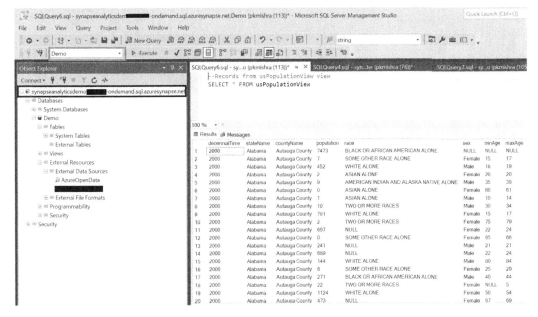

Figure 8.22 – Displaying the result set of the usPopulationView view in SSMS

Now that we have created a `usPopulationView` view in a serverless SQL pool, we will try bringing data from this view to Power BI Desktop:

5. Open the Power BI Desktop application and select **Get data**:

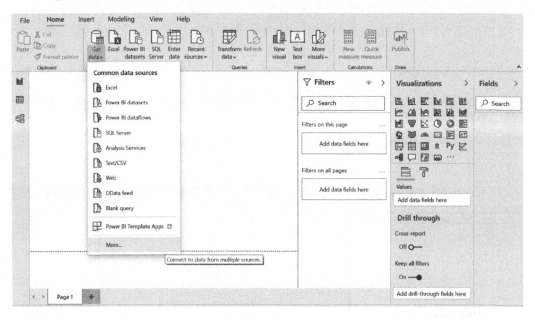

Figure 8.23 – A screenshot of Power BI Desktop connecting to a data source using the Get data tab

6. Select **Azure SQL Database** from the list of all data sources available.

7. Type the serverless SQL endpoint in the **Server** field, and then type the database name. Select the **Import** option and then select **OK**.

8. Select the preferred authentication method. In this example, we will select **Database**. Type your details into the **User name** and **Password** fields for the authentication and then click on **Connect**:

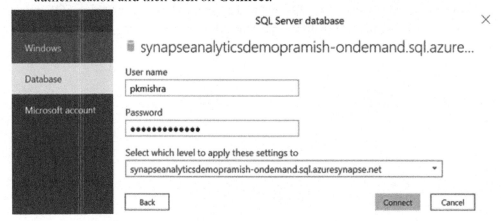

Figure 8.24 – Providing authentication details for connecting a serverless SQL pool to Power BI

9. Select your view, and then click on **Load**.

10. Wait for the operation to complete, and then a popup will appear stating **There are pending changes in your queries that haven't been applied**. Select **Apply changes**.

11. Wait for the **Apply query changes** dialog box to disappear, which may take a few minutes.

12. Once the load completes, select the **Filled map** visualization and then select the **countyName**, **population**, and **stateName** columns in the same order to create the report, as shown in the following screenshot in *Figure 8.25*.

13. After making all the required changes, you can publish this report to your workspace:

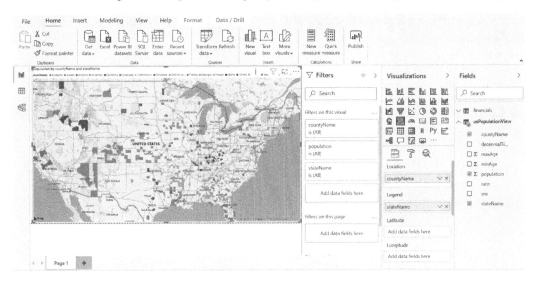

Figure 8.25 – A screenshot of the Power BI report generated by using the view created in a SQL serverless pool

> **Important note**
> As of now, you cannot connect Synapse Spark data to Power BI.

Summary

In this chapter, we learned how to integrate Power BI with Azure Synapse. Azure Synapse has made it really convenient to keep data, analysis, and visualizations together. Now, we do not need to go to the Power BI tool to generate a report using Synapse data.

Aside from a dedicated SQL pool, Synapse also enables us to create reports by using serverless SQL pool data as well. Thus, by using Azure Synapse, we can read the data directly from Azure Data Lake Gen2, create a view on top of that data, and create visualizations in Power BI, in just a couple of minutes. In this chapter, not only did we learn about integrating the Power BI workspace with your Synapse workspace, but also how to create or modify reports directly in Synapse Studio. This chapter also outlined how to create visualizations for the data stored in Synapse SQL pools.

In the next chapter, we are going to learn how to use Azure Synapse to perform real-time analytics on streaming data.

9
Perform Real-Time Analytics on Streaming Data

Azure Synapse has various built-in features that allow us to perform end-to-end analysis on our data. One of the best features is the integration of Azure Synapse with Azure Cosmos DB via Azure Synapse Link. It removes the pain of bringing data from transactional data stores to analytical data stores using an ETL tool. You can read more about this in *Chapter 5*, *Using Synapse Link with Azure Cosmos DB*. In this chapter, we are going to use this feature to learn how to perform real-time analytics on streaming data in Azure Synapse. We are also going to learn how to use **Azure Stream Analytics** jobs to copy streaming data from **Event Hubs** to **Azure Data Lake Storage Gen2**. There is also a brief section in this chapter on Azure Databricks. We will create a simple C# application to generate streaming data that will be ingested in a Cosmos DB transactional store, and finally, we will access this data in Synapse through the analytical store of Cosmos DB. We will also learn how to generate Power BI reports using data on Synapse.

The topics covered in this chapter will help you perform end-to-end real-time data analysis and are as follows:

- Understanding the architecture and components
- Bringing data to Azure Synapse
- Implementation of real-time analytics on streaming data

Technical requirements

Before you start orchestrating your data, here are the prerequisites that you need to meet:

- You should have access to your Azure subscription or any other subscription with contributor-level access.
- Create a Synapse workspace using your subscription. You can follow the instructions from *Chapter 1, Introduction to Azure Synapse,* to create your Synapse workspace.
- Create a Spark pool and SQL pool on Azure Synapse. This has been covered in *Chapter 2, Considerations for Your Compute Environment.*
- You should have already created your Azure Cosmos DB account; make sure you have enabled your analytical store using your Azure Cosmos DB account. To learn more about this, you can refer to *Chapter 5, Using Synapse Link with Azure Cosmos DB.*
- Download Power BI Desktop to your machine and make sure you have access to the Power BI workspace, where you can publish your Power BI Desktop file.

Understanding various architecture and components

Azure provides various data services that can be used to perform real-time analytics in different ways. In this section, we will learn about two different architectures and how different components are stitched together in both of these architectures to deliver the end result.

There are various use cases for real-time analytics, including the following:

- **Anomaly detection**: This technique is used to identify unusual behavior or patterns that raises suspicions because of a significant difference from the rest of the data.

- **Supply chain analytics**: This process is used to increase operational effectiveness by using data and quantitative methods for decision making.

- **Real-time personalization**: This technique is used to gather information about the user visiting your website and engage that user by providing tailored content on the website based on their company, location, digital behavior, and so on.

The architecture seen in the following screenshot can be used for any of the use cases mentioned in the preceding list. This architecture consists of a data ingestion layer, a data storage layer, and a visualization layer:

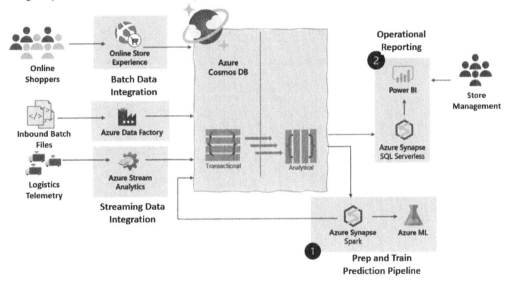

Figure 9.1 – Architecture for real-time analytics on Azure by using Azure Synapse Link

You can use an online application, Azure Data Factory or Azure Stream Analytics, to stream the data to the Azure Cosmos DB transactional store. If you have enabled the analytical store on your Azure Cosmos DB account, then your analytical store will automatically be kept in sync with your transactional store in Azure Cosmos DB. The next step is to connect Azure Synapse with the analytical store of your Azure Cosmos DB container. You can refer to the following link (`https://docs.microsoft.com/ en-us/azure/cosmos-db/synapse-link-use-cases#supply-chain- analytics-forecasting--reporting`) to learn more about this architecture. However, we will try to implement this architecture end to end in the upcoming *Implementation of real-time analytics on streaming data* section.

We can use a different approach for real-time analytics by using Synapse. Instead of feeding data to the Azure Cosmos DB account, we can ingest the data to Azure Data Lake Storage Gen2. We can also use Azure Databricks to access the data stored on Azure Data Lake Storage Gen2 and implement business logic on that data before sending it to Azure Synapse. The architecture in the following screenshot displays the overall journey of the data, from one end to the other. You can learn more about this architecture by using the following link: `https://docs.microsoft.com/en-us/azure/architecture/solution-ideas/articles/real-time-analytics`:

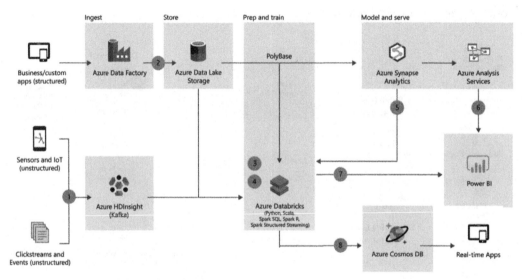

Figure 9.2 – Architecture for real-time analytics using Azure Databricks, Cosmos DB, and Synapse

Both the architectures shown in *Figure 9.1* and *Figure 9.2* are just examples; you can use Azure services the way your business demands.

In the next section, we will find different ways to bring data to Azure Synapse, and later, we will see an end-to-end implementation of the first architecture that we saw in *Figure 9.1* in this section.

Bringing data to Azure Synapse

In the *Understanding the architecture and components* section, we saw how architectures use different Azure services to perform real-time analytics on Azure. In this section, our main focus is to bring data from all data sources to Azure Synapse. We are going to learn about bringing data to Azure Synapse by using Azure Stream Analytics jobs, and later we will see how we can use Azure Databricks to copy data to Azure Synapse.

Using Azure Stream Analytics

Azure Stream Analytics is a real-time analytics engine that is designed to process a large volume of streaming data from various sources to various targets. Within Azure Stream Analytics, you can create an Azure Stream Analytics job that consists of an input, a query, and an output. You can use the Stream Analytics job to ingest data directly from the source to the target as is, or you can perform certain aggregation operations on the input data before sending it to the target.

These are the following instructions to ingest data to **Azure Synapse Analytics (formerly SQL DW)** using Azure Stream Analytics:

1. Go to the Azure portal at `https://portal.azure.com`, and click on the **Create a resource** link.

2. Search for *Stream Analytics job* in the search bar and select it from the drop-down list of the search bar.

3. You can go through the overview of the Stream Analytics job on the next screen before clicking on the **Create** button.

4. Provide an appropriate **Job name** value for your Stream Analytics job, and select your **Subscription**, **Resource Group**, and **Location** values.

5. In this example, we are going to use **Cloud** for **Hosting Environment**, but feel free to use **Edge** as per your business needs.

6. Enter the appropriate value for **Streaming units** as per your requirements and click on **Create**:

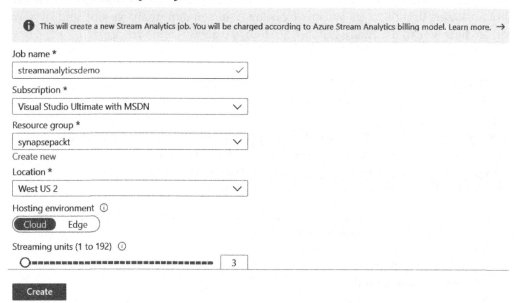

New Stream Analytics job   ...

> ⓘ This will create a new Stream Analytics job. You will be charged according to Azure Stream Analytics billing model. Learn more. →

Job name *

streamanalyticsdemo   ✓

Subscription *

Visual Studio Ultimate with MSDN   ∨

Resource group *

synapsepackt   ∨

Create new

Location *

West US 2   ∨

Hosting environment ⓘ

(Cloud   Edge)

Streaming units (1 to 192) ⓘ

O■■■■■■■■■■■■■■■■■■■■■■■■■■■■■■■■■   3

Create

Figure 9.3 – Creating the Stream Analytics job in the Azure portal

7. It will take a couple of seconds to create the Stream Analytics job, after which we are going to add details to this job. Go to your Stream Analytics job, click on the **Inputs** tab, and click on **+ Add stream input**.

8. You can select **Event Hub**, **IoT Hub**, or **Blob storage/ADLS Gen2** from the dropdown list; for this example, let's select **Event Hub**:

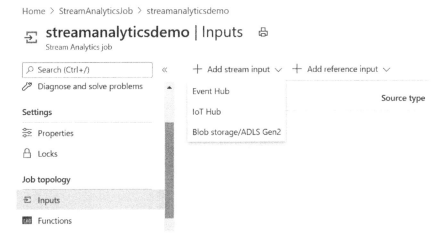

Figure 9.4 – Providing input for the Stream Analytics job

9. Next, provide connection details for **Event Hub** and click on **OK**.

10. Now, let's create an output for this job. Click on the **Outputs** tab on your **Stream Analytics job** and click on **+Add**.

11. Select **Azure Synapse Analytics (formerly SQL DW)** from the drop-down list. However, you can send data directly to **ADLS Gen2** as well:

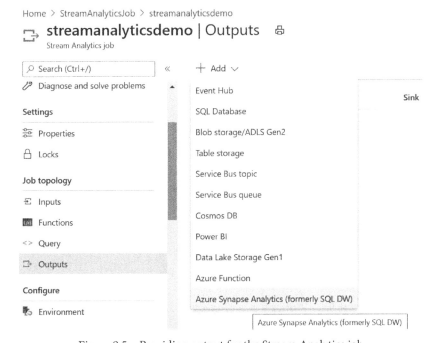

Figure 9.5 – Providing output for the Stream Analytics job

12. Next, provide an appropriate **Output alias** value.

13. Provide details for **Subscription**, **Database**, **Table**, **Username**, and **Password**.

14. After verifying all the details, click on **Save**.

15. Now we are all set to run our business logic in the **Query** tab. Click on the **Query** tab of your Stream Analytics job, and you will see the following script already created for you:

```
SELECT
    *
INTO
    [YourOutputAlias]
FROM
    [YourInputAlias]
```

16. You can change the name of YourOutputAlias and YourInputAlias as per your business needs:

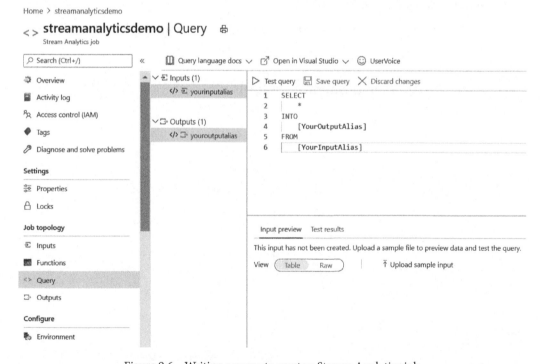

Figure 9.6 – Writing a query to create a Stream Analytics job

Now that your data has come to Azure Synapse, you can perform various operations, such as transformations, analytics operations, and more, on this data, which is now residing within Azure Synapse.

This is one of the best possible ways to ingest streaming data to Azure Synapse; however, there are a couple of other ways as well that might be better suited for your business needs, and we are going to talk about those options in the following subsection.

Using Azure Databricks

Azure Databricks is a data analytics platform optimized for the Microsoft cloud platform. You can create an Azure Databricks notebook to set up a connection with Event Hubs and read data directly from there. You can perform various operations on the data coming from Event Hubs, such as calculating aggregations, plotting charts, running Cognitive Services, and so on. You can also ingest the transformed data to Azure Synapse to be consumed further by Azure Analysis Services and Power BI.

In the previous section, we learned how to use an Azure Stream Analytics job to bring data to Azure Synapse Analytics, and now, in this section, we will learn how can we use Azure Databricks to access data from Event Hubs and write it to Azure Synapse using Structured Streaming in Scala and Python notebooks.

We need the following in order to access Event Hubs from Azure Databricks:

- An Azure Event Hubs namespace
- An event hub within the namespace
- A connection string to access the Event Hubs namespace
- A shared access policy name and a policy key for Event Hubs

After capturing all the preceding information, we will fill in the corresponding values in the following **Scala** code snippet:

```scala
import org.apache.spark.eventhubs._
    import com.microsoft.azure.eventhubs._


    // Build connection string with the above information
    val namespaceName = ''<EVENT HUBS NAMESPACE>''
    val eventHubName = ''<EVENT HUB NAME>''
    val sasKeyName = ''<POLICY NAME>''
    val sasKey = ''<POLICY KEY>''
```

```
    val connStr = new com.microsoft.azure.eventhubs.
ConnectionStringBuilder()
                    .setNamespaceName(namespaceName)
                    .setEventHubName(eventHubName)
                    .setSasKeyName(sasKeyName)
                    .setSasKey(sasKey)

    val customEventhubParameters =  \
    EventHubsConf(connStr.toString()).setMaxEventsPerTrigger(5)

    val incomingStream = spark.readStream.
format(''eventhubs'').options(customEventhubParameters.toMap).
load()
    incomingStream.printSchema
    // Sending the incoming stream into the console.
    // Data comes in batches!      incomingStream.writeStream.
outputMode(''append'').format(''console'').option(''truncate'',
false).start().awaitTermination()
```

You can learn more about this by going through the following link (`https://docs.microsoft.com/en-us/azure/databricks/scenarios/databricks-stream-from-eventhubs`), where Twitter data has been used as a use case for streaming data into Azure Databricks using Event Hubs.

You can write data to Azure Synapse from Azure Databricks by using Structured Streaming in Scala and Python notebooks. **PolyBase** or **COPY** are used by the Azure Synapse connector to transfer high volumes of data between a Databricks cluster and an Azure Synapse instance. Let's go through the following steps to ingest the data from Databricks to Azure Synapse. You can modify the Python code snippet as per your environment:

1. Set up the blob storage account access key in the notebook session config:

```
    spark.conf.set(
      ''fs.azure.account.key.<your-storage-account-name>.
    blob.core.windows.net'',
      ''<your-storage-account-access-key>'')
```

2. Prepare the streaming source; this could be Kafka or a simple rate stream:

```
df = spark.readStream \
  .format(''rate'') \
  .option(''rowsPerSecond'', ''100000'') \
  .option(''numPartitions'', ''16'') \
  .load()
```

3. Apply some transformations to the data and then use the Structured Streaming API to continuously write the data to a table in Azure Synapse:

```
df.writeStream \
  .format(''com.databricks.spark.sqldw'') \
  .option(''url'', ''jdbc:sqlserver://<the-rest-of-the-
connection-string>'') \
  .option(''tempDir'', ''wasbs://<your-container-
name>@<your-storage-account-name>.blob.core.windows.
net/<your-directory-name>'') \
  .option(''forwardSparkAzureStorageCredentials'',
''true'') \
  .option(''dbTable'', ''<your-table-name>'') \
  .option(''checkpointLocation'', ''/tmp_checkpoint_
location'') \
  .start()
```

To learn more about this connector, you can refer to the following link: `https://docs.databricks.com/data/data-sources/azure/synapse-analytics.html`.

After learning about the architecture and various components that make real-time analytics possible on the Azure platform, it's time to learn how to implement this solution end to end in your environment.

Implementation of real-time analytics on streaming data

In this section, we are going to learn about a step-by-step process for implementing real-time analytics using Azure Synapse. We are taking *Figure 9.1* as our reference architecture. There are various stages involved in implementing this architecture, and we will go through all these steps in this section. We will learn how to configure all the required resources according to your environment.

Before jumping to the analytics part, we will learn how to ingest data to an Azure Cosmos DB account.

Ingesting data to Cosmos DB

There are various ways to ingest streaming data to Azure Cosmos DB; however, in this section, we are going to use an online application sample to ingested streaming data to the Azure Cosmos DB account.

Follow the instructions to start streaming the data to your Cosmos DB account:

1. Go to your Azure Cosmos DB account in the Azure portal and click on the **Data Explorer** tab.

2. Click on the **New Container** tab at the top of the screen and create a new container called **CovidData** with **demodb** as the database ID and **/country** as **Partition key**. Next, click on the **Provision dedicated throughput for this container** checkbox, and make sure that the **Analytical store** radio button is set to **On**:

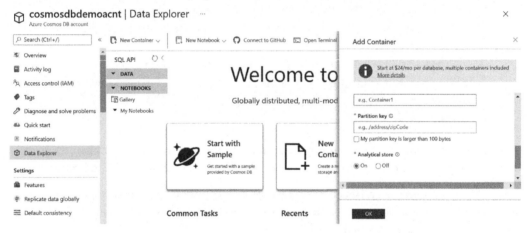

Figure 9.7 – Creating a new container in Azure Cosmos DB

3. Download the solution ZIP file from the following link and extract all the files and save them on your local machine: `https://github.com/PacktPublishing/Limitless-Analytics-with-Azure-Synapse/blob/master/Chapter%2009%20-%20StreamToCosmos.zip`.

4. Open Visual Studio on your machine and click on **File | Open | Project/Solution** to open the solution file that you extracted in the preceding step.

5. Right-click on your project and click on **Build** to build your project.

6. Double-click on the `Program.cs` file to open this file in Visual Studio:

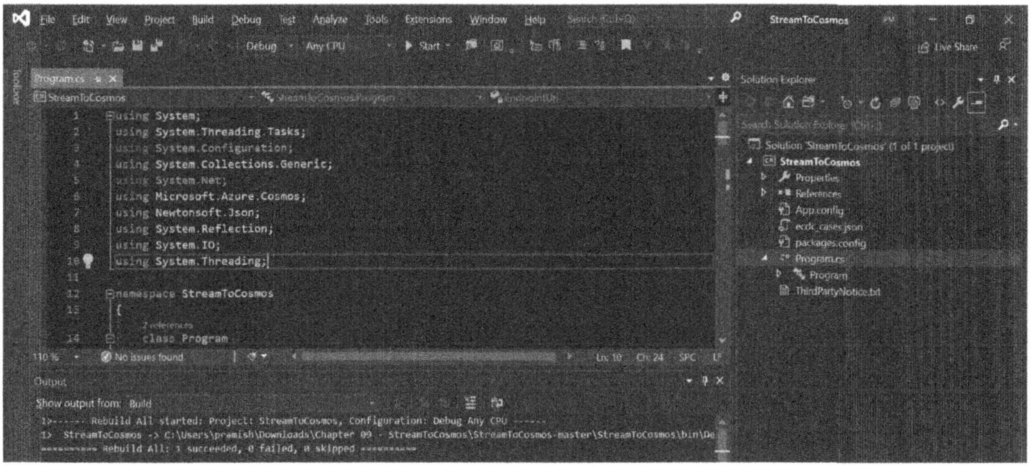

Figure 9.8 – A screenshot of the StreamToCosmos project open in Visual Studio

7. Copy `EndPointURI` and the primary `AccessKey` from your Cosmos DB account and paste them in the following code:

```
    // The Azure Cosmos DB endpoint for running this
sample.
    private static readonly string EndpointUri =
''<end point URL>'';
    // The primary key for the Azure Cosmos account.
    private static readonly string PrimaryKey =
''<primarykey>'';
```

8. After making the changes, build the project once again and click on the **Start** button, which is at the top of the Visual Studio screen.

> **Important note**
>
> We have used COVID sample data (`https://pandemicdatalake.blob.core.windows.net/public/curated/covid-19/ecdc_cases/latest/ecdc_cases.json`) to feed into this application. It has 60,000 records and the application has been set to push each record at a 1-second interval, so the application will keep running for 60,000 seconds until stopped manually.

You can see that the application is running on Visual Studio and the data is being copied to the Cosmos DB account in the following screenshot:

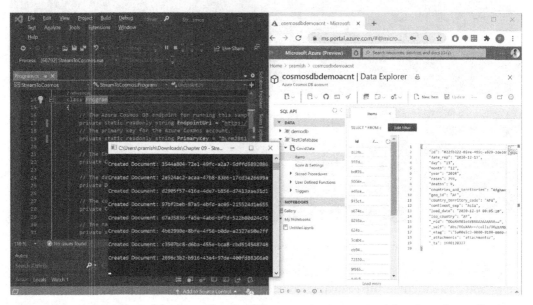

Figure 9.9 – A screenshot of the Azure Cosmos DB account having received data from the application

Now you can go to your Cosmos DB account to verify whether data is being pushed there correctly.

This is only an example of how to stream data to your Cosmos DB account; however, feel free to use Data Factory, Stream Analytics, or any other method to stream the data to your Azure Cosmos DB account. But one important thing that we should always keep in mind is that an analytical store must be enabled for this Cosmos DB account.

Next, we will see how to make sure that data is in sync between the transactional and analytical stores of your Azure Cosmos DB account.

Accessing data from the Azure Cosmos DB analytical store in Azure Synapse

We're about halfway through the steps, and now it's time to read Cosmos DB data from the Synapse notebook. We will be using the OPENROWSET function to read the data from the Cosmos DB container.

You can follow these instructions to query your data using Synapse:

1. Go to your Synapse workspace in the Azure portal and click on **Synapse Studio**.

2. Click on the **Develop** tab and click on the + icon to create a new SQL script.

3. Paste the following code in this cell and replace the values for `SECRET` and `CONNECTION` with the corresponding values of your Azure Cosmos DB account:

```
SELECT TOP 10 *
FROM OPENROWSET(
        'CosmosDB',
        'Account=cosmosdbdemoacnt;Database=
demodb;Key=DLrm2Bt1uKj2rb4TU49qxzvsBJrgD1yzECnkh
pIQObmLTzBxsZxM0PtlhtbS407ceMLYkMdFdBTFwO9PwPgCIw==',
        CovidData
    ) with ( date_rep varchar(20), cases bigint, geo_
id varchar(6) ) as rows
```

In the following screenshot, you can see the data in Synapse Studio directly, which is streaming in from the Azure Cosmos DB account from the .NET console application:

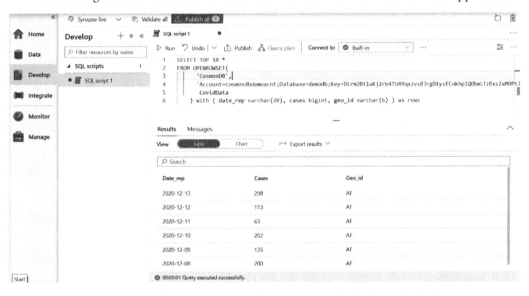

Figure 9.10 – A screenshot of the COVID data in Synapse Studio being fetched from the Cosmos DB account

Now that you have got the data in Azure Synapse, you can perform **machine learning** operations on it. But we will be learning how to use Azure Machine Learning with Azure Synapse in our next chapter, *Chapter 10, Generate Powerful Insights on Azure Synapse Using Azure Machine Learning*.

Loading data to a Spark DataFrame

The following Python syntax can be used to load Cosmos DB data to a **Spark DataFrame** without impacting the transactional store:

```
df = spark.read.format(''cosmos.olap'')\
    .option(''spark.synapse.linkedService'', ''<enter linked
service name>'')\
    .option(''spark.cosmos.container'', ''<enter container
name>'')\
    .load()
```

You can visualize the data directly in Synapse notebooks; however, you can generate Power BI reports to visualize your data as well. If you have the Power BI Premium license, you will be able to share these reports with other colleagues as well.

Creating visualizations

You can create Power BI reports using the data transformed in your Synapse dedicated SQL pool or Synapse Serverless SQL pool; however, as of now, you cannot create Power BI reports against your Synapse Spark pool.

I suggest that you go through *Chapter 8, Integrating a Power BI Workspace with Azure Synapse*, before you proceed further in this section.

Make sure that you have access to the Power BI workspace before we proceed further. You can go through the following instructions to visualize the report on Power BI Desktop:

1. Go to your Synapse workspace and copy the Serverless Copy endpoint to your clipboard. We could create a view directly in Synapse Studio; however, we will perform the same operation using the **SQL Server Management Studio** (**SSMS**) tool instead.

2. Open SSMS on your machine and connect to the Serverless endpoint that you copied in the preceding step.

3. Open a new query window and run the following script to create a new DemoDB database:

```
CREATE DATABASE DemoDB
```

4. Right-click on the **demodb** database from **Object Explorer** and click on **New Query**:

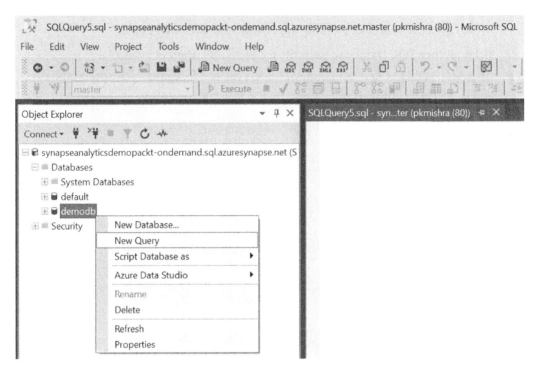

Figure 9.11 – Creating a new database using SSMS

5. Paste the following script and execute this script to create a vwCovidData view, but do not forget to change the Cosmos DB account name and the corresponding access key:

```
CREATE OR ALTER VIEW vwCovidData
AS
SELECT *
FROM OPENROWSET(
        'CosmosDB',
```

```
        'Account=cosmosdbdemoacnt;Database=demodb
;Key=DLrm2Bt1uKj2rb4TU49qxzvsBJrgD1yzECnkhpIQO
bmLTzBxsZxM0PtlhtbS407ceMLYkMdFdBTFwO9PwPgCIw==',
        CovidData
    ) with ( date_rep varchar(20), cases bigint, geo_id
varchar(6) ) as rows
```

6. Now that we have created the view, we will be creating the reports on top of this view. Open the Power BI Desktop application and select **Get data**.

7. Select **Azure SQL Database** from the list of all data sources available.

8. Type the serverless SQL endpoint in the **Server** field, and then type the database name. Select the **Import** option and then select **OK**:

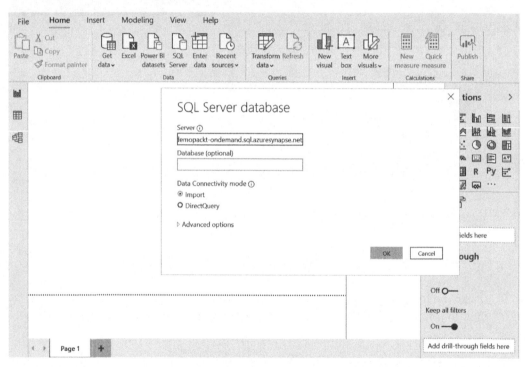

Figure 9.12 – Providing serverless SQL pool details to Power BI

9. Select the preferred authentication method; in this example, we will select **Database**. Fill in **User name** and **password** for authentication and click on **Connect**:

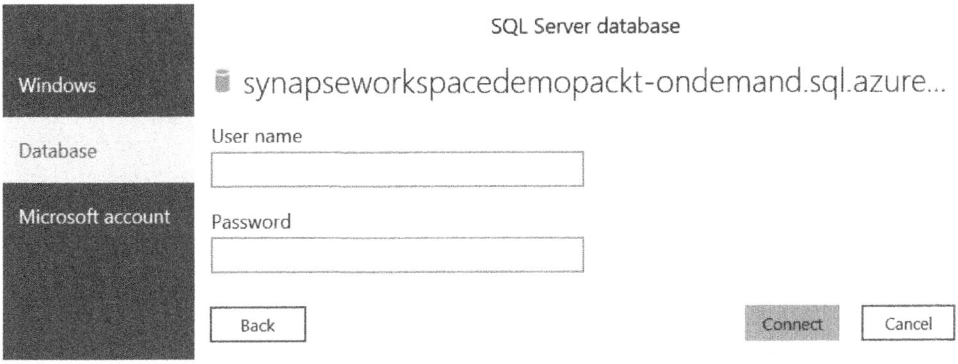

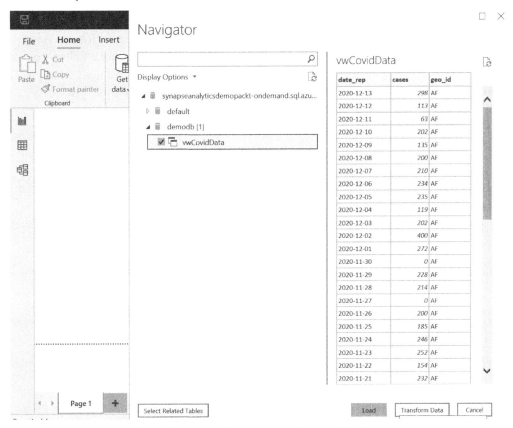

Figure 9.13 – Providing authentication details to connect a serverless SQL pool to Power BI

10. Select your view under the **demodb** database, and then click on **Load**:

Figure 9.14 – Loading the data to Power BI Desktop

11. Wait for the operation to complete, and then a popup will appear stating **There are pending changes in your queries that haven't been applied**. Select **Apply changes**.

12. Wait for the **Apply query changes** dialog box to disappear, which may take a few minutes.

13. Once the load completes, select **Table** visualization and select the **geo_id**, **date_rep**, and **cases** columns, in that order, to create the report.

14. After making all the required changes, you can publish this report to your workspace.

Now we are able to visualize our data directly on Power BI Desktop, and this visualization can be published to Power BI Service as well. Here, we added just one visualization. However, you can create multiple visualizations on the same dashboard, which could bring some meaningful insights for your data.

Summary

In this chapter, we learned how to perform real-time analytics using Azure Synapse. We learned how to bring data to Azure Synapse by using Azure Stream Analytics and Azure Databricks. We also learned how to create a view in a serverless SQL pool and how to use this view to connect to Power BI Desktop for data visualizations. We used a sample application in this chapter to stream data to an Azure Cosmos DB account by using a sample JSON file. You can download and use this application if you want to perform a proof of concept on this particular topic yourself.

In the next chapter, we are going to learn how to use Azure Machine Learning with Azure Synapse. It is important to have prior knowledge of Azure Machine Learning before plunging to the next chapter. You will also learn how to use machine learning models with Azure Synapse SQL and Spark pools.

10

Generate Powerful Insights on Azure Synapse Using Azure ML

Machine Learning (ML) has become an integral part of the data ecosystem now and Azure enables you to build powerful, cloud-based ML applications by using the Azure Machine Learning service. Azure ML provides you with options to create supervised or unsupervised ML models and its integration with Azure Synapse has opened a wide ocean for data scientists.

In this chapter, we are going to learn about the integration of Azure Synapse with the Azure ML service, and how we can leverage this unique feature to generate powerful insights into our data.

We will cover the following topics in order to understand how we can bring better insight to our data using machine learning capabilities in Azure Synapse:

- Preparing the environment
- Creating an Azure ML linked service in Synapse
- Machine learning capabilities in Azure Synapse
- Use cases with Cognitive Services

Technical requirements

Before you start orchestrating your data, here are some of the prerequisites that you should meet:

- You should have an Azure subscription or access to any other subscription with contributor-level access.
- Create your Synapse workspace on this subscription. You can follow the instructions from *Chapter 1, Introduction to Azure Synapse*, to create your Synapse workspace.
- Create a Spark pool on Azure Synapse. This was covered in *Chapter 2, Consideration for Your Compute Environment*.
- You should have already created your Azure Cosmos DB account. Make sure you have enabled analytical storage in your Azure Cosmos DB account. To learn more about this, you can refer to *Chapter 5, Using Synapse Link with Azure Cosmos DB*.

Preparing the environment

Before we can start learning about Azure ML integration with Azure Synapse, we need to prepare the environment to run ML operations on Azure Synapse, by creating some resources on Azure.

Creating a Text Analytics resource in the Azure portal

Text analytics is an AI service that is used to discover insights such as sentiment, entities, key phrases, and so on, in unstructured text. This resource will be used for performing sentiment analysis on data using a Synapse Spark pool in the *Sentiment analysis* section.

You can go through the following steps to create a Text Analytics resource in the Azure portal:

1. Log in to the Azure portal, at `https://portal.azure.com`.

2. Click on + **Create a resource** and select **Text Analytics** from the list of all available resources.

3. You can see the overview of this service. Click on **Create**:

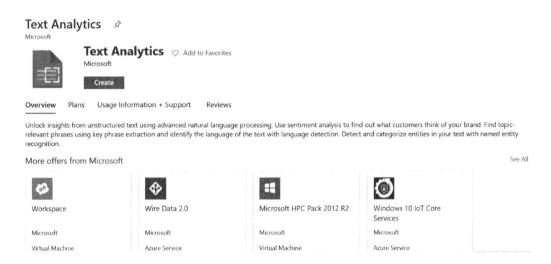

Figure 10.1 – Creating a Text Analytics resource in the Azure portal

4. Fill in the values for **Subscription**, **Resource group**, **Region**, **Name**, and **Pricing tier**.

5.   You can leave the default values for the remaining fields and click on
     Review + create:

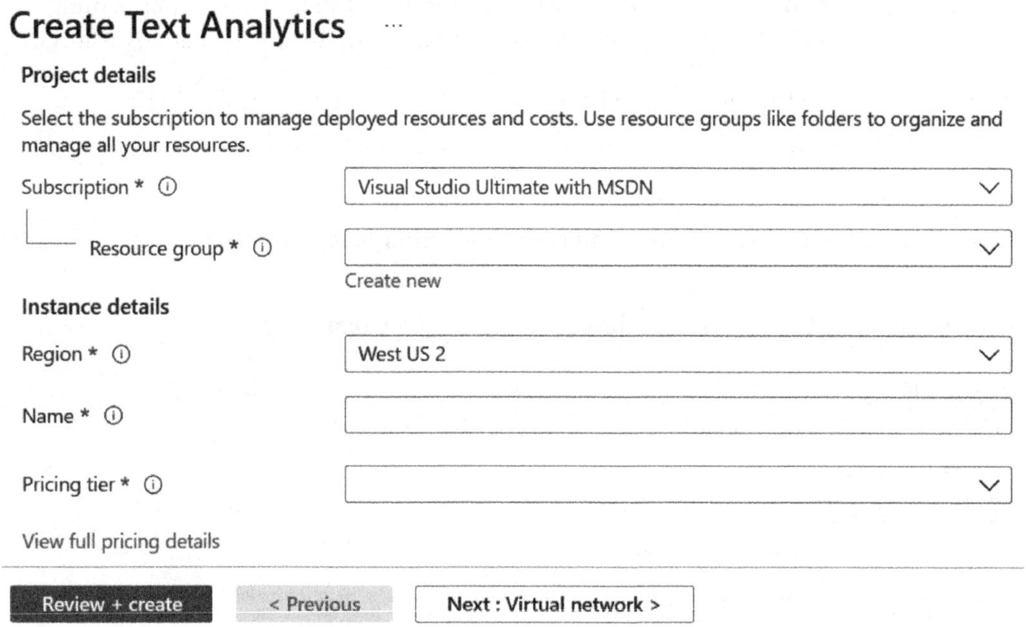

Create Text Analytics   ...

Project details

Select the subscription to manage deployed resources and costs. Use resource groups like folders to organize and manage all your resources.

Subscription * ⓘ

    Visual Studio Ultimate with MSDN   ⌄

└──── Resource group * ⓘ

                                                                            ⌄

    Create new

Instance details

Region * ⓘ

    West US 2   ⌄

Name * ⓘ

Pricing tier * ⓘ

                                                                            ⌄

View full pricing details

[Review + create]   [< Previous]   [Next : Virtual network >]

Figure 10.2 – Providing the required details to create a Text Analytics resource in the Azure portal

Now that we have created a Text Analytics resource in the Azure portal, next we will be creating an anomaly detector in the Azure portal.

Creating an Anomaly Detector resource in the Azure portal

Anomaly detection is the process of identifying unexpected behavior of data as compared to the rest of the records. We are going to use this resource to perform anomaly detection on our data stored in the *Anomaly detection* section.

You can go through the following steps to create an anomaly detector in the Azure portal:

1.   Log in to the Azure portal, at https://portal.azure.com.

2.   Click on **+ Create a resource** and select **Anomaly Detector** from the list of all available resources:

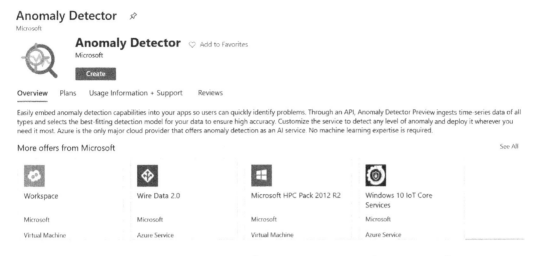

Anomaly Detector 📌
Microsoft

Anomaly Detector ♡ Add to Favorites
Microsoft

[Create]

Overview   Plans   Usage Information + Support   Reviews

Easily embed anomaly detection capabilities into your apps so users can quickly identify problems. Through an API, Anomaly Detector Preview ingests time-series data of all types and selects the best-fitting detection model for your data to ensure high accuracy. Customize the service to detect any level of anomaly and deploy it wherever you need it most. Azure is the only major cloud provider that offers anomaly detection as an AI service. No machine learning expertise is required.

More offers from Microsoft   See All

Workspace	Wire Data 2.0	Microsoft HPC Pack 2012 R2	Windows 10 IoT Core Services
Microsoft	Microsoft	Microsoft	Microsoft
Virtual Machine	Azure Service	Virtual Machine	Azure Service

Figure 10.3 – Creating an Anomaly Detector resource in the Azure portal

3. You can see the overview of this service. Click on **Create**.

4. Fill in the values for **Subscription**, **Resource group**, **Region**, **Name**, and **Pricing tier**.

5. You can leave the default values for the remaining fields and click on **Review + create**:

Create Anomaly Detector   ⋯

Select the subscription to manage deployed resources and costs. Use resource groups like folders to organize and manage all your resources.

Subscription * ⓘ   [Visual Studio Ultimate with MSDN   ⌄]

└── Resource group * ⓘ   [⌄]
                                   Create new

Instance details

Region * ⓘ   [West US 2   ⌄]

Name * ⓘ   [   ]

Pricing tier * ⓘ   [⌄]

View full pricing details

[Review + create]   [< Previous]   [Next : Virtual network >]

Figure 10.4 – Providing the required details to create an anomaly detector resource in the Azure portal

The Text Analytics and Anomaly Detector resources are both created now, and we are going to use both of these resources later in this chapter.

Now it's time to create a key vault in the Azure portal. It will be used while creating linked services in Synapse Studio.

Creating an Azure key vault

Azure Key Vault is a cloud service that is used to store secrets securely, such as passwords, API keys, certificates, and so on. In this section, we are going to create an Azure key vault and then we will learn how to use it for creating linked services in Synapse Studio:

1. Log in to the Azure portal, at `https://portal.azure.com`.

2. Click on **+ Create a resource** and select **Key Vault** from the list of all available resources.

3. Fill in the values for **Subscription**, **Resource group**, **Region**, **Name**, and **Pricing tier**.

4. You can leave the default values for the remaining fields and click on **Review + create**:

Create key vault ⋯

trail for compliance.

Project details

Select the subscription to manage deployed resources and costs. Use resource groups like folders to organize and manage all your resources.

Subscription *	Visual Studio Ultimate with MSDN ⌄
Resource group *	⌄
	Create new

Instance details

Key vault name * ⓘ	Enter the name
Region *	East US ⌄
Pricing tier * ⓘ	Standard ⌄

Review + create		< Previous	Next : Access policy >

Figure 10.5 – Creating a key vault in the Azure portal

5. Once the key vault is created, go to the **Access policies** tab in your key vault and click on **+ Add Access Policy**:

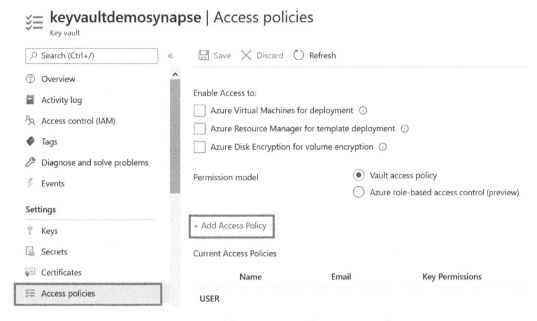

Figure 10.6 – Adding an access policy in Key Vault

6. Select **Key, Secret, & Certificate Management** from the drop-down list of the **Configure from template (optional)** field.

7. Select your **Synapse** workspace as the principal to grant permissions to read secrets from the Azure key vault:

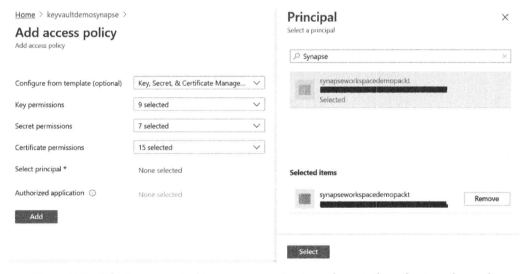

Figure 10.7 – Selecting a principal to grant permission to read secrets from the Azure key vault

8. Go to your **Cognitive Services** resource, for example, **Anomaly Detector | Keys and Endpoint**, and copy either of the two keys to the clipboard:

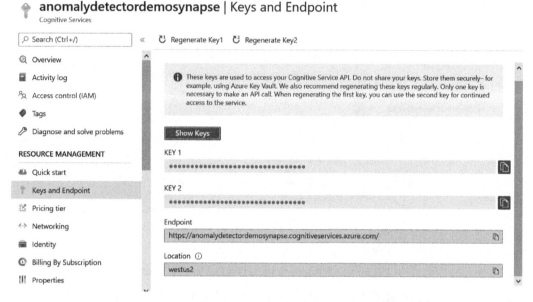

Figure 10.8 – Copying a key from the anomaly detector resource on the Azure portal

9. Go to your key vault (**keyvaultdemosynapse**)| **Secret to create a new secret**. Specify the name of the secret, and then paste the key from *Step 7* into the **Value** field. Finally, click **Create**:

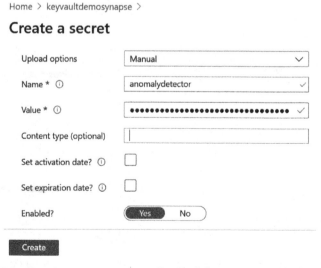

Figure 10.9 – Creating a secret in Azure Key Vault by using anomaly detector keys

10. Next, go to Synapse Studio in the Azure portal and navigate to **Linked services** under the **Manage** tab and click on **+ New** to create a **New linked service**.

11. Select **Key Vault** from the list of all available Azure resources, fill in the required details, and click on **Create**:

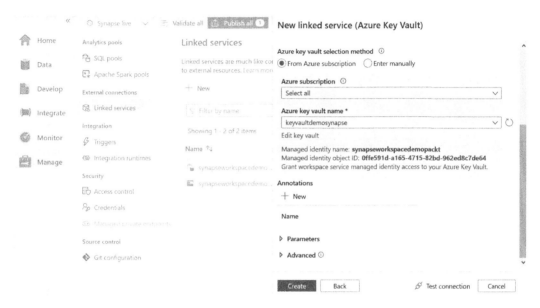

Figure 10.10 – Creating a linked service for a key vault in Azure Synapse

In order to use Azure ML services within Azure Synapse, we need to create a linked service for Azure ML in Azure Synapse. The next section will cover this topic in detail.

Creating an Azure ML linked service in Azure Synapse

Azure ML is a cloud-based service that can be used to create and manage machine learning solutions. You can easily link an Azure Synapse Analytics workspace with an Azure Machine Learning workspace in order to leverage various ML features within Azure Synapse. With this linked service created within your Azure Synapse workspace, you can directly bring a machine learning model from the Azure ML model registry and score the model in the Synapse SQL pool.

Most importantly, you can run your Azure Machine Learning pipelines directly from Azure Synapse by creating a Synapse pipeline and linking it to the ML linked service created in Azure Synapse. We will go through the required steps in this section.

For now, we will be creating an ML linked service in Azure Synapse, but before we do that, we need to register an application on Azure Active Directory. So, go through the following steps to complete the pre-requisites for creating ML linked services:

1. Log in to the Azure portal, at `https://portal.azure.com`.

2. Go to **App registrations** under **Azure Active Directory** in the Azure portal:

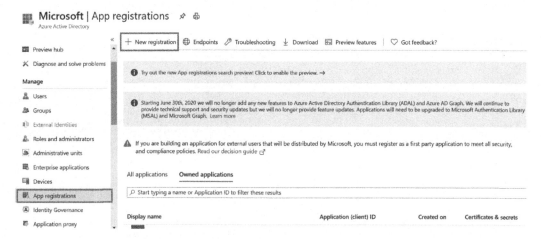

Figure 10.11 – A screenshot of the App registrations page of Azure Active Directory

3. Click on the **New registration** tab.

4. Next, provide an appropriate user-facing display name. Select **Supported account types** as per your business need and click on **Register**:

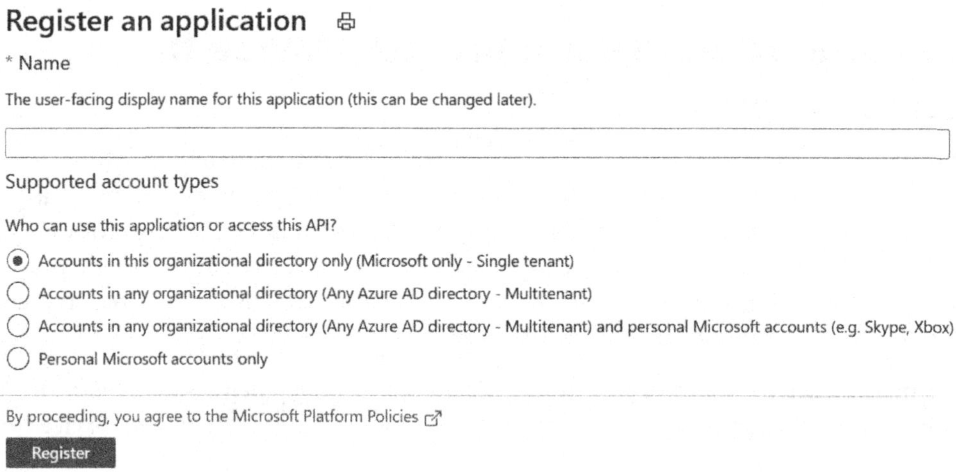

Register an application

* Name

The user-facing display name for this application (this can be changed later).

Supported account types

Who can use this application or access this API?

(●) Accounts in this organizational directory only (Microsoft only - Single tenant)

( ) Accounts in any organizational directory (Any Azure AD directory - Multitenant)

( ) Accounts in any organizational directory (Any Azure AD directory - Multitenant) and personal Microsoft accounts (e.g. Skype, Xbox)

( ) Personal Microsoft accounts only

By proceeding, you agree to the Microsoft Platform Policies

Register

Figure 10.12 – Registering an application in Azure Active Directory

5.   After the application is registered, generate a secret for the application. Go to **Your application | Certificates & secrets**, and click on **Add a client secret** to generate a secret. Save the secret in a notepad as it will be used later:

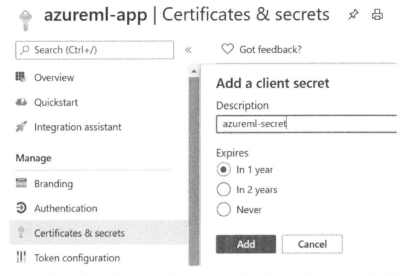

Figure 10.13 – Generating a client secret for a registered application in Azure Active Directory

Now that we have completed the prerequisite phase, we will go through the following steps to create our ML linked services:

1.   Launch Synapse Studio from your Synapse workspace and go to the **Management** tab.

2.   Click on the **Linked services** tab and click on the **+ New** tab:

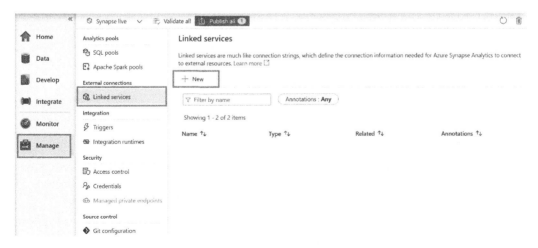

Figure 10.14 – Creating linked services for Azure ML

3. Select **Azure Machine Learning** from the list of all available resources and click on **Continue**.

4. Fill in the details for **Service principal ID** and **Service principal key** in the corresponding fields and click on **Create**:

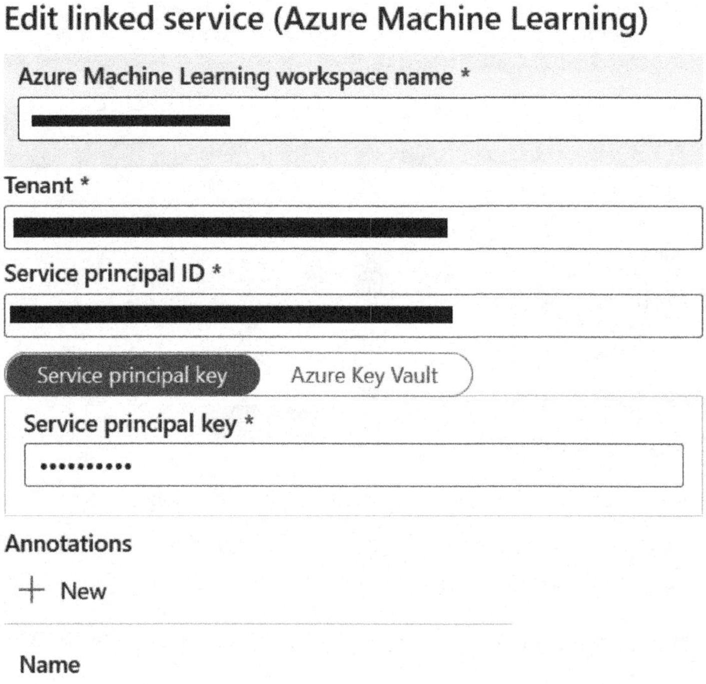

Figure 10.15 – Creating a linked service for an Azure Machine Learning workspace

So, now we have completed the first step of using Azure ML services with Azure Synapse to analyze our data at scale. Next, we will learn which capabilities of the Azure Machine Learning service can be used on Azure Synapse.

Machine learning capabilities in Azure Synapse

Data analysis is not a standalone process that can be executed without getting help from other counterpart services. Before we learn how to use Azure ML services with Azure Synapse, it's important to understand the various steps involved in any data analysis process, such as data collecting, transforming, cleaning, and modeling data.

We are going to learn about these steps in brief in the following subsections.

Data ingestion and orchestration

This section is focused on the data collection and transformation process. In this section, we are going to learn how to create a Synapse pipeline for data ingestion and how to use notebooks for data orchestration.

Azure Synapse pipelines provide a variety of data sources to ingest data from. An Azure Synapse pipeline is an integrated part of Azure Synapse used to **Extract, Transform, and Load** (ETL) data. To learn more about Azure Synapse pipelines, you can refer to *Chapter 4, Using Synapse Pipelines to Orchestrate Your Data*.

It's very easy to create a Synapse pipeline in Synapse Studio. You just need to go to the **Integrate** hub in Synapse Studio and click on the + icon to create a new pipeline as shown in the following screenshot:

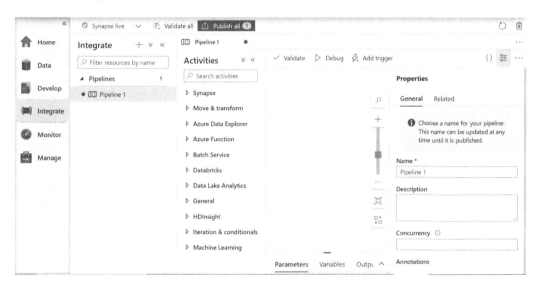

Figure 10.16 – Creating Azure Synapse pipelines in Synapse Studio

Azure Synapse provides various options to orchestrate your data as per the business need. After bringing the data to Azure Synapse, you can proceed to the next stage in the data analysis process.

Data preparation and exploration

Azure Synapse offers you different options to explore your data depending upon where the data is stored or which tool you want to use for data exploration. You can use a Spark pool or Serverless SQL pool in Azure Synapse to explore and visualize your data. We will learn more about these options in the following sections.

Azure Synapse Spark pools

It becomes really difficult when you are trying to transform and analyze data at scale, but Spark pools provide capabilities to deal with this problem. Spark pools provide you with the option to choose the tool for your data processing. Now it does not matter whether you are comfortable with PySpark, Scala, or you just know .NET, Spark pools let you choose whichever you are comfortable with.

We already saw in *Chapter 7, Working with R, Python, Scala, .NET, and Spark SQL in Azure Synapse*, how to read data from data lake directly and use different libraries to transform the data as per the business need. You can go to the following link if you need a quick-start guide to start analyzing data using Spark pools: https://docs.microsoft.com/en-us/azure/synapse-analytics/get-started-analyze-spark.

Azure Synapse Serverless SQL pool

Similar to Synapse Spark pools, you can also use Synapse Serverless SQL pool to analyze your data. Using the OPENROWSET function is the easiest approach to begin with, however, you can use T-SQL to transform and analyze your data very efficiently in Serverless SQL pool.

If you want to learn about Serverless SQL pool, you can refer to *Chapter 2, Considerations for Your Compute Environment*. The following code snippet is just an example of reading data by using the OPENROWSET function:

```
SELECT
    TOP 100 *
FROM
    OPENROWSET(
        BULK' https://azureopendatastorage.blob.core.windows.
net/nyctlc/yellow/puYear=*/puMonth=*/*.parquet',
        FORMAT = 'parquet'
    ) AS [result];
```

> **Important note**
> You can go through the following quick-start link if you are new to this topic: https://docs.microsoft.com/en-us/azure/synapse-analytics/get-started-analyze-sql-on-demand.

Once your data preparation is done, we can jump to the next section to learn about training our machine learning models using this data.

Training machine learning models

Sometimes just visualizing data is not sufficient; we need to understand our data to predict the future or to detect anomalous behavior in data. We can learn the trends and behavior of our existing data, which can help us understand the nature of futuristic data. But to understand millions and billions of records our life may pass by, so we define some training data and train a model on various parameters by using this training data. In simple terms, this process is called machine learning and a file that has been trained to recognize certain types of patterns is called a machine learning model.

In this section, we will learn how to train a model with **Automated ML (AutoML)** and MLlib.

Azure enables you with a resource called **Azure Machine Learning** that can be used to train, deploy, automate, manage, and track ML models. Now, the integration of Azure ML with Synapse has opened up a new world for our data to be explored and visualized without much effort.

You can train your ML models either by using **AutoML**, which is also known as **AutoML** or you can use **Apache Spark MLlib** to create your machine learning application. We will learn about both options in the following sections.

Training models with Azure Machine Learning AutoML

The process of automating the iterative tasks of machine learning model development is called AutoML. We can build highly scalable, efficient, and productive ML models using AutoML. We can use Automated ML for classification, regression, or forecasting tasks as per our business needs.

In this section, we will learn how to use automated machine learning in Azure Synapse Analytics Studio. First, let's try to create our first model without writing any code in Azure Synapse. Let's go through the following steps. You do not need to be an expert in data science to perform these steps:

1. Log in to the Azure portal at `https://portal.azure.com`.

2. Go to your Synapse workspace and click on **Synapse Studio** to launch it.

3. If your data is residing in your storage account, you can use the following script to create a Spark table:

```
blob_account_name = ''yourstorageaccountname''
blob_container_name = ''containername''
from pyspark.sql import SparkSession
```

```
sc = SparkSession.builder.getOrCreate()

token_library = / sc._jvm.com.microsoft.azure.synapse.
tokenlibrary.TokenLibrary

blob_sas_token = token_library.
getConnectionString(''AzureBlobStorage'')


spark.conf.set(
    'fs.azure.sas.%s.%s.blob.core.windows.net' % (blob_
container_name, blob_account_name),
    blob_sas_token)

df = / spark.read.load('wasbs://containername@
yourstorageaccountname.blob.core.windows.net/sample.csv',
format='csv'

##If header exists uncomment line below

, header=True

)

spark_df.write.mode(''overwrite'').saveAsTable(''default.
sample'')
```

4. But if you are new to machine learning, you can use sample data for NYC Yellow Taxi from **Azure Open Datasets** to create our Spark table. Go to the following link to download a sample notebook: https://go.microsoft.com/fwlink/?linkid=2149229.

5. Go to the **Develop** tab of Synapse Studio and click on **+** then **Import** to import the downloaded notebook:

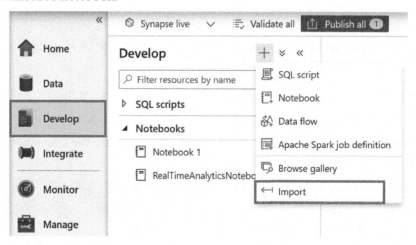

Figure 10.17 – Importing a sample notebook from the local machine

6. Select the Spark pool you want to use and click on **Run all** to run all the code sections available in this notebook:

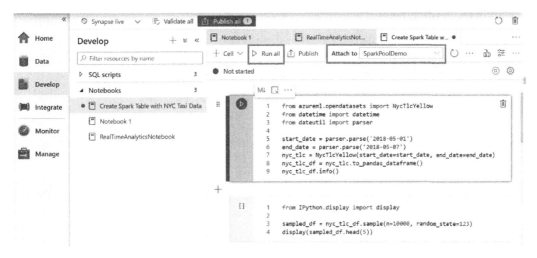

Figure 10.18 – Running all the cells in the imported notebook

7. Now let's go to the **Data** tab to validate that the Spark table has been created under the default Spark database after the notebook run has completed.

8. Right-click on the Spark table (**nyc_taxi**) that got created in *Step 6*, select **Machine Learning** from the dropdown and click on **Enrich with new model**:

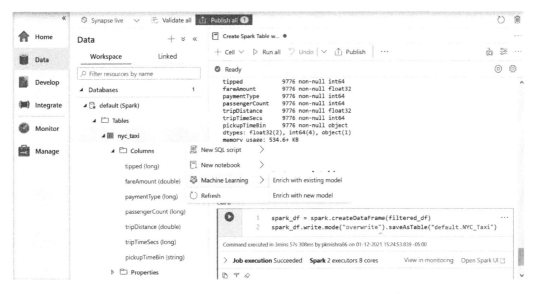

Figure 10.19 – Using Machine Learning on a Spark table created in Synapse

9. Select your **Azure Machine Learning workspace** that you want to use for this model.

10. Provide an appropriate **Experiment name** and **Best model name** in the corresponding fields.

11. Select your **Target column** from the drop-down list.

12. Select your **Apache Spark pool** and click on **Continue**:

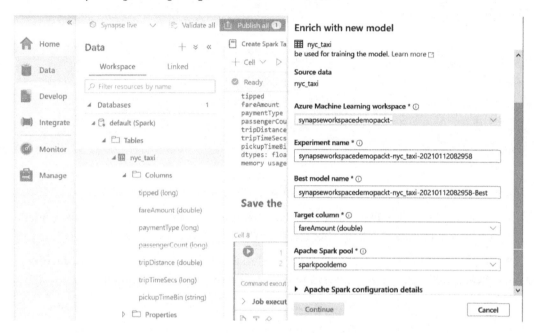

Figure 10.20 – A screenshot of enriching data with a new model

13. On the next screen, choose **Regression** as your task type and click on **Continue**:

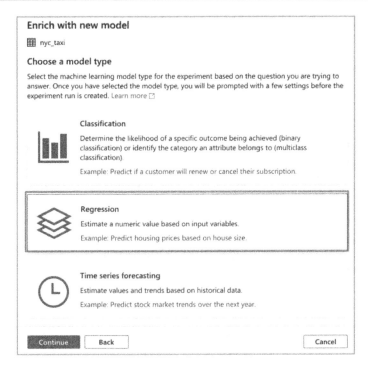

Figure 10.21 – Selecting the model type for the nyc_taxi data in Azure Synapse

14. You can leave the remaining fields with the default settings and click on **Create run**. Instead of running it directly, you can click on **Open in notebook** and run all the cells manually:

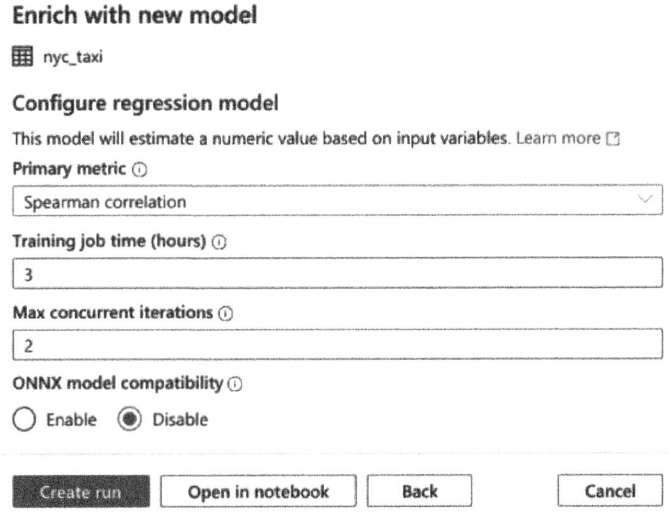

Enrich with new model

nyc_taxi

Configure regression model

This model will estimate a numeric value based on input variables. Learn more

Primary metric ⓘ

Spearman correlation

Training job time (hours) ⓘ

3

Max concurrent iterations ⓘ

2

ONNX model compatibility ⓘ

○ Enable   ⦿ Disable

Create run   Open in notebook   Back   Cancel

Figure 10.22 – Creating a run automatically in Azure Synapse

Now we know how to enrich our data with a new or existing model, however, we can use Python code as well to perform the same operation.

The following script can be used to configure your Azure ML workspace:

```python
from azureml.core import Workspace
# Enter your workspace subscription, resource group,
name, and region.
subscription_id = ''<enter your subscription ID>'' #you
should be owner or contributor
resource_group = ''<enter your resource group>'' #you
should be owner or contributor
workspace_name = ''<enter your workspace name>'' #your
workspace name
workspace_region = ''<enter workspace region>'' #your
region

ws = Workspace(workspace_name = workspace_name,
               subscription_id = subscription_id,
               resource_group = resource_group)
```

Pass the training settings to an `AutoMLConfig` object:

```python
from azureml.train.automl import AutoMLConfig

automl_config = AutoMLConfig(task='regression',
                    debug_log='automated_ml_errors.log',
                    training_data = dataset_training,
                    spark_context = sc,
                    model_explainability = False,
                    label_column_name =''fareAmount'',**automl_settings)
```

> **Important note**
>
> You can download the complete notebook from the following link: `https://github.com/PacktPublishing/Limitless-Analytics-with-Azure-Synapse/blob/master/Chapter%2010-%20Sample%20Notebooks.zip`. This notebook will use the NYC Taxi sample data to create the regression model.

Now that we have learned how to use Spark AutoML to train our models, let's try to learn about training models using Spark MLlib.

Training models on Spark pools with MLlib

MLlib is Spark's machine learning library, it provides various tools to make practical machine learning scalable and easy. These libraries can be used for any common learning algorithms, such as classification, regression, clustering, and so on. Moreover, it provides utilities for linear algebra, statistics, data handling, and more.

First, we need to import the model types required to use Spark MLlib libraries:

```
from pyspark.ml.classification import LogisticRegression
from pyspark.mllib.evaluation import
BinaryClassificationMetrics
from pyspark.ml.evaluation import BinaryClassificationEvaluator
```

In the preceding code section, we imported three different model types:

- `LogisticRegression`: Logistic regression is used to predict a categorical response. Logistic regression is a statistical model that can be used to calculate the probability of a certain class or a binary event occurring such as win/loss, healthy/sick, present/not present, and so on.

- `BinaryClassificationMetrics`: An evaluator for binary classification.

- `BinaryClassificationEvaluator`: An evaluator for binary classification. It accepts two parameters, label and prediction. The prediction column can be of type double or vector.

Once the training and test DataFrames are ready, you can create your model formula to run it against the training DataFrame and validate it against the testing DataFrame.

Let's go through the following steps to perform evaluation on the test data:

1. Create a new `LogisticRegression` object for the model:

   ```
   logReg = LogisticRegression(maxIter=10, regParam=0.3,
   labelCol = 'tipped')
   ```

2. Here's the formula for the model:

   ```
   classFormula = RFormula(formula=''tipped ~ pickupHour +
   weekdayVec + passengerCount + tripTimeSecs + tripDistance
   + fareAmount + paymentType+ trafficTimeBinsVec'')
   ```

3. Undertake the training and create a logistic regression model:

```
lrModel = Pipeline(stages=[classFormula, logReg]).
fit(train_data_df)
```

4. Saving the model is optional but it's another form of intersession cache:

```
datestamp = datetime.now().strftime('%m-%d-%Y-%s')
fileName = ''lrModel_'' + datestamp
logRegDirfilename = fileName
lrModel.save(logRegDirfilename)
```

5. Predict tip 1/0 (yes/no) on the test dataset, and run the evaluation using AUROC:

```
predictions = lrModel.transform(test_data_df)
predictionAndLabels = predictions.
select(''label'',''prediction'').rdd
metrics = BinaryClassificationMetrics(predictionAndLabels)
print(''Area under ROC = %s'' % metrics.areaUnderROC)
```

> **Important note**
>
> You can download the complete notebook from the following link: `https://github.com/PacktPublishing/Limitless-Analytics-with-Azure-Synapse/blob/master/Chapter%2010-%20Sample%20Notebooks.zip`. This notebook has been created by using the NYC Taxi sample data to create a regression model.
>
> To learn more about this example, please go to the following link: `https://docs.microsoft.com/en-us/azure/synapse-analytics/spark/apache-spark-machine-learning-mllib-notebook`.

So far in this chapter, we have seen a couple of examples using different ML models on our data, and in the next section, we will learn about some of the common use cases for Azure Synapse with Cognitive Services.

Use cases with Cognitive Services

Cognitive Services are Microsoft-developed **machine learning** algorithms to solve problems in the field of artificial intelligence. Cognitive Services are categorized into five main categories:

- Vision
- Speech
- Language
- Decision
- Search

Azure Cognitive Services are cloud-based services with REST APIs. You can build intelligent applications using client library SDKs. Go to the following link to learn about all supported APIs for different categories of Cognitive Services: `https://docs.microsoft.com/en-us/azure/cognitive-services/what-are-cognitive-services`.

Cognitive Services can be used to solve many day-to-day life problems without worrying about creating a new ML model from scratch. One of the best examples is extracted and enhanced texts from typewritten and handwritten notes, photos and diagrams, and other unstructured data from the **John F. Kennedy (JFK)** files, which contain over 34,000 pages of documents about the CIA investigation into the 1963 JFK assassination.

Azure Synapse enables you to easily enrich your data in Azure Synapse with existing Cognitive Services models. As of now, you can see two existing models to enrich your data, **sentiment analysis** and **anomaly detector**. We will learn about both these options in the following sections.

Sentiment analysis

You can perform sentiment analysis on your text data with the existing models available on Azure Synapse. But first, you need to have your data loaded to a Spark table. Make sure your file is uploaded to the Azure Data Lake Gen2 account that is configured as the default storage for your Azure Synapse Analytics workspace. You need to make sure that you have the contributor level permission on the Azure Data Lake Gen2 filesystem where your data is residing:

1. Go to the **Data** tab on your Azure Synapse Studio and expand your **default (Spark)** database.

2. Right-click on your Spark table, select **Machine Learning** from the drop-down list, and click on **Enrich with existing model**:

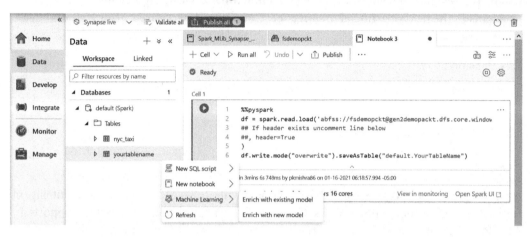

Figure 10.23 – A screenshot of enriching your data in a Spark table

3. Select **Text Analytics - Sentiment Analysis** from the list of existing models and click on **Continue**:

Enrich with existing model

⊞ yourtablename

This experience allows you to enrich the selected dataset with pre-trained Azure Cognitive Services models. Learn more ☐

Azure Cognitive Services

Name

Anomaly Detector ⓘ

Text Analytics - Sentiment Analysis ⓘ

Continue		Cancel

Figure 10. 24 – Selecting Text Analytics - Sentiment Analysis for enriching data in Azure Synapse

4. Provide the details for the **Azure Cognitive Services account** and **Azure Key Vault linked service** fields:

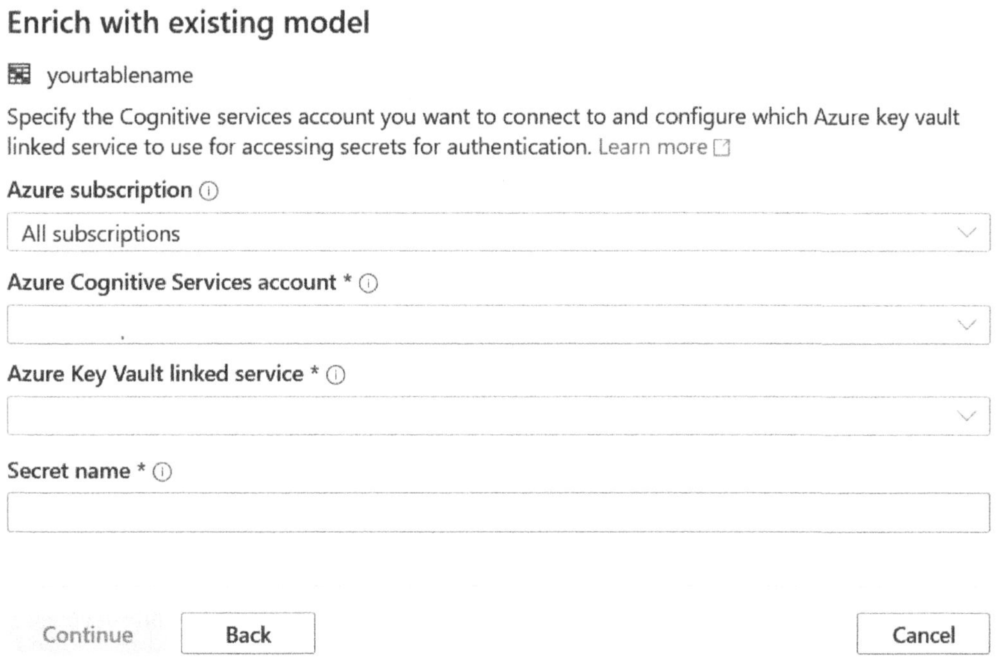

Enrich with existing model

▦ yourtablename

Specify the Cognitive services account you want to connect to and configure which Azure key vault linked service to use for accessing secrets for authentication. Learn more ⬎

Azure subscription ⓘ

All subscriptions	⌄

Azure Cognitive Services account * ⓘ

.	⌄

Azure Key Vault linked service * ⓘ

	⌄

Secret name * ⓘ

Continue   Back   Cancel

Figure 10.25 – Providing configuration for your Cognitive Services account

5. Next, we just need to select the **Language** and **Text** columns that will be used for sentiment analysis and click on **Open notebook**.

6. Now, click on **Run All** to run all the cells of the notebook and you will see the result.

We have learned how to perform sentiment analysis on your data in Azure Synapse with just a couple of steps. Next, we will learn how to perform anomaly detection on your data.

Anomaly detection

Anomaly detection is a process of identifying data that shows unexpected behavior as compared to the rest of the data. These anomalies might point out unusual bank transactions, unusual network traffic, or dirty data that requires cleansing, and so on.

You can go through the following steps to perform anomaly detection on your data:

1. Go to the **Data** tab of your Azure Synapse Studio and expand the **default (Spark)** database:

2. Right-click on your Spark table, select **Machine Learning** from the drop-down list, and click on **Enrich with existing model**.

3. Select **Anomaly Detector** from the list of existing models and click on **Continue**:

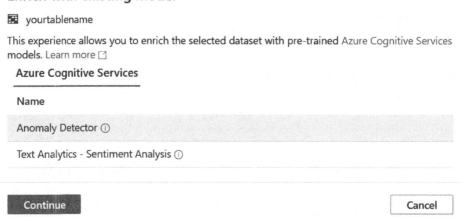

Figure 10. 26 – Selecting Anomaly Detector to enrich data in Azure Synapse

4. Provide the details for **Cognitive Services** and **Azure Key Vault linked services**.

5. Next, we need to fill in the values for **Granularity**, **Timestamp column**, **Timeseries value column**, and **Grouping column**, as shown in the following screenshot:

Figure 10.27 – Providing details for Anomaly Detector

6. Now, click on **Run All** to run all the cells on the notebook and you will see the result.

Now we have learned how we can use an existing ML model to enrich our data with just a couple of steps. It would not be possible to cover all the topics on the Azure ML service and its integration with Azure Synapse in just one chapter, but we have covered most of the important topics that will help in exploring the benefits and usage of the Azure ML service's integration with Azure Synapse.

Summary

In this chapter, we learned how to create a linked service for machine learning in Azure Synapse and how to use a key vault to store secrets for cognitive services. We also learned how to use Azure ML with Azure Synapse in order to use new or existing ML models to enrich our data. We then learned how can we use Cognitive Services directly on our data without writing even a single line of code. There are various steps involved before we can start using Cognitive Services on our data and we went through all these technical requirements. Sample notebooks were also provided to understand the approach to using **Spark AutoML** and **Spark MLlib** on the data.

With this chapter, we've covered and understood all the concepts of Azure Synapse. In the next chapter, we will learn different ways to perform backup and restore operations in Azure Synapse.

Section 4: Best Practices

The objective of this section is to guide you in terms of the best practices related to security, coding, managing, and monitoring Azure Synapse.

This section comprises the following chapters:

- *Chapter 11, Performing Backup and Restore in Azure Synapse Analytics*
- *Chapter 12, Securing Data on Azure Synapse*
- *Chapter 13, Managing and Monitoring Synapse Workloads*
- *Chapter 14, Coding Best Practices*

11

Performing Backup and Restore in Azure Synapse Analytics

High-availability solutions ensure that your data is never lost, even in the case of unplanned events, such as underlying hardware, software, or network failures. Azure Synapse Analytics uses database screenshots to provide the high availability of dedicated SQL pools. These screenshots create several restore points that can be used to recover your data to a previous state.

In this chapter, you will learn about backup and restore operations on Azure Synapse Analytics. We will begin this chapter by creating restore points for Azure Synapse Analytics; we are also going to create geo-redundant restores using PowerShell. Then, we will learn about the geo-backup and disaster recovery of Synapse SQL pools.

To learn more about these concepts, the following topics will be covered in this chapter:

- Creating restore points
- Geo-backups and disaster recovery
- Cross-subscription restore

Technical requirements

Before you start orchestrating your data, there are certain prerequisites to meet:

- You should have an Azure subscription or access to any other subscription with contributor-level access.

- Create your Synapse workspace on this subscription. You can follow the instructions from *Chapter 1, Introduction to Azure Synapse*, to create your Synapse workspace.

- Create a SQL pool on Azure Synapse. This has been covered in *Chapter 2, Considerations for Your Compute Environment*.

- Install Azure PowerShell on your machine.

Creating restore points

Azure Synapse Analytics creates various restore points throughout the day by using screenshots. These restore points are available for 7 days and we do not have the luxury of modifying this retention period. But we do have the luxury of creating a new SQL pool in the primary region, by using any of the screenshots taken within the last 7 days. We can create our own restore points as well. Let's learn about both types of restore points in the following sections.

Automatic restore points

By using an automatic restore point, we can select any date and time within the range of the last 7 days to restore the SQL pool in our primary region. This is a built-in feature, so we do not need to enable this feature manually. However, if we pause our dedicated SQL pool very frequently, then these automatic restore points cannot be generated. Users do not have the privilege of deleting these restore points.

It takes just a couple of steps to create and restore a SQL pool, so let's go through the following steps to restore your own SQL pool:

1. Log in to the Azure portal at `https://portal.azure.com`.

2. Navigate to your Synapse workspace and click on your dedicated SQL pool.

3. Click on the **Restore** link highlighted in the following screenshot:

Figure 11.1 – Restoring a dedicated SQL pool on the Azure portal

4. Select the **Automatic restore points** radio button for **Restore point type**.

5. Provide an appropriate value for a new dedicated SQL pool name.

6. Select the date and time for your restore point. It must not be older than 7 days.

7. Select your Synapse workspace name from the list of available workspaces in the drop-down list.

8. Select the performance level as per your compute needs and click on **Review + Restore**:

Figure 11.2 – Selecting an automatic restore point to restore the dedicated SQL pool on the Azure portal

9. Review all the details and click on **Create dedicated SQL pool – Restore database**.

> **Important note**
> Screenshots are not taken when a dedicated SQL pool is paused.

Within a couple of minutes, a new dedicated SQL pool will be created for you. It will have all the data available from the restore point that you selected. Once the pool is created, you can log in to this SQL pool by using the dedicated SQL endpoints in **SQL Server Management Studio (SSMS)** or Azure Data Studio to validate that you have got all the required data in your new SQL pool.

You can run the following query on your dedicated SQL pool to see when the last screenshot was created:

```
select    top 1 *
from      sys.pdw_loader_backup_runs
order by run_id desc
```

You can see the name of the last restore point in the following screenshot:

Figure 11.3 – A screenshot of query output on the SSMS tool showing the last restore point for the SQL pool

Similarly, we can use user-defined restore points to restore a dedicated SQL pool. We will learn about this in the next section.

User-defined restore points

If you need to pause your dedicated SQL pool frequently, automatic restore points may not get created sometimes. In such circumstances, it is better to create user-defined restore points every time before you pause your SQL pool. Otherwise, you are at risk of losing your data in the case of any failures.

Unlike automatic restore points, first you need to create your own restore points in order to restore your dedicated SQL pool, by using user-defined restore points. Go to your dedicated SQL pool, click on **+ New restore point**, and provide a name for your restore point, as shown in *Figure 11.4*. It is best to append a date and time to the SQL pool name, for example, `sqlpooldemo_01272021_0740`:

Figure 11.4 – Creating a new restore point for the dedicated SQL pool on the Azure portal

We will go through the following steps to create a restore point for the dedicated SQL pool:

1. Log in to the Azure portal at `https://portal.azure.com`.

2. Navigate to your Synapse workspace and click on your dedicated SQL pool.

3. Click on the **Restore** link.

4. Select the **User-defined restore points** radio button for **Restore point type**.

5. Provide an appropriate value for a new dedicated SQL pool name.

6. Select the restore point that you have already created, that is, **sqlpooldemo_01272021_0740PM**.

7. Select your Synapse workspace name from the list of available workspaces in the drop-down list.

8. Select the performance level as per your compute needs and click on
   Review + Restore:

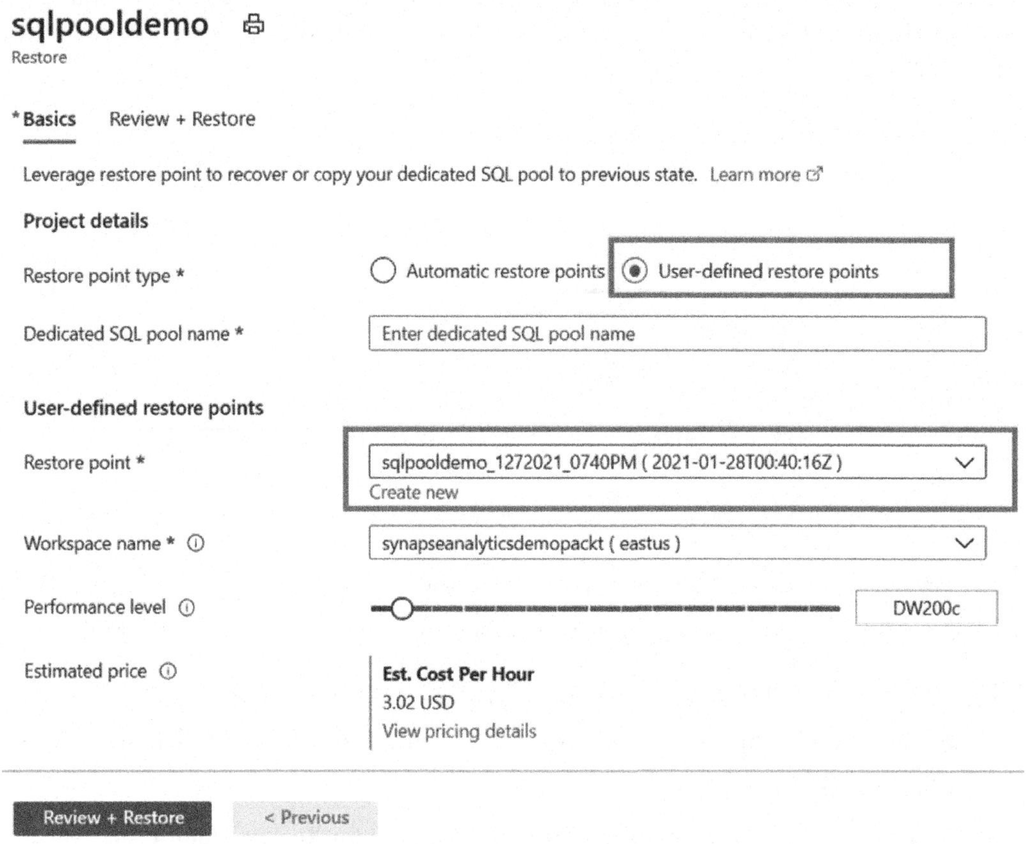

sqlpooldemo 🖶
Restore

* Basics   Review + Restore

Leverage restore point to recover or copy your dedicated SQL pool to previous state. Learn more ⬀

Project details

Restore point type *   ◯ Automatic restore points   ⦿ User-defined restore points

Dedicated SQL pool name *   Enter dedicated SQL pool name

User-defined restore points

Restore point *   sqlpooldemo_1272021_0740PM (2021-01-28T00:40:16Z)   ⌄
                                         Create new

Workspace name * ⓘ   synapseanalyticsdemopackt (eastus)   ⌄

Performance level ⓘ   ●─○───   DW200c

Estimated price ⓘ   **Est. Cost Per Hour**
                                        3.02 USD
                                        View pricing details

[Review + Restore]   [< Previous]

Figure 11.5 – Restoring the dedicated SQL pool by using user-defined restore points on the Azure portal

> **Important note**
> Restore points in a dedicated SQL pool will be automatically deleted when they
> hit the 7-day retention period and when there are at least 42 restore points.
> These restore points include user-defined and automatic restore points as well.

Again, a new dedicated SQL pool will be created in just a couple of minutes with all the
data available from the restore point that you selected. Both the options are easy and
straightforward; you can decide which option works better for you.

The following section outlines how to create geo-backups for implementing disaster
recovery solutions for dedicated SQL pools in Azure Synapse.

Geo-backups and disaster recovery

Synapse performs a geo-backup once per day to a paired data center automatically, and that's why the option to enable a geo-backup policy for your dedicated SQL pool is disabled. The **Recovery Point Objective** (**RPO**) for a geo-backup is 24 hours. This geo-backup can be used to restore your SQL pool if the restore points in the primary region are not available.

In this section, we are going to create geo-redundant restore points using the Azure portal and PowerShell script as well. This PowerShell script can be used for any dedicated SQL pool just by providing correct values for the parameters in the script.

As shown in the following screenshot, we cannot create a geo-backup policy for a dedicated SQL pool because the SQL pool is automatically backed up to the region pair. You can read about region pairs at the following link—`https://docs.microsoft. com/en-us/azure/best-practices-availability-paired-regions`:

Figure 11.6 – A screenshot of a geo-backup policy for a dedicated SQL pool on the Azure portal

We can restore the dedicated SQL pool from an Azure geographical region through the Azure portal or PowerShell. We will learn about this in detail in the following sections.

Geo-redundant restore through the Azure portal

You can restore a dedicated SQL pool by using the most recent backup of any dedicated SQL pool in the subscription.

Go through the following steps to create a new SQL pool using the geo-backup of any SQL pool in your subscription:

1. Log in to the Azure portal at `https://portal.azure.com`.

2. Go to the Synapse workspace in your primary region.

3. Click on the **SQL pools** tab in your Synapse workspace.

4. Click on **+ New** to create a new dedicated SQL pool.

5. Provide a name for your dedicated SQL pool and go to the **Additional settings** tab.

6. For the **Use existing data** property under **Data source**, select **Backup**.

7. Select the backup file from the drop-down list of the **Backup** property that you want to restore and click on **Review + create**.

8. Finally, after reviewing all the details, click on **Create**:

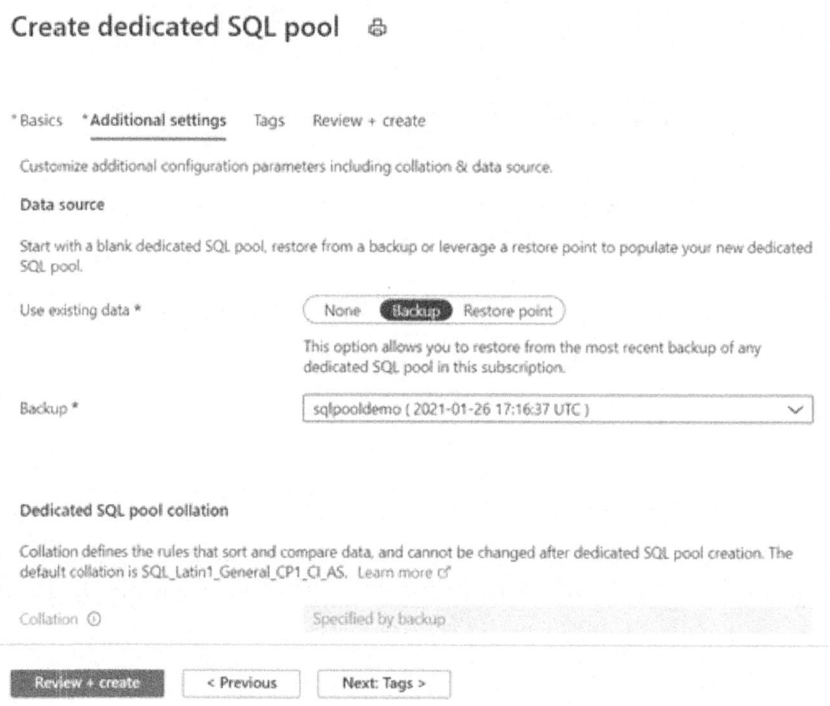

Figure 11.7 – Creating a dedicated SQL pool using geo-backup through the Azure portal

So, we learned that even if our restore points are not available in the primary region, we can restore our dedicated SQL pool using a geo-backup that is created automatically.

Geo-redundant restore through PowerShell

In order to maintain a screenshot of your dedicated SQL pool in any other region than your primary region, it is important to have the geo-restore option. In the case of unplanned events in your primary region, you can switch to another region.

You can restore a dedicated SQL pool by using PowerShell script as well, but you need to have Azure PowerShell installed on your machine.

Before running the PowerShell script, we need to have the following information available:

- **Subscription name**: The subscription name of your Azure subscription where the Azure Synapse workspace has been created.

- **Source resource group name**: The resource group name where your source Azure Synapse workspace is created.

- **Source server name**: The dedicated SQL endpoint of your Azure Synapse workspace where you have created your source dedicated SQL pool.

- **Source database name**: The name of your source dedicated SQL pool.

- **Target resource group name**: The resource group name where your target Azure Synapse workspace is created.

- **Target server name**: The dedicated SQL endpoint of your Azure Synapse workspace where you have created your target dedicated SQL pool.

- **Target database name**: The name of your target dedicated SQL pool.

- **Target service objective**: The service objective for your target SQL pool, for example, dw200.

You should be able to gather all these details if you go to your source and target Synapse workspace on the Azure portal. The following screenshot highlights all the key parameters that you will need to run the PowerShell script:

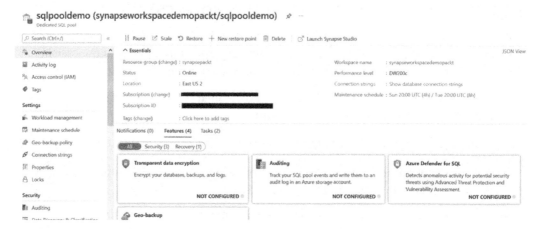

Figure 11.8 – A screenshot of the dedicated SQL pool on the Azure portal

Now that you have gathered all the required information, you can modify the values accordingly in the following PowerShell script before running it:

```
$SubscriptionName="<YourSubscriptionName>"
$ResourceGroupName="<YourResourceGroupName>"
$ServerName="<YourServerNameWithoutURLSuffixSeeNote>"
# Without database.windows.net
$TargetResourceGroupName="<YourTargetResourceGroupName>"
# Restore to a different server.
$TargetServerName="<YourtargetServerNameWithoutURL
SuffixSeeNote>"
$DatabaseName="<YourDatabaseName>"
$NewDatabaseName="<YourDatabaseName>"
$TargetServiceObjective="<YourTargetServiceObjective-DWXXXc>"

Connect-AzAccount
Get-AzSubscription
Select-AzSubscription -SubscriptionName $SubscriptionName
Get-AzureSqlDatabase -ServerName $ServerName

# Get the data warehouse you want to recover
```

```
$GeoBackup = Get-AzSqlDatabaseGeoBackup -ResourceGroupName
$ResourceGroupName -ServerName $ServerName -DatabaseName
$DatabaseName
```

```
# Recover dedicated SQL pool
$GeoRestoredDatabase = Restore-AzSqlDatabase -FromGeoBackup
-ResourceGroupName $TargetResourceGroupName -ServerName
$TargetServerName -TargetDatabaseName $NewDatabaseName -
ResourceId $GeoBackup.ResourceID -ServiceObjectiveName
$TargetServiceObjective
```

```
# Verify that the geo-restored data warehouse is online
$GeoRestoredDatabase.status
```

So, now we know various ways to restore our dedicated SQL pools in the same region or a different region. The next important topic is cross-subscription restore. Let's try to learn more about this feature in Azure Synapse in the following section.

Cross-subscription restore

As of the time of writing, **cross-subscription restore** is not supported in Azure Synapse. However, there have been various requests submitted for this particular feature, hence the Synapse team might consider this request for the next release cycle.

In the future, whenever this feature becomes available in Azure Synapse, we will capture it in the book.

With this, we have learned everything about the backup and restoration of Azure Synapse dedicated SQL pools, along with their limitations and usages.

Summary

In this chapter, we learned how data warehouse (dedicated SQL pool) screenshots create various restore points automatically to provide high-availability solutions in Azure Synapse. Apart from this, we also learned how can we create our own restore points in Azure Synapse and when we would need to create these restore points. Later, we learned how to leverage these restore points to restore our dedicated SQL pool within the same primary region or to any other region. In this chapter, we covered both of the ways to restore our SQL pool, through the Azure portal and PowerShell script as well.

In the next chapter, we are going to explore the security aspects of Azure Synapse. We will learn how Azure Synapse protects our data, and about all the layers of security that Azure Synapse provides us to protect our data.

12
Securing Data on Azure Synapse

Data is the new gold, so you have got to protect your wealth. Azure Synapse Analytics provides a relational database service for the cloud. Azure provides multiple security measures to access any data in Azure Synapse Analytics. However, it is important for the user to be aware of all these security measures and how to use them appropriately. In this chapter, we are going to learn about the different layers of security options provided by Azure Synapse Analytics. We will learn how to secure the network to protect our data, and the access management section will outline SQL authorization and Active Directory integration. We are also going to learn about some of the advanced features provided by Azure, including threat protection and information protection.

The following diagram represents the different layers of security surrounding customer data:

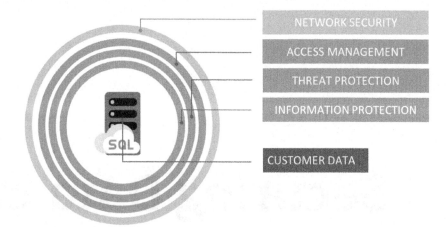

Figure 12.1 – Different layers of enterprise-grade security in Synapse

Understanding all these security layers in detail will help us learn the importance of security measures, and how we can implement them in our Synapse environment. In this chapter, we will cover the following topics:

- Implementing network security
- Understanding access control
- Enabling threat protection
- Understanding information protection

Implementing network security

Azure Synapse Analytics helps protect your data by using IP firewall rules. We can also use the **managed workspace virtual network** to isolate one workspace from another. We are going to learn about these options in the following sections.

Managed workspace virtual network

Azure Synapse provides you with the option to enable **a managed workspace virtual network** while creating your Synapse workspace. It ensures that your workspace is isolated from another workspace. If you have enabled a managed workspace virtual network in your Synapse workspace, then data integration and Spark resources are also deployed in the same virtual network; however, SQL pools (dedicated or serverless) reside outside this managed virtual network.

You can go through the following steps to enable a managed workspace virtual network on your Synapse workspace while creating it:

1. Log in to the Azure portal at `https://portal.azure.com`.

2. Click on the **+ Create a resource** tab, select **Azure Synapse Analytics** from the list of all available Azure resources, and then click on **Create**.

3. On the **Basics** tab, provide all the required information and then click on **Next** to go to the **Security** tab.

4. On the **Security** page, provide information about your admin username and password for your SQL pools and then click on **Next**.

5. Now, on the **Networking** page, we can enable a managed virtual network. Click on the checkbox for **Enable managed virtual network** in the **Managed virtual network** section:

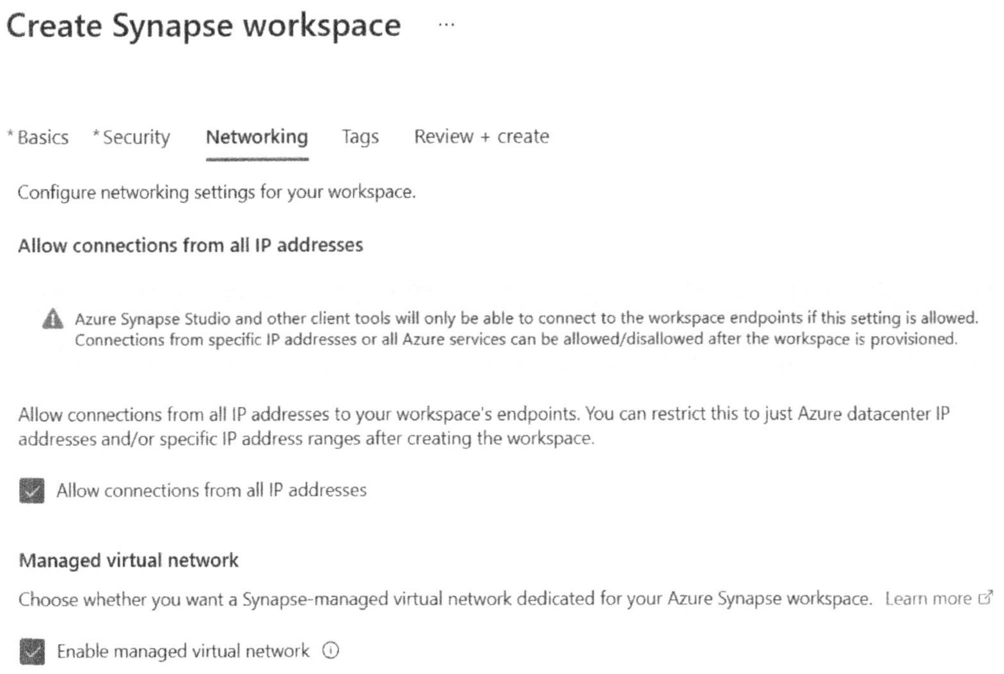

Create Synapse workspace   ⋯

*Basics   *Security   **Networking**   Tags   Review + create

Configure networking settings for your workspace.

Allow connections from all IP addresses

⚠ Azure Synapse Studio and other client tools will only be able to connect to the workspace endpoints if this setting is allowed. Connections from specific IP addresses or all Azure services can be allowed/disallowed after the workspace is provisioned.

Allow connections from all IP addresses to your workspace's endpoints. You can restrict this to just Azure datacenter IP addresses and/or specific IP address ranges after creating the workspace.

☑ Allow connections from all IP addresses

Managed virtual network

Choose whether you want a Synapse-managed virtual network dedicated for your Azure Synapse workspace. Learn more ↗

☑ Enable managed virtual network ⓘ

Figure 12.2 – Enabling a managed virtual network in an Azure Synapse workspace

6. Next, you need to decide whether you want to **Allow outbound data traffic only to approved targets**. Select **No** to allow outbound traffic from the workspace to any target; however, you can select **Yes** if you want to limit outbound traffic from a managed workspace virtual network to any limited target through **managed private endpoints**. We will learn about managed private endpoints in the following section.

7. If you selected **Yes** in the preceding step, then click on **+Add** to create a private managed endpoint in an **Azure Active Directory (AAD)** tenant that differs from the one that your subscription belongs to.

8. You can either select an **AAD tenant** from the dropdown or manually enter the AAD tenant's ID:

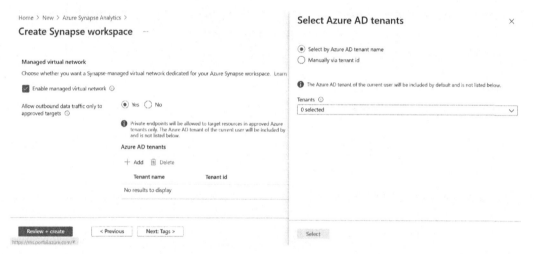

Figure 12.3 – Selecting AAD tenants to set up private endpoints for Azure Synapse

9. Next, click on **Review + create**.

10. Review all the details, and then click on **Create** to create the Azure Synapse workspace.

Now that we have enabled a managed workspace virtual network, it's time to learn about managed private endpoints.

Private endpoint for SQL on-demand

A private endpoint is used to provide secure connectivity between your storage and the clients on the virtual network using a private IP address from your virtual network. It is a network interface that enables you to connect to a service securely powered by Azure Private Link. You can go to the following link (`s://docs.microsoft.com/en-us/azure/private-link/private-endpoint-overview`) to understand Private Link in detail.

You can configure a private endpoint for Azure Synapse SQL on-demand by using **Private endpoint connections** in the workspace blade within the Azure portal:

1. Log in to the Azure portal at `https://portal.azure.com`.

2. Navigate to the Synapse workspace by typing the service name (or resource name) directly into the search bar.

3. Click on the workspace where you want to create your SQL pool.

4. Click on **Private endpoint connections** in the workspace blade:

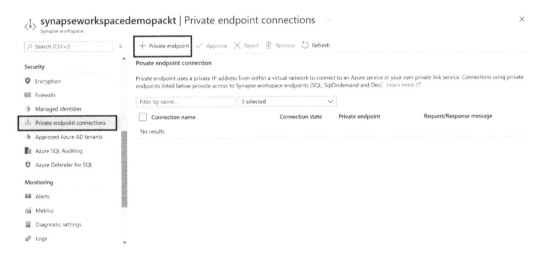

Figure 12.4 – A screenshot highlighting private endpoint connections in the workspace blade

5. Click on **+ Private endpoint** and provide appropriate information to create a new private endpoint for SQL on-demand:

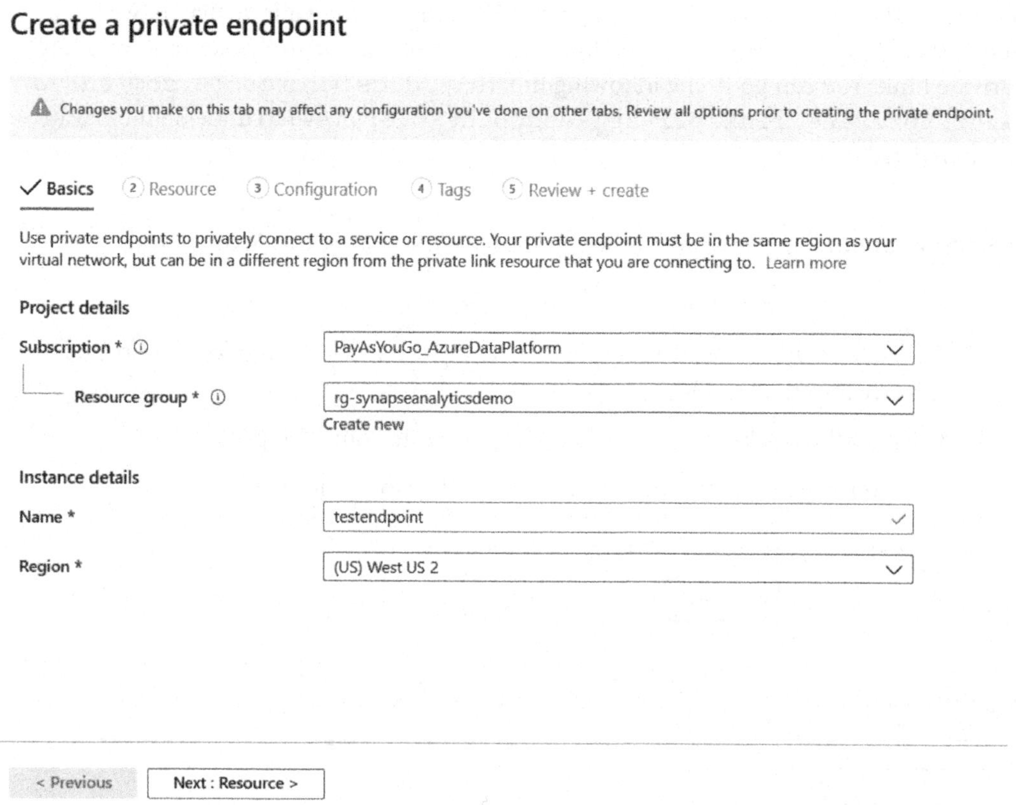

Create a private endpoint

⚠ Changes you make on this tab may affect any configuration you've done on other tabs. Review all options prior to creating the private endpoint.

✓ **Basics**   ② Resource   ③ Configuration   ④ Tags   ⑤ Review + create

Use private endpoints to privately connect to a service or resource. Your private endpoint must be in the same region as your virtual network, but can be in a different region from the private link resource that you are connecting to. Learn more

Project details

Subscription * ⓘ

| PayAsYouGo_AzureDataPlatform | ⌄ |

Resource group * ⓘ

| rg-synapseanalyticsdemo | ⌄ |
Create new

Instance details

Name *

| testendpoint | ✓ |

Region *

| (US) West US 2 | ⌄ |

< Previous | Next : Resource > |

Figure 12.5 – A screenshot of the Basics tab to create a private endpoint

6. Fill in all the details on the **Basics** page to create a private endpoint and then click on the **Next: Resource >** link.

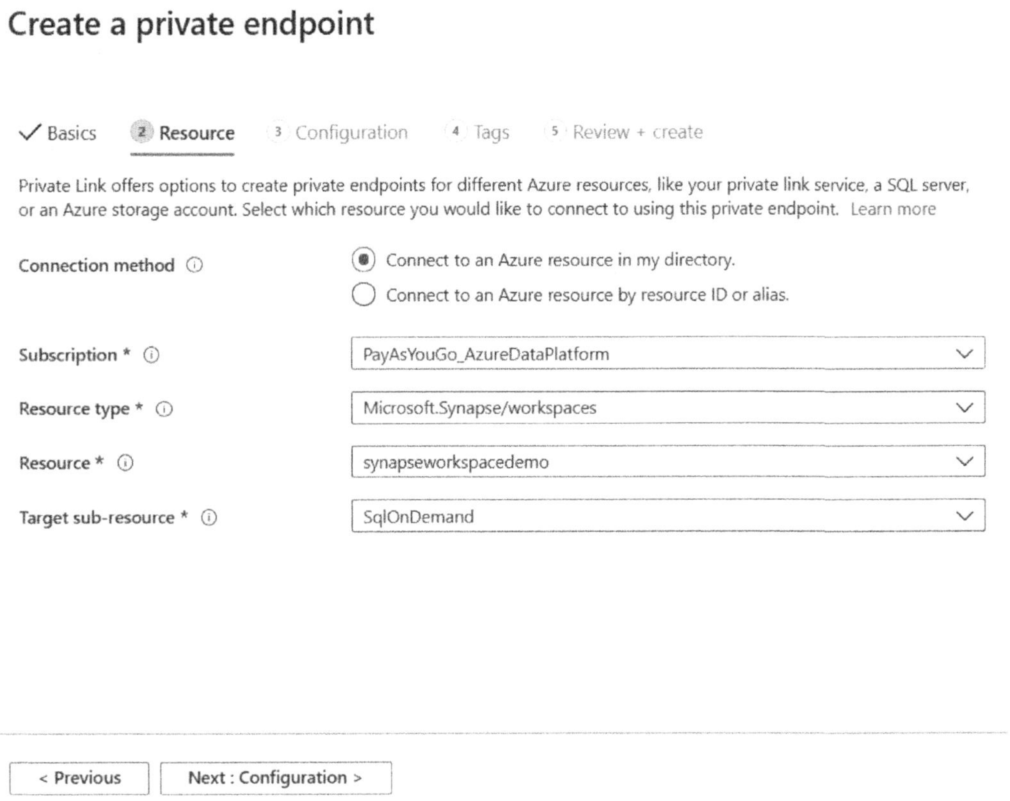

Create a private endpoint

✓ Basics   ② **Resource**   ³ Configuration   ⁴ Tags   ⁵ Review + create

Private Link offers options to create private endpoints for different Azure resources, like your private link service, a SQL server, or an Azure storage account. Select which resource you would like to connect to using this private endpoint. Learn more

Connection method ⓘ   ⦿ Connect to an Azure resource in my directory.
                              ◯ Connect to an Azure resource by resource ID or alias.

Subscription * ⓘ | PayAsYouGo_AzureDataPlatform   ⌄ |

Resource type * ⓘ | Microsoft.Synapse/workspaces   ⌄ |

Resource * ⓘ | synapseworkspacedemo   ⌄ |

Target sub-resource * ⓘ | SqlOnDemand   ⌄ |

[< Previous]   [Next : Configuration >]

Figure 12.6 – A screenshot of the Resource tab for creating a private endpoint

7. After completing all the information in the **Resources** tab, go to the **Configuration** tab and then select the **Virtual network** option from the dropdown that you want to use here:

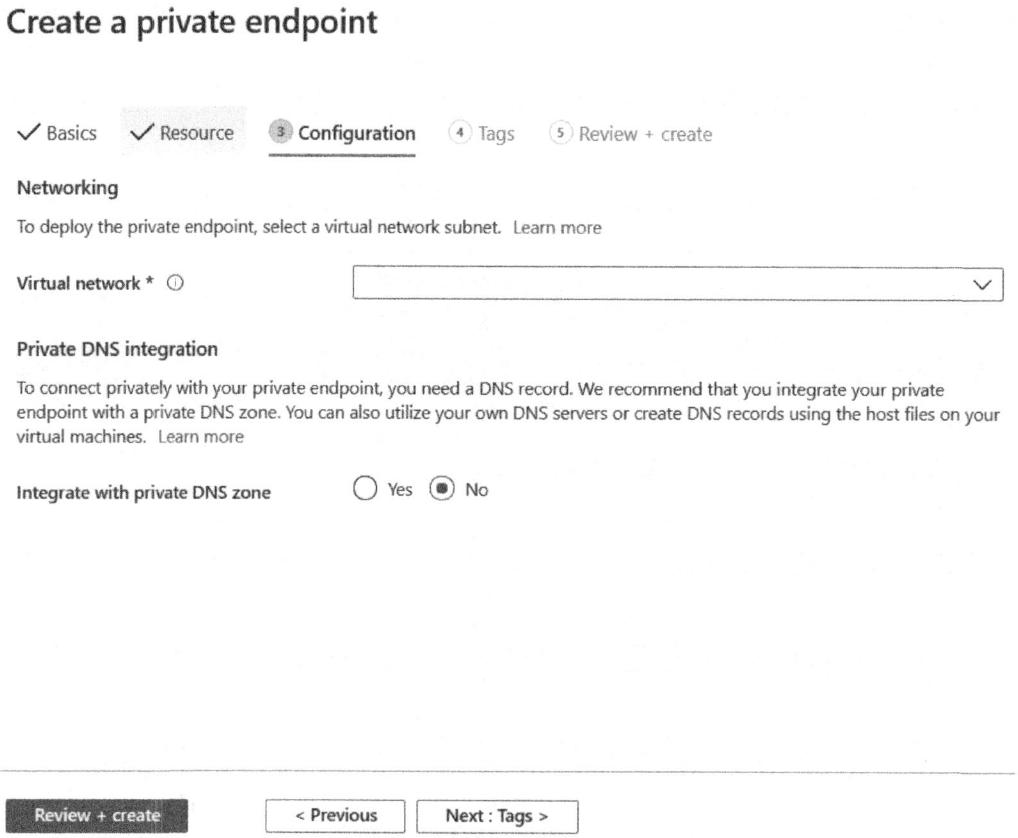

Create a private endpoint

✓ Basics   ✓ Resource   ③ **Configuration**   ④ Tags   ⑤ Review + create

Networking

To deploy the private endpoint, select a virtual network subnet. Learn more

Virtual network * ⓘ   [∨]

Private DNS integration

To connect privately with your private endpoint, you need a DNS record. We recommend that you integrate your private endpoint with a private DNS zone. You can also utilize your own DNS servers or create DNS records using the host files on your virtual machines. Learn more

Integrate with private DNS zone   ◯ Yes   ◉ No

[Review + create]   [< Previous]   [Next : Tags >]

Figure 12.7 – A screenshot of the Configuration tab to create a private endpoint

After providing the configuration details, you can create new tags and then click on **Review + create** after reviewing all the details.

After setting up a virtual network, next we need to add IP firewall rules to the Azure Synapse workspace to provide another layer of security for our data.

IP firewall rules

IP firewall rules enable you to access SQL pools from the IP addresses that are whitelisted in these IP firewall rules. If your IP address has not been added to the IP firewall rules, then you will get the following error while connecting to the SQL pool using an SSMS tool:

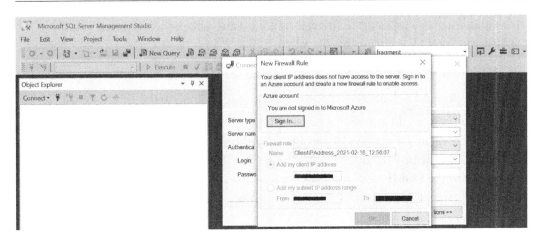

Figure 12.8 – A screenshot of the IP firewall error on the SSMS tool while connecting
to the dedicated SQL pool

If you checked the box for allowing connections from all IP addresses while creating your
Synapse workspace under the **Security** settings tab, then it will automatically set up an IP
firewall rule for your Synapse workspace that will permit access from any IP within the
range **0.0.0.0** to **255.255.255.255** and you will be able to connect to the SQL pool from
any IP address:

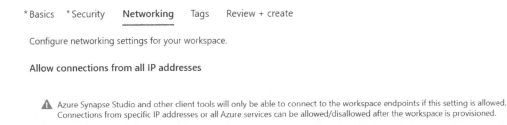

Figure 12.9 – Allowing connections from all IP connections under the Networking tab

There is another way to set up IP firewall rules for your Synapse workspace if your Synapse workspace has already been created:

1. Go to the **Firewalls** tab of your Azure Synapse workspace within the Azure portal.

2. Click on + **Add client IP** to add your current IP address to the IP firewall rules.

3. If you want to add just one IP address to the IP firewall rule, add the same IP address value in the **Start IP** and **End IP** fields. However, if you want to add a range, provide a starting IP address value in the **Start IP** field and an ending IP address value in the **End IP** field and click on **Save** to save your changes.

> **Important note**
> Make sure you have deleted the **allowAll** rule, which allows all IP addresses, starting from **0.0.0.0** to **255.255.255.255**, if you want to provide access to only limited IP addresses that can be connected to your Synapse workspace.

The following screenshot displays the firewall rules associated with your Synapse workspace:

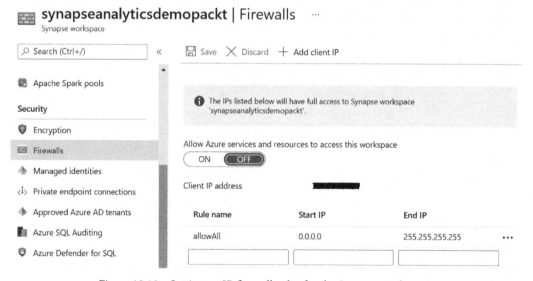

Figure 12.10 – Setting up IP firewall rules for the Synapse workspace

Now that we have provided an IP firewall restriction to our Synapse workspace, we will try to learn how we can control access to the Synapse workspace through authorization and authentication in the following section.

Understanding access control

The Azure Synapse workspace provides you with the option to create a SQL admin for your SQL pools and, along with that, you get to provide permissions using AAD. In this section, we are going to learn how to access Synapse SQL pools using SQL authentication and Azure Active Directory. We will also learn how to implement RBAC in Azure Synapse SQL pools toward the end of this section.

You can find the reference to this diagram at the following link: `https://docs.microsoft.com/en-us/azure/synapse-analytics/sql/active-directory-authentication#administrator-structure`.

Now we are going to learn about the SQL authorization and AAD authorization techniques in detail in the following sections.

SQL authorization

Synapse SQL needs to have an administrative account that will have full access to the Synapse SQL pool. However, you can also create a non-administrative account that can provide access to SQL pools with limited access.

While creating the Synapse workspace, you need to provide a username and password for your SQL pool. SQL Server creates this account as a **login** in the **master** database. You can have only one of these accounts in your Synapse workspace.

Administrative accounts can add or remove members to the `dbmanager` and `loginmanager` roles. This account has access to create, alter, or drop databases, logins, users, and server-level IP firewall rules.

In the following screenshot, we can see how to create SQL administrator credentials while creating a Synapse SQL pool:

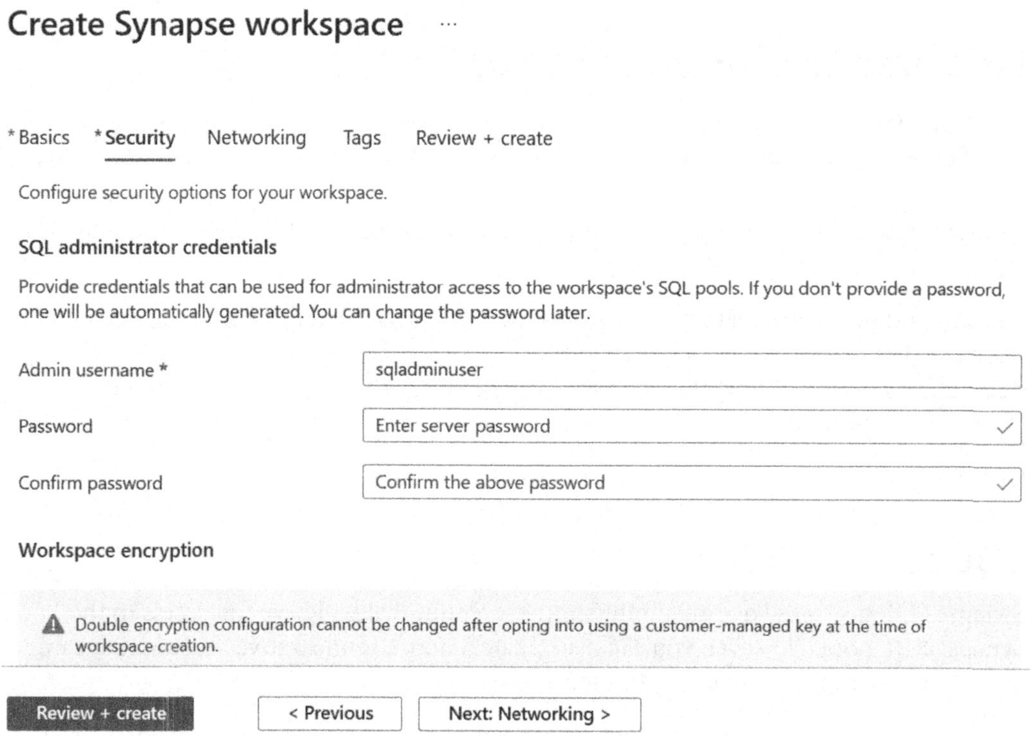

Create Synapse workspace   ...

* Basics   * **Security**   Networking   Tags   Review + create

Configure security options for your workspace.

SQL administrator credentials

Provide credentials that can be used for administrator access to the workspace's SQL pools. If you don't provide a password, one will be automatically generated. You can change the password later.

Admin username *	sqladminuser
Password	Enter server password
Confirm password	Confirm the above password

Workspace encryption

⚠ Double encryption configuration cannot be changed after opting into using a customer-managed key at the time of workspace creation.

| Review + create | | < Previous | Next: Networking > |

Figure 12.11 – Providing SQL administrator credentials for Azure Synapse Analytics

By using an administrative account, we can create a SQL Server login in the master database and then we can create a user based on this SQL Server login. Let's perform the following steps to create a new SQL Server login and a new user:

1. Open SSMS or Azure Data Studio on your machine.

2. Using the administrator account, connect to the master database.

3. Run the following script in a new query window to create a SQL Server authentication login:

```
CREATE LOGIN PacktLogin WITH PASSWORD = '<password>';
```

4. Now, run the following script on the SSMS tool against the master database to create a SQL Server authentication-contained database user:

```
CREATE USER PacktUser WITH PASSWORD = '<password>';
```

5. You can run the following SQL script to create a SQL Server user based on the SQL Server authentication login:

```
CREATE USER PacktUser FROM LOGIN PacktLogin;
```

6. We need to add the user to the dbmanager database role so that this user can create databases. Run the following script after creating a SQL Server user as mentioned in the preceding step:

```
EXEC sp_addrolemember 'dbmanager', 'PacktMember';
```

You can connect to your dedicated SQL pool by using Azure Active Directory authentication as well, and we will learn about this in the section that follows.

Azure Active Directory authorization

Azure Synapse provides you with an alternative option to use identities in Azure Active Directory for authentication. The Azure Active Directory user or group can be an Azure Active Directory administrator login, and the group administrator account can be used by any group member.

Synapse SQL pools can be connected from **SSMS** by using **Active Directory Universal Authentication**. Active Directory Universal Authentication supports two non-interactive and one interactive authentication methods as listed here:

- **Active Directory - Password**
- **Active Directory - Integrated**
- **Active Directory - Universal with MFA**

The following screenshot displays all the authentication methods available on SSMS to connect to Synapse SQL pools:

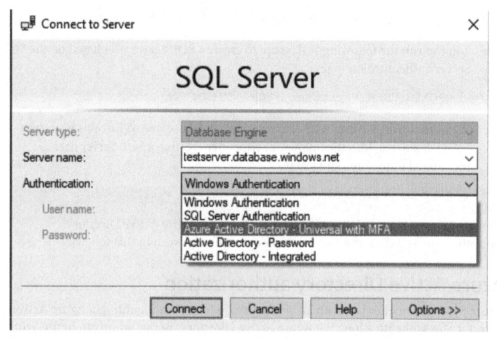

Figure 12.12 – Selecting the authentication type to connect to a Synapse dedicated
SQL pool on the SSMS tool

All users invited from other AADs are called guest users. All these users must enter their Azure Active Directory domain name or tenant ID if they need to be authenticated by using universal authentication; for example, `prashant@packt.onmicrosoft.com`.

After learning about various authentication mechanisms in SQL pools, we will now learn how to authorize a user to view the records in the following section.

Implementing RBAC in a Synapse SQL pool

RBAC stands for **role-based access control**, and only the Synapse administrator can assign the Synapse RBAC role to any user. Synapse RBAC can be used to manage the following permissions:

- For publishing and viewing code artifacts
- To execute code on Synapse Spark pools

- To access linked services
- To access the integration runtime for monitoring job execution and execution logs

Synapse RBAC can be managed by using **Access control** tools in the **Manage** hub of Synapse Studio:

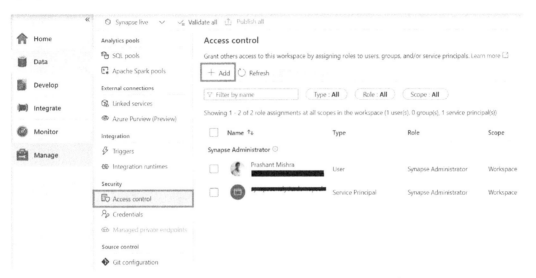

Figure 12.13 – Managing access control in Synapse Studio

We need to perform the following steps to create a new role assignment:

1. Go to the **Access control** tools in the **Manage** hub of Synapse Studio.

2. Click on **+ Add**, as highlighted in the preceding screenshot, to create a new role assignment.

3. Select a **Scope** option to add a role assignment. We can select **Workspace** or **Workspace item** as the scope. There are four workspace item types available to choose from, namely, **Apache Spark pool**, **Integration runtime**, **Linked service**, and **Credential**:

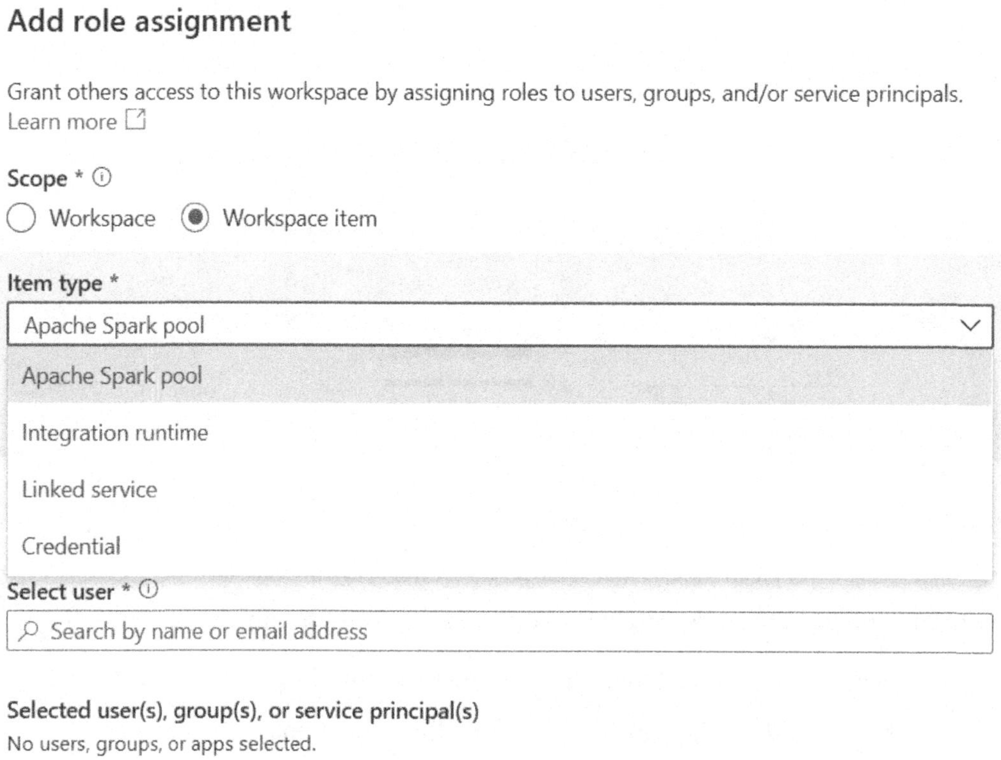

Add role assignment

Grant others access to this workspace by assigning roles to users, groups, and/or service principals. Learn more ☐

Scope * ⓘ

◯ Workspace   ⦿ Workspace item

Item type *

Apache Spark pool	⌄

Apache Spark pool
Integration runtime
Linked service
Credential

Select user * ⓘ

🔍 Search by name or email address

Selected user(s), group(s), or service principal(s)

No users, groups, or apps selected.

Figure 12.14 – Different workspace item types to define the scope for new role assignments

4. If you selected **Workspace item** as the scope, you need to select the workspace item for the type selected.

5. Next, we need to select a **Role** option from the list of all available roles for a particular scope:

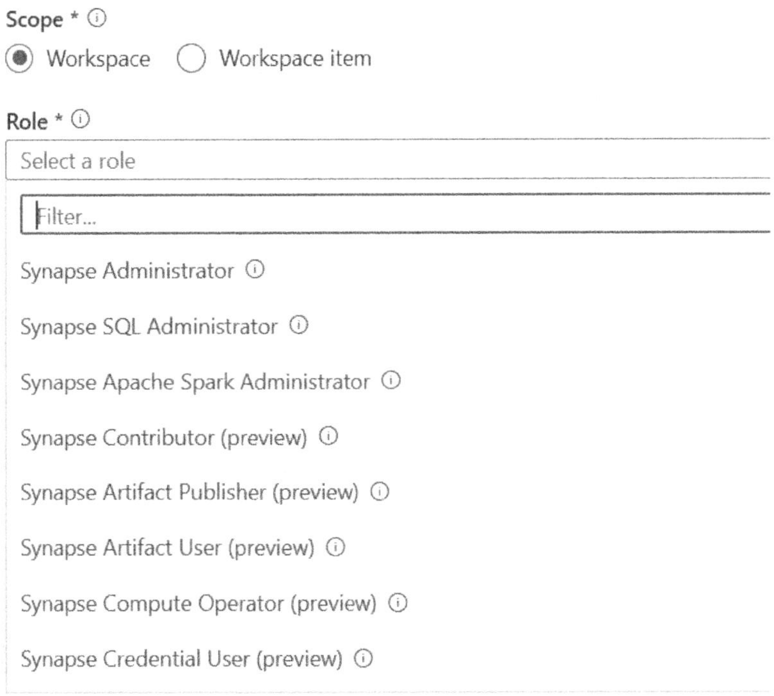

Scope * ⓘ

◉ Workspace   ○ Workspace item

Role * ⓘ

Select a role

Filter...

Synapse Administrator ⓘ

Synapse SQL Administrator ⓘ

Synapse Apache Spark Administrator ⓘ

Synapse Contributor (preview) ⓘ

Synapse Artifact Publisher (preview) ⓘ

Synapse Artifact User (preview) ⓘ

Synapse Compute Operator (preview) ⓘ

Synapse Credential User (preview) ⓘ

Figure 12.15 – Selecting a role to create a new role assignment in Synapse Studio

6. And finally, we need to provide a value for the **Select User** field. This could be either users, groups, or service principals.

7. After providing all the details, click on **Apply** and your new role assignment is created.

> **Important note**
> You can learn more about roles, actions, and the scope of Synapse RBAC at the following link: https://docs.microsoft.com/en-us/azure/synapse-analytics/security/synapse-workspace-synapse-rbac-roles.

Even after securing your data on a SQL pool, it's important to keep eye on our data to protect it from any sort of threat. Next, we are going to learn about some of the threat protection measures in the following section.

Enabling threat protection

It is important to protect our data from any anomalous activities that could be potentially harmful attempts to exploit our databases. Synapse provides you with two ways to protect your data against any threat. The first one is **SQL auditing**, which captures the activities related to all the changes to security, access to tables, and many more activities besides, to protect your data. The second is **Azure Defender**, which checks the vulnerability of your SQL pools and provides advanced data security for your data.

Let's learn a little more about Azure SQL auditing in the next subsection.

Azure SQL auditing

Azure SQL auditing captures all the events in a Synapse SQL pool and writes them to an audit log in your Azure Storage account. These audit logs can be used to analyze anomalous activities or unexpected behavior in the SQL pool.

This feature will be disabled by default, but you can enable it on the **Azure SQL Auditing** tab of your Azure Synapse workspace:

Figure 12.16 – Enabling Azure SQL auditing for your Synapse workspace

You can store these audit log files in the storage account for as many days as you provide a value for with **Retention (Days)** while selecting a storage account for the audit logs:

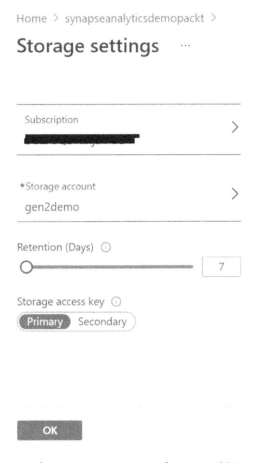

Figure 12.17 – Selecting a storage account for storing SQL audit log files

Once this feature is enabled, you can track events in the storage account that you selected while enabling this feature. Make sure that nobody can delete these log files manually, otherwise you may lose important data.

> **Important note**
> A storage account that has **hierarchical namespace** enabled is not supported for Azure SQL auditing in Synapse.

Along with the SQL auditing feature, Azure enables you to protect your data using Azure Defender. We will learn about this feature in the following section.

Azure Defender for SQL

Azure Defender for SQL is a unified package for the vulnerability assessment of SQL pools and advanced SQL security capabilities. Azure Defender for SQL provides protection just for dedicated SQL pools in Azure Synapse, and there is an additional charge, apart from the storage and compute cost, for leveraging this feature.

In this section, we will be learning about Azure Defender for SQL and how we can use it for our Synapse SQL pools. Then, we will dive into transparent data encryption.

You can go to the **Azure Defender for SQL** tab in your Synapse workspace to enable this feature for your dedicated SQL pools:

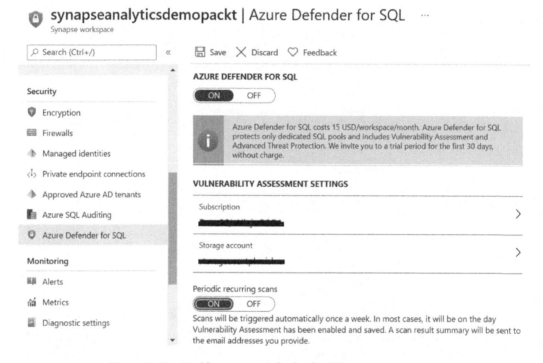

Figure 12.18 – Enabling Azure Defender for SQL in Azure Synapse

When we enable this feature for Synapse dedicated SQL pools, we need to provide settings for vulnerability assessment and advanced threat protection.

So, let's try to learn a little bit more about vulnerability assessment in the following section.

Vulnerability assessment

Vulnerability assessment is a service provided by Azure that provides insight into the security of dedicated SQL pools and recommends to you actionable steps to resolve security issues, if any.

We need to provide subscription and storage account details so that these assessment results can be stored. Azure Synapse also provides us with the option for periodic recurring scans; these scans are triggered automatically once a week. These scan summary results are sent to the email addresses that you provide while enabling this feature in your Azure Synapse workspace.

The following screenshot shows how to use **Azure Defender for SQL** for your Synapse SQL pools:

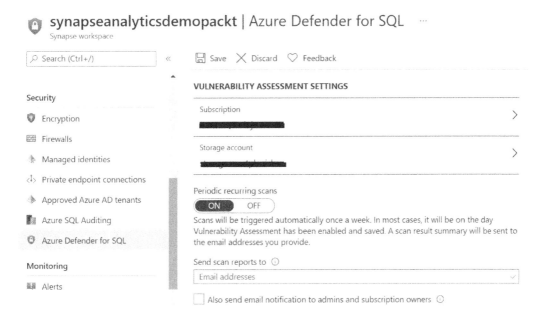

Figure 12.19 – Providing setting information for a vulnerability assessment of an Azure Synapse dedicated SQL pool

These scan reports can also be sent to the admins and subscription owners by clicking on the checkbox right below the **Email addresses** field.

Similar to the vulnerability assessment feature, now we will learn about the Advanced Threat Protection feature in Azure Synapse dedicated SQL pools.

Advanced Threat Protection

The Advanced Threat Protection feature for Azure Synapse dedicated SQL pools detects unusual activities that could be potentially harmful attempts to access or exploit databases. You need to provide the email addresses of the users who should be receiving the alerts in case of any unusual activity in the SQL pool. You can click on the checkbox right below the **Email addresses** field if you want to send the alert to admins and subscription owners:

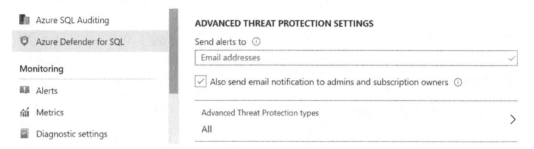

Figure 12.20 – Providing settings for Advanced Threat Protection in your Azure Synapse workspace

There are six different **Advanced Threat Protection** types. As shown in the following screenshot, you can select any or all of these types while enabling this feature for your Azure Synapse dedicated SQL pool:

Advanced Threat Protection types

Learn more - Advanced Threat Protection alerts ☐

☑ All

☑ SQL injection ⓘ

☑ SQL injection vulnerability ⓘ

☑ Data exfiltration ⓘ

☑ Unsafe action ⓘ

☑ Brute Force ⓘ

☑ Anomalous client login ⓘ

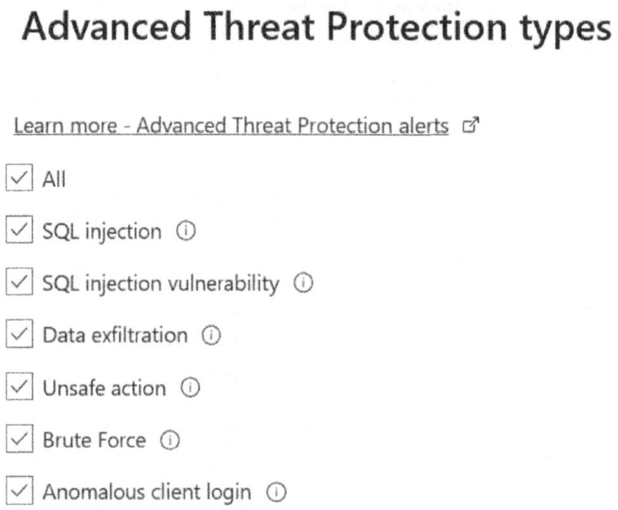

Figure 12.21 – Different types of Advanced Threat Protection in an Azure Synapse dedicated SQL pool

So far, we have learned about the various security layers of the Azure Synapse SQL pool, and last, but by no means least, we are going to learn about the information protection layer in the following section.

Understanding information protection

Sometimes, just storing data securely is not sufficient. We need to protect data even when it is in motion and in use. Azure provides different security features to protect your data at any given time so that you can meet all the data-related compliances. These are as follows:

- **Encryption-in-flight (Transport Layer Security – TLS)**: The Synapse SQL pool secures your data by encrypting data in motion with TLS.

- **Encryption-at-rest (Transparent Data Encryption – TDE)**: TDE encrypts your databases, backups, and logs at rest. This setting is specific to one particular SQL pool. If you create another SQL pool in your Synapse workspace, then you need to enable this setting separately for that pool.

   The following screenshot shows how to enable data encryption for your Synapse SQL pools:

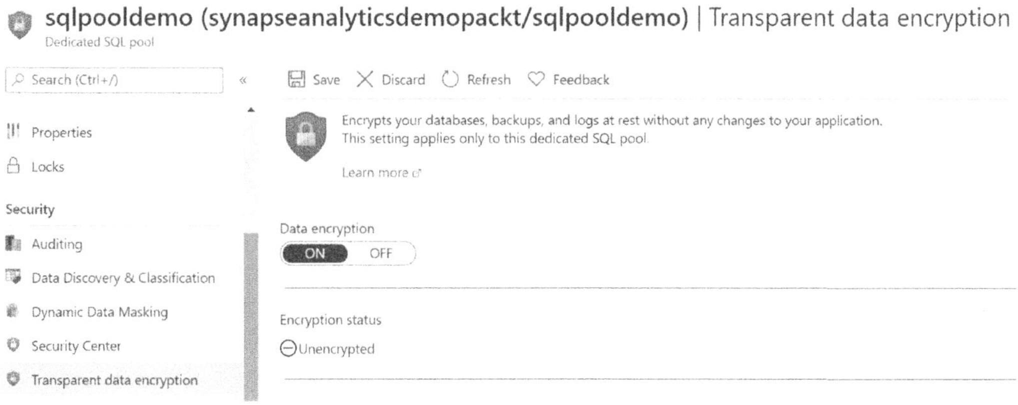

Figure 12.22 – Enabling TDE for the dedicated SQL pool in Azure Synapse

- **Encryption-in-use (always encrypted)**: The always encrypted feature is designed to protect sensitive data; it only makes the data available to client-side applications, and the data will not be visible to administrators either.

In this section, we learned how to keep our data secure when data is at rest, in motion, or in use. Aside from this, you need to make sure that your data is secured while accessing from your application side as well.

Summary

In this chapter, we learned about different ways of securing our data in an Azure Synapse SQL pool. We got to learn how to implement network security, access management, threat protection, and information protection. We learned how to use SQL authorization and AAD authorization for connecting to the dedicated SQL pool.

We also learned how to send alerts to any specific user in case of any malicious activity in the SQL pool. Although we now know all the various layers of security in a SQL pool, we need to be careful to implement these forms of security properly in order to secure our data from all possible threats.

In the next chapter, we will learn how to manage and monitor various resources of your Azure Synapse workspace using Synapse Studio.

13
Managing and Monitoring Synapse Workloads

Microsoft Azure **Platform as a Service (PaaS)** enables users to manage their resources on the cloud efficiently and with minimal effort. Azure Synapse Analytics provides you with a centralized experience to manage and monitor all the resources and workloads in your Synapse workspace.

In this chapter, we are going to learn how to manage pools, connections, pipelines, security, and source control, all in a single unified space – Synapse Studio. We will also learn how we can monitor different activities happening across the Synapse workspace.

The following topics will be covered in this chapter in order to understand how we can manage and monitor Synapse workloads:

- Managing Synapse resources
- Monitoring Synapse workloads
- Managing maintenance schedules
- Creating alerts for Azure Synapse Analytics

Technical requirements

Before you start orchestrating your data, here are certain prerequisites that you should meet:

- You should have your Azure subscription, or access to any other subscription, with contributor-level access.

- Create your Synapse workspace on this subscription. You can follow the instructions from *Chapter 1, Introduction to Azure Synapse*, to create your Synapse workspace.

- Create your SQL pool on Azure Synapse. This has been covered in *Chapter 2, Consideration for Your Compute Environment*.

- Create the logic app in the Azure portal, which is required to create the alert rule. Please refer to the following link (`https://docs.microsoft.com/en-us/azure/logic-apps/logic-apps-overview`) to explore Logic Apps if you have never used it before.

- You must have an Azure DevOps account created in order to configure source control for Azure Synapse Analytics.

Managing Synapse resources

The **Manage** hub within Azure Synapse Studio allows you to manage your workspace within a unified experience. It gives you the option to create a new pool, pause an existing provisioned pool, or delete your provisioned pools. You can also manage linked services, triggers, and integration runtimes here.

You can also set up Synapse RBAC within the **Manage** hub on Synapse Studio and you can manage Git configuration for your code artifacts as well. We are going to learn about all these topics in the following sections.

Although we have already covered how to create a SQL or Spark pool in our previous chapters, in the following section, we will try to learn how we can create these pools using Synapse Studio.

Analytics pools

Azure Synapse supports two types of analytics pool, namely, SQL and Spark pools. These pools are basically two different compute environments that can be used independently as per business requirements. We will learn how to manage both types of pools in this section.

SQL pool

If you have not created a SQL pool yet, you can only see a built-in serverless SQL pool available under the **SQL pools** tab of the **Manage** hub.

You can create multiple SQL pools within the same Synapse workspace, and you can view, pause, or delete all these pools in the **Manage** hub itself.

The following is a screenshot of the **Manage** hub in Synapse Studio:

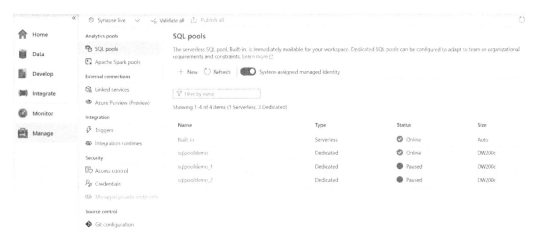

Figure 13.1 – A screenshot of SQL pools under the Manage hub of Synapse Studio

You cannot have more than one serverless SQL pool, so you do not get any option for doing so. However, you can click on the **+New** link to create a new dedicated SQL pool, as seen in *Figure 13.1*:

Figure 13.2 – Creating a new SQL pool using Synapse Studio

You may not need to run these SQL pools all the time, hence you may want to pause them when not in use in order to save on the total cost of ownership. If you click on the three dots (**…**) next to your SQL pool, you get options to **Pause**, **Scale**, **Assign tags**, and **Delete** the SQL pool, which we can see in the following screenshot:

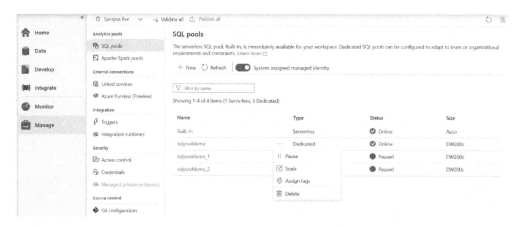

Figure 13.3 – Options to pause, scale, assign tags, or delete the SQL pool

Let's go through all these options one by one:

- **Pause**: You can pause your SQL pool by selecting this option, but if your SQL pool is already in a paused state, you will not see this option appearing on this list. However, you will see the option to resume your SQL pool.

- **Scale**: Any time you need more or less computation power in your SQL pool, you can click on the **Scale** option to change the performance level of your SQL pool:

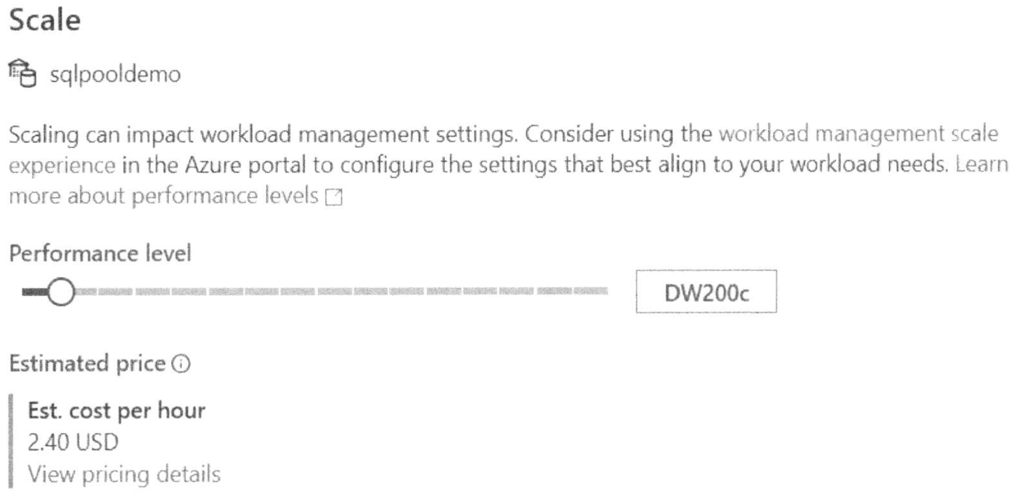

Scale

 sqlpooldemo

Scaling can impact workload management settings. Consider using the workload management scale experience in the Azure portal to configure the settings that best align to your workload needs. Learn more about performance levels ☐

Performance level

DW200c

Estimated price ⓘ

Est. cost per hour
2.40 USD
View pricing details

Figure 13.4 – Changing the performance level of a SQL pool to modify its computational power

- **Assign tags**: You can assign tags to your SQL pools in order to group some of the pools together for billing purposes.

- **Delete**: The last option is to delete your SQL pool. When you no longer need your SQL pool, you can click on this option to delete your SQL pool permanently.

Now that we have already learned how we can manage SQL pools in Synapse Studio, let's learn about managing Spark pools in Synapse Studio.

Spark pool

Similar to a SQL pool, you can also manage all your Spark pools within the **Manage** hub of Synapse Studio. Click on the **+New** link to create a new Spark pool, and if you already have a Spark pool, you can click on the three dots (**…**) next to your Spark pool to view all the available options to manage your pool.

In this following screenshot, you can see all the Spark pools in the **Manage** hub of Synapse Studio:

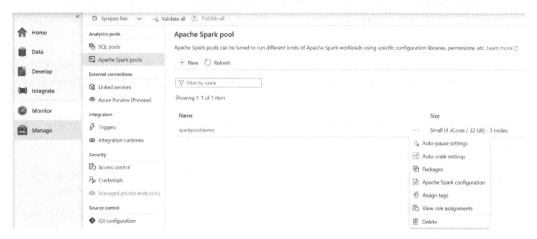

Figure 13.5 – A screenshot of Apache Spark pools in Synapse Studio

This allows performance of the following operations on your Spark pool:

- **Auto-pause settings**: While creating an Apache Spark pool in Synapse, you get the option to enable auto-pause settings. You can see all of your Spark pools in the **Apache Spark pools** tab under the **Manage** hub of **Synapse Studio**. Click on the three dots (**…**) next to the Spark pool and select **Auto-pause** settings to modify the auto-pause settings of your Spark pool:

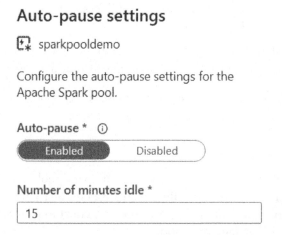

Figure 13.6 – Modifying the auto-pause settings of a Spark pool

- **Auto-scale settings**: Similar to auto-pause settings, we can modify **Auto-scale settings** for the Spark pool as well. Click on the three dots (…) next to your Spark pool and select **Auto-scale settings** from the list of available options to modify the settings:

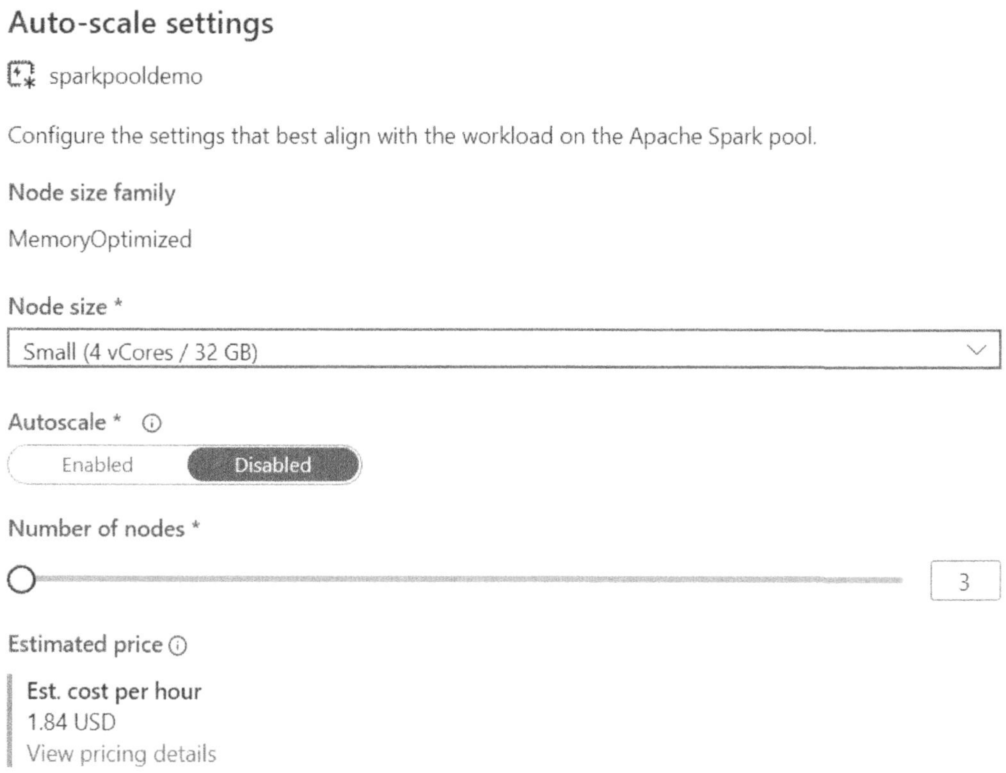

Auto-scale settings

sparkpooldemo

Configure the settings that best align with the workload on the Apache Spark pool.

Node size family

MemoryOptimized

Node size *

| Small (4 vCores / 32 GB) | ⌄ |

Autoscale * ⓘ

| Enabled | **Disabled** |

Number of nodes *

○——————————————————————————————— | 3 |

Estimated price ⓘ

Est. cost per hour
1.84 USD
View pricing details

Figure 13.7 – Modifying the auto-scale settings of an Apache Spark pool in Synapse Studio

- **Packages**: You can customize your Apache Spark pools with additional libraries by uploading library requirement files:

Manage packages

⌞⌝ sparkpooldemo

Apache Spark pools can be customized with additional libraries by providing a library requirements file. Learn more ⌐

↑ Upload   ⟳ Refresh

NAME	SIZE	DATE

No requirement files have been specified.

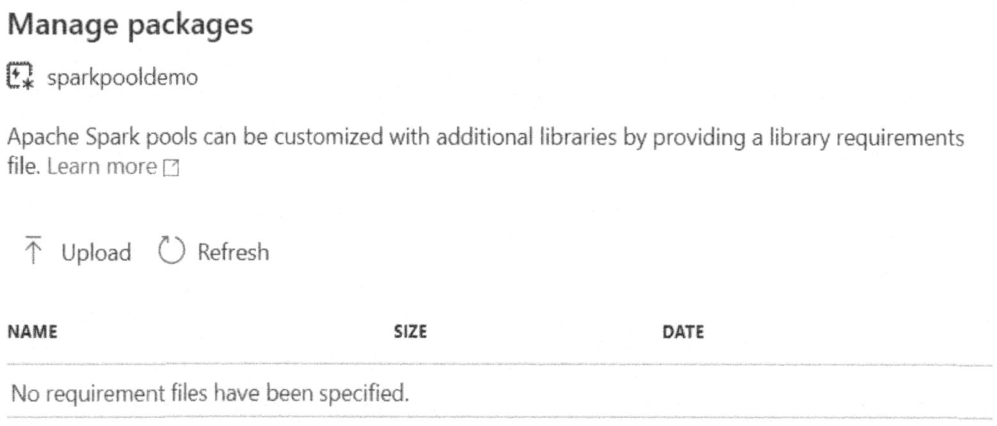

Figure 13.8 – Uploading environment configuration files to the Apache Spark pool

You can find more detailed information on managing libraries in a Synapse Spark pool in the following article: `https://docs.microsoft.com/en-us/azure/synapse-analytics/spark/apache-spark-azure-portal-add-libraries`.

- **Apache Spark configuration**: Similar to the preceding option, you can upload library requirement files using this option as well.

- **Assign tags**: You can use this option to add tags to your Apache Spark pool to categorize it with other resources if you wish to view the consolidated billing of all the resources with this tag:

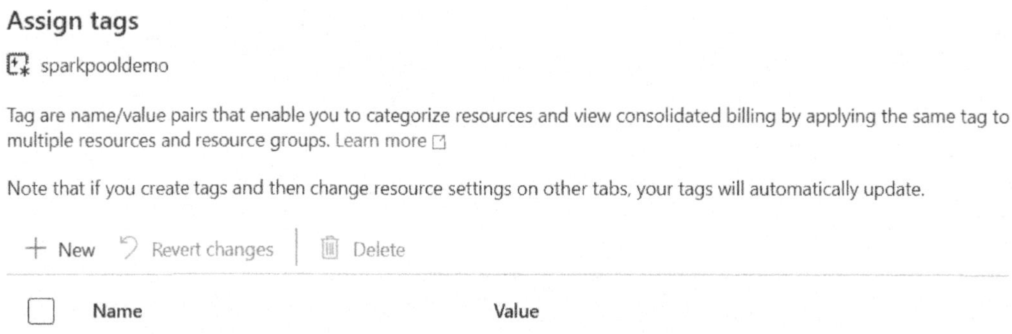

Assign tags

⌞⌝ sparkpooldemo

Tag are name/value pairs that enable you to categorize resources and view consolidated billing by applying the same tag to multiple resources and resource groups. Learn more ⌐

Note that if you create tags and then change resource settings on other tabs, your tags will automatically update.

+ New   ⟲ Revert changes | 🗑 Delete

☐   Name   Value

Figure 13.9 – Assigning tags to the Apache Spark pool in Synapse Studio

- **View role assignment**: You can view all the role assignments specific to your Synapse workspace, but you will not be able to add any new role assignments here. You must navigate to the **Access control** tab under the **Manage** hub in order to add a new role assignment:

View role assignment

⬚ sparkpooldemo

    ℹ To manage these pools, users need sufficient Azure RBAC permissions on this workspace, such as the Owner or Contributor role. Learn more ⤴

Synapse role assignments on this Apache Spark pool allow users to submit jobs. All Workspace users can view this pool. Learn more ⤴

| ▽ Filter by name | Type : **All** | Role : **All** |

Showing 1 - 2 of 2 role assignments (1 user(s), 0 group(s), 1 service principal(s))

Name ↑↓	Type	Scope
Synapse Administrator ⓘ		
Prashant Mishra Prashant.Mishra	User	Workspace (Inherited)
synapseanalytics	Service Principal	Workspace (Inherited)

Figure 13.10 – Viewing role assignments for the workspace in Synapse Studio

- **Delete**: Click on this option if you want to delete your Apache Spark pool permanently.

Next, we will see how we can manage external connections in Synapse Studio.

External connections

Synapse Studio enables you to define the connection information needed for Azure Synapse Analytics to connect to external resources. You can either create linked services or connect to your Azure Purview account within the **Manage** hub of Synapse Studio. This section outlines how to manage linked services within Synapse Studio. We will also learn about integrating Azure Purview with Azure Synapse Analytics.

Linked services

Linked services are created to register external data repositories within Azure Synapse Analytics. You can create linked services for Azure Machine Learning, a Power BI workspace, a storage account, and so on.

Click on the +**New** link on the **Linked services** tab and follow the instructions to create a new linked service. These linked services can be leveraged further in order to do the following:

- Create Synapse pipelines
- Create a new Power BI report
- Create or use machine learning models

You can see all the linked services listed in Synapse Studio as shown in the following screenshot:

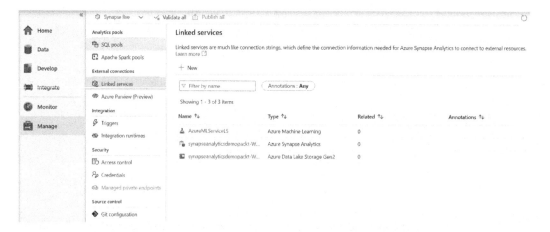

Figure 13.11 – A screenshot of linked services displaying under the Manage hub of Synapse Studio

Other than linked services, you can also use Azure Purview to establish an external connection. In the following section, we will learn how we can connect an Azure Synapse workspace to the Azure Purview account.

Azure Purview (preview)

You can connect your Azure Synapse workspace to your Azure Purview account. The Azure Purview service is a unified data governance service that can be used for the following purposes:

- To register your data to expand your governance and cataloging scope
- For relevant data discovery through a global search bar based on keywords and advanced filtering

> **Important note**
>
> We can connect Azure Purview data to our Synapse workspace to analyze the data. The following link will help you to understand this topic in detail: https://docs.microsoft.com/en-us/azure/purview/overview.

The following screenshot shows Azure Purview within Synapse Studio:

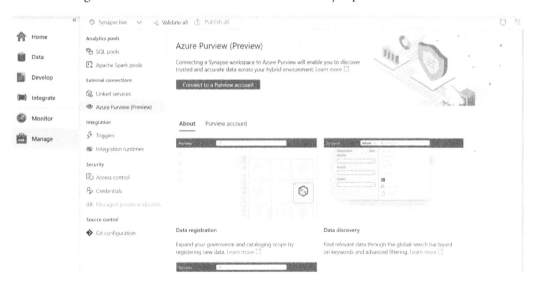

Figure 13.12 – A screenshot of Azure Purview in Synapse Studio

In the following section, we are going to learn how to manage triggers and integration runtimes that are used within Synapse pipelines for data integration.

Integration

Synapse pipelines are an integral part of the Azure Synapse workspace. We covered Synapse pipelines in detail in *Chapter 4, Using Synapse Pipelines to Orchestrate Your Data*. Synapse Studio provides you with a centralized experience to manage triggers and integration runtimes in the same place. In this section, we will learn about the different types of integration runtimes supported by Synapse pipelines. We will also learn how we can manage triggers within Synapse Studio.

Integration runtimes

Pipelines use integration runtimes as the compute infrastructure to provide data integration capabilities across different network environments. You can select Azure as your network environment for running pipeline activities in a fully managed, serverless compute in Azure. However, you can select **Self-Hosted** for running activities in an on-premises or private network, as seen in the following screenshot:

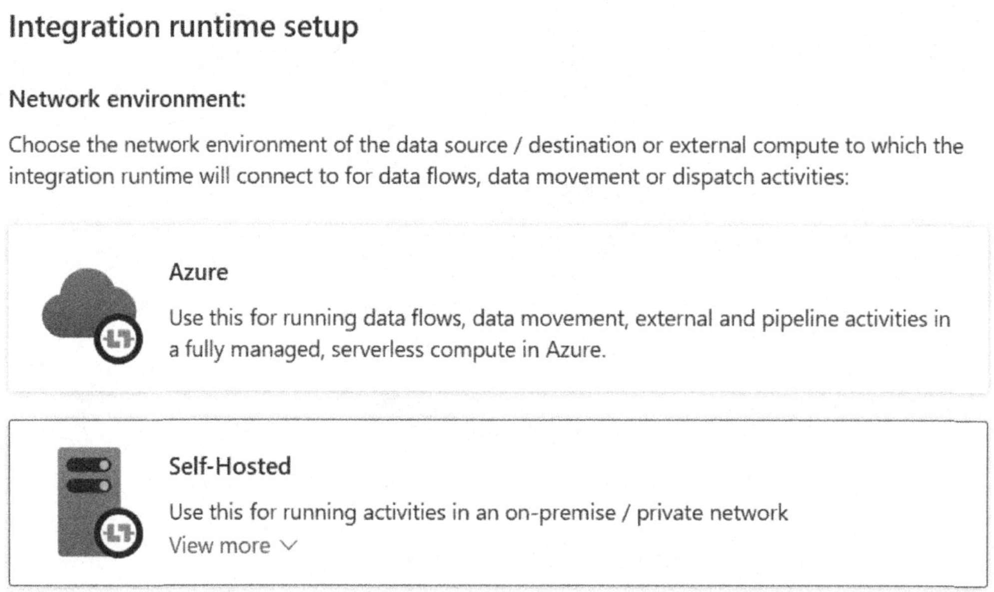

Integration runtime setup

Network environment:

Choose the network environment of the data source / destination or external compute to which the integration runtime will connect to for data flows, data movement or dispatch activities:

Azure

Use this for running data flows, data movement, external and pipeline activities in a fully managed, serverless compute in Azure.

Self-Hosted

Use this for running activities in an on-premise / private network
View more ∨

Figure 13.13 – A screenshot of the integration runtime in Synapse Studio

You need to follow all the instructions to create an integration runtime. You can go through the *Creating linked services* section of *Chapter 4, Using Synapse Pipelines to Orchestrate Your Data*, to create your linked services. You will be able to view all the integration runtimes in the **Manage** hub of Synapse Studio. You can also view role assignments associated with your integration runtimes:

Figure 13.14 – A screenshot of the integration runtimes in Synapse Studio

Now let's have a look at how to manage Synapse pipeline triggers in the **Manage** hub of Synapse Studio.

Triggers

You can execute a Synapse pipeline either manually (on-demand) or by using a trigger. Synapse supports a schedule trigger, a tumbling window trigger, and an event-based trigger. You can create all these types of triggers within the **Manage** hub of Synapse Studio. We have covered all these trigger types in detail in *Chapter 4, Using Synapse Pipelines to Orchestrate Your Data*.

A **Schedule** or **Event** trigger can be used by multiple pipelines, but a **Tumbling window** trigger can only be used with one pipeline. Click on the **+New** link in the **Triggers** tab of the **Manage** hub, and provide all the required details in the corresponding field to create a new trigger, as shown in the following screenshot:

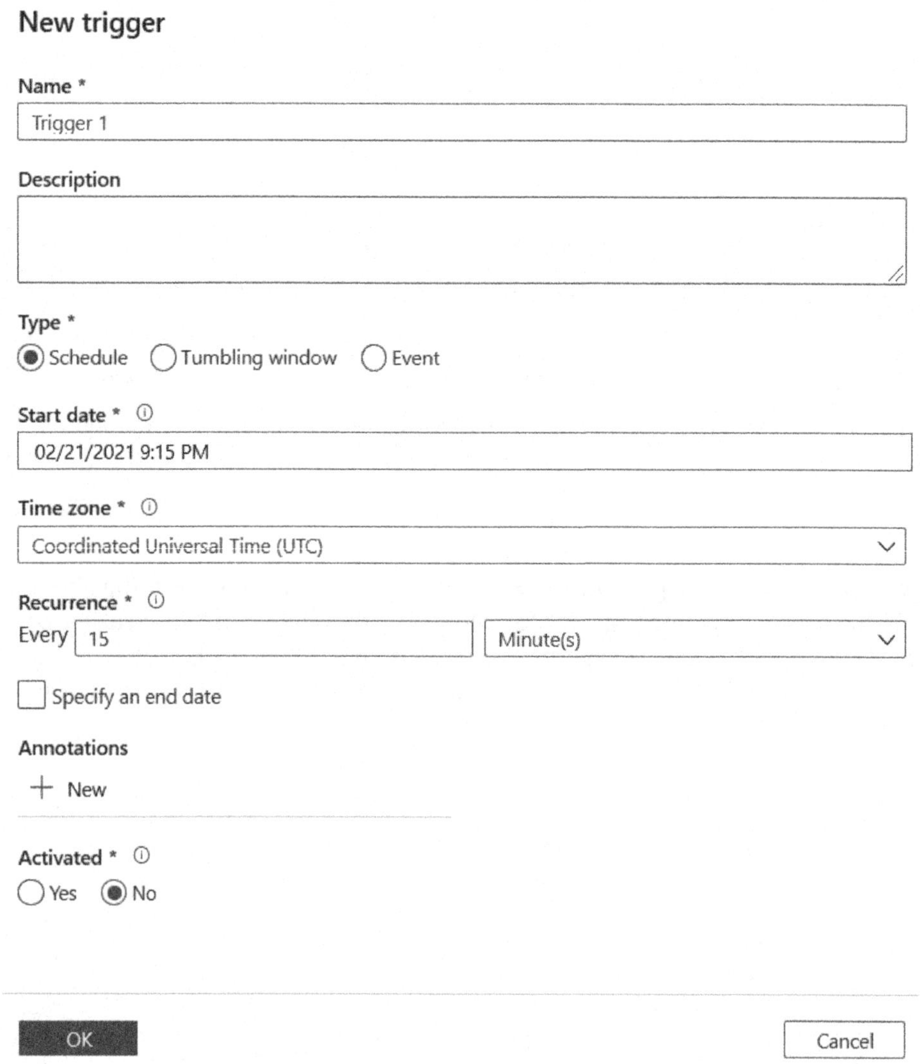

New trigger

Name *

> Trigger 1

Description

>

Type *

(●) Schedule   ( ) Tumbling window   ( ) Event

Start date * ⓘ

> 02/21/2021 9:15 PM

Time zone * ⓘ

> Coordinated Universal Time (UTC)   ⌄

Recurrence * ⓘ

Every | 15 | | Minute(s)   ⌄ |

[ ] Specify an end date

Annotations

+ New

Activated * ⓘ

( ) Yes   (●) No

| OK | | Cancel |

Figure 13.15 – Creating a trigger for Synapse pipelines in the Manage hub of Synapse Studio

We learned different ways to secure data in Azure Synapse Analytics in the preceding chapter. We can manage access to the Synapse workspace within the **Manage** hub of Synapse Studio.

In the next section, we are going to learn how we can manage data security within Synapse Studio.

Security

We learned in *Chapter 12, Securing Data on Azure Synapse*, that Azure provides multiple security measures to access data on Azure Synapse Analytics. In this section, we are going to learn how we can secure data using access controls and credentials within the **Manage** hub of Synapse Studio. This section also outlines managing credentials for Azure Synapse Analytics within Synapse Studio.

Access control

Access control can be used to grant others access to the Synapse workspace by assigning roles to users, groups, or service principals. Synapse RBAC can be used to manage permissions for publishing and viewing the code artifacts, to execute code on Synapse Spark pools, to access linked services, and to access integration runtimes for monitoring job execution and execution logs. Only Synapse administrators can assign any role to users or service principals.

You can perform the following steps to create a new role assignment:

1. Go to the **Access control** tools in the **Manage** hub of Synapse Studio.

2. Click on **+Add**, as you can see in *Figure 13.17*, to create a new role assignment.

3. Select a **Scope** option to add the role assignment. Next, we can select **Workspace** or **Workspace item** as the scope. There are four workspace item types available to choose from, namely, **Apache Spark pool**, **Integration runtime**, **Linked service**, **Credential**, and **Scope pool**.

4. If you selected **Workspace item** as the scope, you need to select a specific item for the selected item type. However, if you selected **Workspace** as the scope, you are granting access to all the items in your Synapse workspace.

5. Next, we need to select a **Role** option from the list of available roles for a
    particular scope:

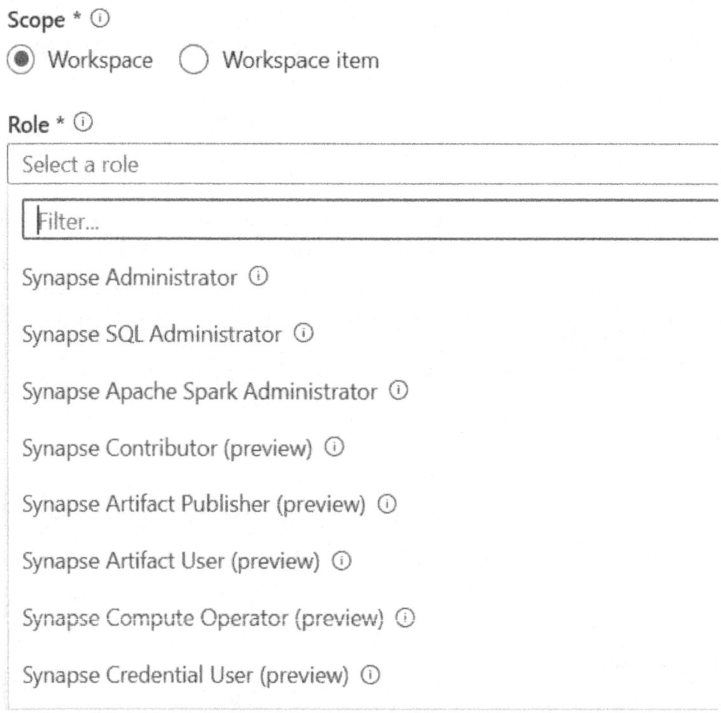

Scope * ⓘ

◉ Workspace   ◯ Workspace item

Role * ⓘ

Select a role

Filter...

Synapse Administrator ⓘ

Synapse SQL Administrator ⓘ

Synapse Apache Spark Administrator ⓘ

Synapse Contributor (preview) ⓘ

Synapse Artifact Publisher (preview) ⓘ

Synapse Artifact User (preview) ⓘ

Synapse Compute Operator (preview) ⓘ

Synapse Credential User (preview) ⓘ

Figure 13.16 – Selecting a role for creating a new role assignment in Synapse Studio

6. And finally, we need to provide the value for the **Select User** field. This could be
    either users, groups, or service principals.

7. After providing all the details, click on **Apply** and your new role assignment
    is created.

You can click on the **Access control** tab in the **Manage** hub to see all of the users and the roles associated with these users:

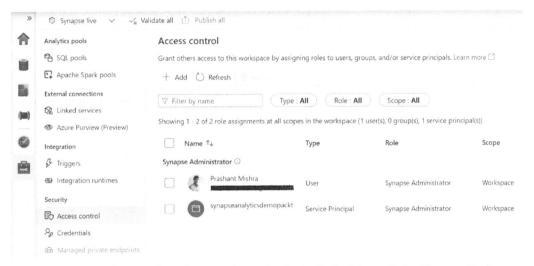

Figure 13.17 – A screenshot of users and associated roles in the Manage hub of Synapse Studio

You can assign multiple roles to the same user, and the same role can be assigned to multiple users; hence, users and roles share many-to-many relationships.

Now, let's see how we can create credentials in Synapse Studio to secure our data.

Credentials

Credentials are used to hold authentication details. These credentials can be used to access data from your Azure Data Lake Storage account or any other data sources.

All the credentials will be listed under the **Credentials** section within the **Manage** hub of Synapse Studio, as seen in the following screenshot:

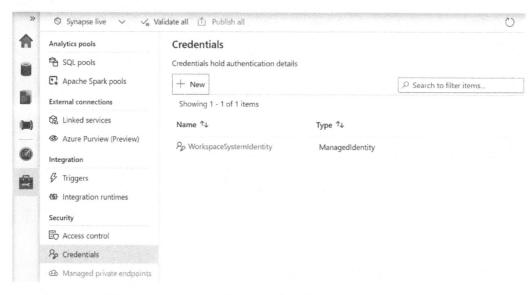

Figure 13.18 – A screenshot of Credentials within Synapse Studio

> **Important note**
>
> You must have a service principal already created before proceeding further in this section. You can go to the following link (`https://docs.microsoft.com/en-us/azure/active-directory/develop/howto-create-service-principal-portal`) to learn about the service principal if you are not already familiar with it.

You need to have the following information in order to create credentials for your Synapse workspace:

- **Tenant ID**: This can be found by going to your Azure Active Directory in the Azure portal. In the **Overview** pane, you will be able to see your tenant ID.

- **Service principal ID**: This is a security identity used by apps or services to access specific Azure resources.

- **AKV linked service**: AKV is an abbreviation for **Azure Key Vault**. You need to add the linked service for AKV from the dropdown. This linked service needs to be created before coming to this step.

- **Secret name**: You can provide the secret name that you created in your AKV services to be used in your Azure Synapse workspace.

- **Secret version**: If you have multiple versions of your secret available in AKV, you can specify the version; otherwise, it will select the latest version automatically.

Having provided all the details, click on **Create** and your credential is created:

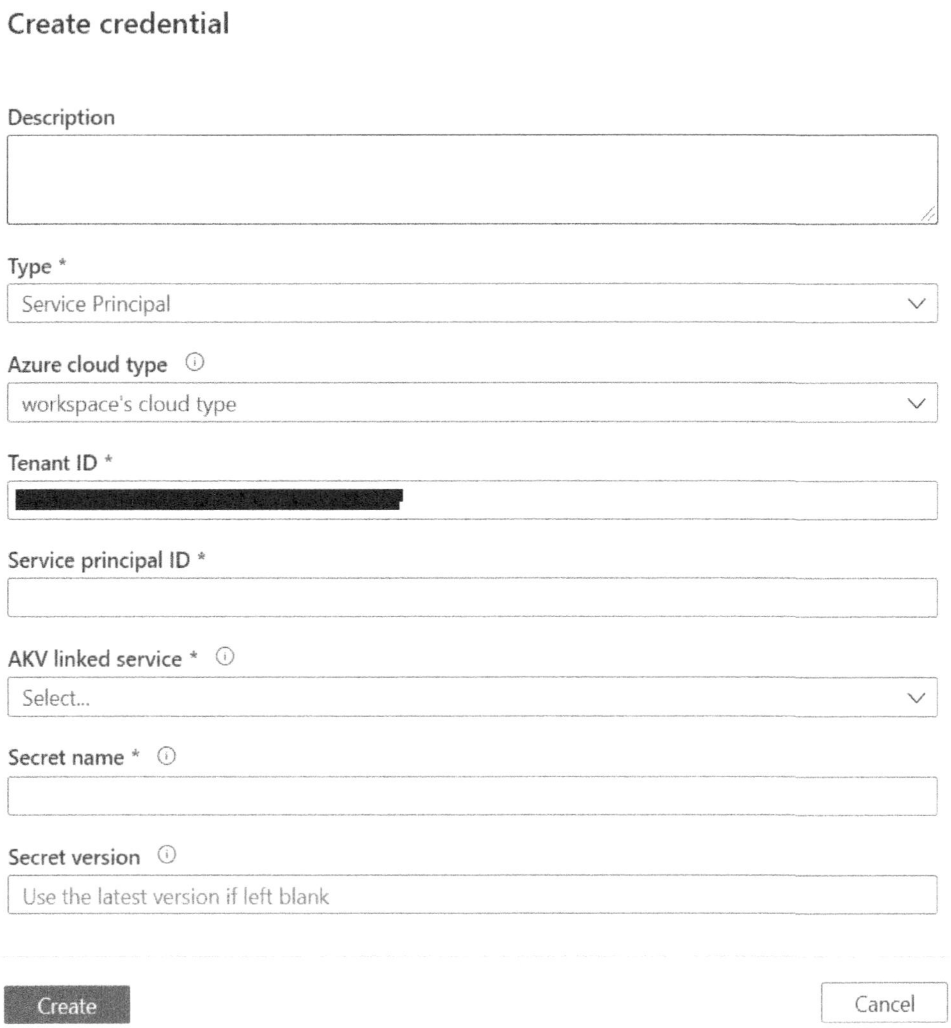

Create credential

Description

Type *

    Service Principal   ∨

Azure cloud type ⓘ

    workspace's cloud type   ∨

Tenant ID *

    ███████████████████████████████████

Service principal ID *

AKV linked service * ⓘ

    Select...   ∨

Secret name * ⓘ

Secret version ⓘ

    Use the latest version if left blank

    Create   Cancel

Figure 13.19 – Creating a new credential in the Manage hub of Synapse Studio

Now, after managing security on a Synapse workspace, it's time to manage our code development. Let's dive further into this topic in the next section.

Source control

This section will outline how to configure and use a Synapse workspace with the Git repository enabled. You can associate your Synapse workspace with Azure DevOps Git or GitHub. If you are using Azure DevOps GitHub as your repository, you need to select your Azure Active Directory associated with your Synapse workspace, but if you are planning to use GitHub as your repository, then you need to provide a GitHub account to configure your repository with your Synapse workspace.

The following screenshot shows both types of repository options available in Azure Synapse:

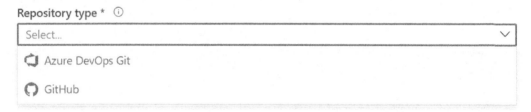

Figure 13.20 – Selecting your repository type for your Synapse workspace

The following sections will cover how to configure your Synapse workspace with both the repository types.

Connecting with an Azure DevOps Git account

Azure DevOps Git enables developers to collaborate on code development. This provides repositories for the source control of your code in the cloud.

> **Important note**
>
> You need to have an Azure DevOps Git repository already in place to follow these steps. If you do not yet have an account, please go to the following link, `https://docs.microsoft.com/en-us/azure/devops/user-guide/sign-up-invite-teammates`, to create your account first.

Azure Synapse provides this feature to configure a repository for your Synapse workspace. Perform the following steps to configure your repository using your Azure DevOps Git account:

1. Go to the **Manage** hub of your Synapse workspace and select **Git configuration** in the **Source control** section.

2. When connecting to the Azure DevOps Git repository, you must select **Azure DevOps Git** as the repository type and then select **Azure Active Directory** from the drop-down list and click on **Continue**.

3. On the next screen, provide the values for **Azure DevOps organization name**, **Project name**, **Repository name**, **Collaboration branch**, **Publish branch**, and **Root folder**.

> **Important note**
>
> When the **Import existing resources to repository** box is checked, your workspace resources (except pools) will be imported into the associated Git repository in JSON format. This action exports each resource individually.

4. And finally, set the working branch that you will be using for making your changes and click on **Apply**:

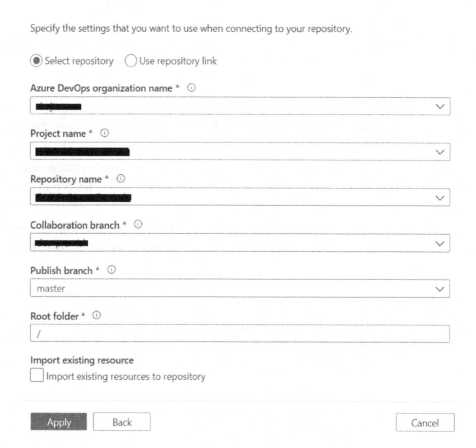

Configure a repository

Specify the settings that you want to use when connecting to your repository.

⦿ Select repository   ◯ Use repository link

Azure DevOps organization name * ⓘ

Project name * ⓘ

Repository name * ⓘ

Collaboration branch * ⓘ

Publish branch * ⓘ

master

Root folder * ⓘ

/

Import existing resource

☐ Import existing resources to repository

[Apply]   [Back]   [Cancel]

Figure 13.21 – Configuring the repository for your Synapse workspace by using
Azure DevOps Git as the repository

If you have a GitHub account instead of an Azure DevOps account, you will still be able to configure the repository for your Synapse workspace. In the next section, we will learn how to configure GitHub for Azure Synapse Analytics.

Connecting with a GitHub account

GitHub also provides you with a repository for source control where you can record or rewind any change to your code to keep all your team members in sync.

Similar to the Azure DevOps Git repository type, you can follow the instructions to configure your repository by using your GitHub account:

1. Go to the **Manage** hub of your Synapse workspace and select **Git configuration** in the **Source control** section.

2. When connecting to the Azure DevOps Git repository, you must select **GitHub** as the repository type, provide the GitHub account name, and then click on **Continue**.

3. Provide corresponding values for **GitHub account**, **Repository name**, **Collaboration branch**, **Root folder**, and **Import resource into this branch**.

4. Next, click on **Apply**.

Next, we are going to learn about monitoring Synapse workloads using Synapse Studio.

Monitoring Synapse workloads

Monitoring workloads is critical for understanding any unexpected behavior with the workload. Synapse pipelines, triggers, integration runtimes, Apache Spark applications, SQL requests, data flow debugging, and analytical pools can be monitored directly on the **Monitor** hub of Synapse Studio. You can also change the time range for certain workloads if you want to monitor workloads for a specific time range. This section is going to cover the monitoring of all activities and workloads within Azure Synapse Analytics.

You can glimpse the **Monitor** hub within Synapse Studio in the following screenshot:

Figure 13.22 – Monitoring various resources of a Synapse workspace in Synapse Studio

Integration is associated with Synapse pipelines, and we will learn how to monitor pipelines, triggers, and integration runtimes in the following section.

Integration

Synapse pipelines has various components that are stitched together to provide one of the best ELT/ETL services in the cloud. Synapse Studio enables you to monitor critical components of Synapse pipelines within the **Monitor** hub of Synapse Studio.

The following activities can be monitored in Synapse Studio with an option to apply date filters if you wish to monitor activities only for that particular day:

- **Pipeline runs**: All the pipeline runs can be monitored here, and we can also find out the error corresponding to any pipeline run failure, in order to investigate the root cause of failure.

- **Trigger runs**: Similar to pipeline runs, we can monitor all the triggers as well. You can monitor which pipelines are executed using these triggers, when these triggers ran for the last time, what type of trigger it is, and so on.

- **Integration runtimes**: You can monitor the health of integration runtimes to determine whether they are in a running state or unavailable.

In the next section, we will learn what types of activities can be monitored under the **Monitor** hub of Synapse Studio.

Activities

We can run Apache Spark applications using various supported languages, or we can run just a simple SQL query on Synapse or just a data flow. We have not spoken much about data flow in this book because in order to cover all the concepts of data flow, we would require a separate book. However, if you want to learn more about data flow, you can go to the following link: `https://docs.microsoft.com/en-us/azure/synapse-analytics/concepts-data-flow-overview`. So, Synapse lets you monitor all these activities in just one place.

The following requests or jobs can be monitored within the **Monitor** hub of Synapse Studio:

- **Apache Spark Applications**: Spark sessions and batch jobs can both be monitored here. It provides us with information regarding the application name, submitter, submit time, status, and pool. We have the option to add filters to narrow down the details as per our business requirements.

- **SQL requests**: Similarly, we can monitor all the SQL requests made in this workspace. We get the Request ID, Request content, Submit time, Duration, Submitter, Status, Queued duration, and Workload group options.

- **Data flow debug**: As data flow is associated with the Synapse pipelines, we can get the information about the current session ID, Started by, Timeout(mins), Integration runtime, Cores, Compute type, Last Activity Time, and Session ID. This information helps in getting to the root cause of the problem in the event of any issue.

The following section outlines how to monitor Analytics pools within a Synapse workspace.

Analytics pools

Synapse provides two separate compute environments; one is a SQL pool and the other is an Apache Spark pool. Azure Synapse has really done an amazing job of providing a monitoring facility for both the compute environments together as a unified experience.

The following bullet points outline the monitoring of SQL and Apache Spark pools within Synapse Studio:

- **SQL pools**: The overall health of SQL pools can be monitored within the **Monitor** hub of Synapse Studio, including **CPU utilization** and **Memory utilization**:

SQL pools

◯ Refresh   ≡≡ Edit columns

(Pool : **All**)

Showing 1 - 4 of 4 items

Pool name ↑↓	Type ↑↓	Status ↑↓	Size ↑↓	CPU utilization % ⓘ ↓	Memory utilization % ⓘ ↑↓	Created o
Built-in	Serverless	✅ Online	Auto	N/A	N/A	N/A
sqlpooldemo	Dedicated	⬤ Paused	DW200c	-	-	12/16/202
sqlpooldemo_1	Dedicated	⬤ Paused	DW200c	-	-	1/27/2021
sqlpooldemo_2	Dedicated	⬤ Paused	DW200c	-	-	1/28/2021

Figure 13.23 – Monitoring SQL pools in the Monitor hub of Synapse Studio

- **Apache Spark pools**: We can monitor **Active users**, **Allocated vCores**, and **Allocated memory (GB)** for Apache Spark pools within the **Monitor** hub of Synapse Studio:

Figure 13.24 – Monitoring Apache Spark pools in the Monitor hub of Synapse Studio

So far, we have learned how to manage and monitor Synapse workloads by using Synapse Studio, but in the following section, we will learn how to manage maintenance schedules of our SQL pools in the Azure Synapse workspace.

Managing maintenance schedules

As soon as the SQL pool deployment is completed, SQL pools have an 8-hour primary and 8-hour secondary maintenance window applied by default. During this maintenance window, all the patch updates will happen internally, and you may not be able to access your resources for the time being. You will be notified when the maintenance job is complete so that you can resume your work after that. Thus, you need to make sure that the maintenance schedule is out of your regular business hours. In order to change the maintenance schedules, perform the following steps:

1. Go to your Synapse workspace in the Azure portal.

2. Click on **SQL pool** and select your SQL pool.

3. Select the **Maintenance schedule** link on the **Overview** blade to open the page for maintenance schedule settings.

4. Select **Primary maintenance window** and **Secondary maintenance window** settings as per your business requirements and then click on **Save** to save your changes.

    The following screenshot displays the maintenance window settings for the selected SQL pool:

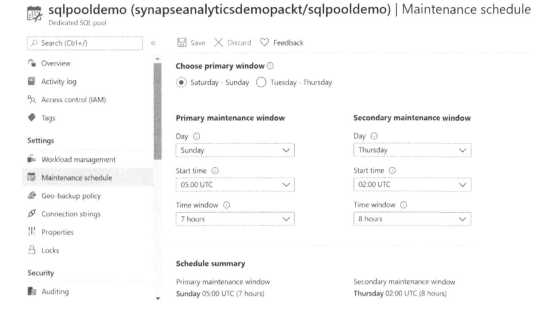

Figure 13.25 – A screenshot of maintenance schedule settings of the selected SQL pool in the Azure portal

During the maintenance window, your SQL pool will not remain offline. Selecting maintenance windows only ensures that the maintenance might take place anytime within this window only. This maintenance activity takes 5-6 minutes to complete, and you will be able to use your SQL pools as this is after the maintenance has been completed. If your SQL pool is paused during this time frame, then maintenance will take place when the pool is resumed.

> **Important note**
> During the maintenance window, your SQL pools may experience multiple brief connection losses if the performance level of your SQL pool is DW400c or lower.

It is a good practice to set up alerts to monitor our workload, as we cannot keep our eyes on the machine 24x7. The following section covers this topic in detail.

Creating alerts for Azure Synapse Analytics

Azure has provided a built-in functionality to set up alerts for monitoring Azure resources efficiently. Alerts can be set up for an individual Azure resource separately, and in this section, we are going to learn how to set up alerts for Azure Synapse Analytics.

To create an alert, we need to select the target resource we need to monitor, which is called the scope. After that, we need to define conditions for the alert, define the actions that will be invoked when the alert rule triggers, and finally provide details on the alert rule.

Perform the following steps to configure an alert rule for your Synapse workspace:

1. Go to your Synapse workspace in the Azure portal.

2. Click on the **Alerts** link of the **Overview** blade of your Synapse workspace.

3. Click on **+New alert rule** to configure a new alert rule:

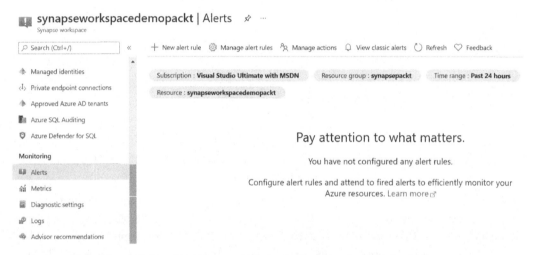

Figure 13.26 – Creating a new alert rule for Azure Synapse Analytics

4. Now we need to establish the scope for the alert rule. Scope is the target resource on Azure that you wish to monitor. In this book, we are talking about Azure Synapse Analytics, so we will restrict our scope to our Synapse workspace. Click on **Edit resource link** under the **Scope** section.

5. Filter your subscription, resource type, and location to select a resource as the scope:

Select a resource   ✕

Select the resource(s) you want to monitor. Available signal types for your selection will show up on the bottom right.

Filter by subscription * ⓘ	Filter by resource type ⓘ	Filter by location ⓘ
Data SQL Ninja POD1 ⌄	Azure Synapse Analytics ⌄	East US ⌄

🔎 Search to filter items...

Resource	Resource type
⌄ ⁆ ▬▬▬▬▬▬▬▬▬	Subscription
⌄ ⌊⁌⌉ ▬▬▬▬	Resource group
⬡ synapseanalyticsdemopackt	Synapse workspace

Figure 13.27 – Selecting a resource to define the scope for creating an alert rule in the Azure portal

6. Next, we need to add a condition to define the logic in terms of when the alert rule should trigger. Click on the **Add condition** link under the **Condition** section.

7. Select a **signal name** from the list of all the available signals. This will take you to the next window:

Figure 13.28 – Selecting a signal name for defining the condition for creating an alert rule in the Azure portal

8. On the next screen, we need to configure the alert logic. Select **Static** or **Dynamic** for the **Threshold** field.

9. Select **Operator**, **Aggregation type**, and **Unit** options for configuring the logic and provide a value for **Threshold value**.

10. Select the appropriate value for **Aggregation granularity (Period)** and **Frequency of evaluation** as per your business requirements and then click on **Done**:

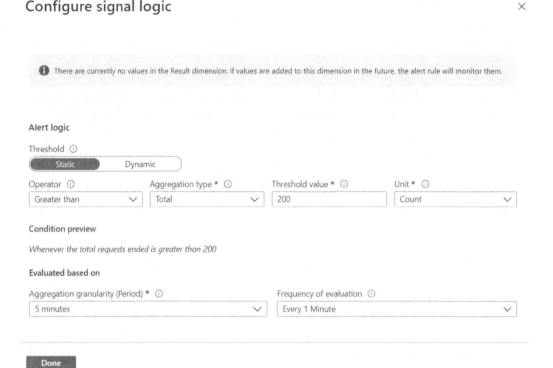

Figure 13.29 – Configuring signal logic to create an alert rule in the Azure portal

11. Now we need to configure **Actions**. Click on the **Add action groups** link. This will take you to a new screen to select an action group to attach to this alert rule.

12. Select an **action group name** if you already have an action group that you want to attach to this alert rule, otherwise click on **+Create action group**.

13. Provide appropriate values for **Action group name** and **Display name** in the **Basics** tab.

14. On the **Notifications** tab, select **Email/SMS message/Push/Voice** as the notification type.

15. Provide the values for **Email** and **Phone number** in the corresponding fields and then click on **OK**:

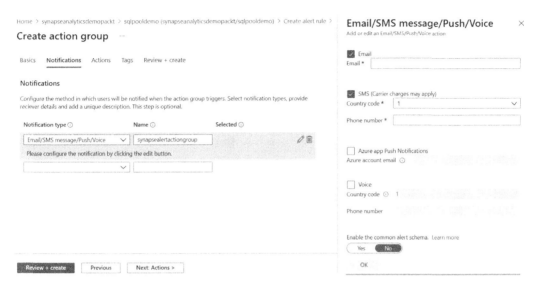

Figure 13.30 – Selecting the notification type and providing corresponding details to configure the alert rule

16. Now, let's go to the **Actions** tab and select an option for **Action type**. In this example, we are going to select **Logic App** as the action type.

17. Provide the corresponding values for **Subscription**, **Resource group**, and **Select a logic app** for the **action type** selected, and then click on **OK**:

Figure 13.31 – Selecting an action type for configuring the alert rule in the Azure portal

18. Now, click on **Review + create** to review all the settings and then click on **Create**.

19. Coming back to the main screen for creating an alert rule, finally, we need to provide appropriate values for **Alert rule name**, **Description**, **Save alert rule to resource group**, and **Severity** in the **Alert rule details** section.

20. Make sure you have checked the box for **Enable alert rule upon creation** and then click on **Create alert rule**:

Alert rule details

Provide details on your alert rule so that you can identify and manage it later.

Alert rule name * ⓘ	Specify the alert rule name
Description	Specify the alert rule description
Save alert rule to resource group * ⓘ	pramish ⌄
Severity * ⓘ	Sev 3 ⌄
Enable alert rule upon creation	☑

Figure 13.32 – Providing alert rule details to create an alert rule in the Azure portal

This was just one example of how to create an alert rule. However, you can create multiple alerts for your Synapse workspace.

Now that we have learned all the possible ways to manage and monitor Synapse workloads, it's time to wrap up this chapter.

Summary

In this chapter, we learned how we can manage different resources on Azure Synapse. We learned how to manage pipelines, triggers, various activities, and analytical pools within an Azure Synapse workspace. We also learned how we can configure a code repository for our workspace. With the built-in monitoring experience provided in Synapse Studio, we learned how to monitor various workloads and integration-related activities. We learned about creating alert rules for the Synapse workspace. We also got to know that we can modify maintenance windows even after creating the SQL pool as per our business requirements.

In the next chapter, we are going to learn about the best practices for using Azure Synapse Analytics.

14
Coding Best Practices

Azure Synapse allows you to create a **Structured Query Language** (**SQL**) pool or an Apache Spark pool with just a couple of clicks, without worrying too much about maintenance and management. However, you need to follow certain best practices in order to utilize these pools effectively and efficiently.

This chapter is crucial to the production environment. When you need to create a SQL or Spark pool in your production environments, you must follow the coding or development best practices. This chapter is mainly focused on the best practices for coding, development, workload management, and cost management, for both SQL and Spark pools on Azure Synapse.

In this chapter, we will cover the following topics:

- Implementing best practices for a Synapse dedicated SQL pool

- Implementing best practices for a Synapse serverless SQL pool

- Implementing best practices for a Synapse Spark pool

Technical requirements

To follow the instructions in the next sections, there are certain prerequisites before we proceed, outlined here:

- You should have your Azure subscription, or access to any other subscription with contributor-level access.

- Create your Synapse workspace on this subscription. You can follow the instructions from *Chapter 1, Introduction to Azure Synapse,* to create your Synapse workspace.

- Create a SQL pool and a Spark pool on Azure Synapse. This has been covered in *Chapter 2, Consideration of Your Compute Environments.*

Implementing best practices for a Synapse dedicated SQL pool

In the previous chapters, we learned many things about Synapse dedicated SQL pools. In this section, we will only learn about the best practices to maintain your dedicated SQL pool and keep it healthy from a computational or storage point of view.

In order to get better performance, we need to have optimized code, but along with that we need to consider various other factors as well. You may have sometimes experienced that your query had been performing well until last week and then suddenly, its performance dropped drastically. So, how do you avoid such kinds of hiccups in your production environment? In the following section, we are going to learn about a couple of features or implementations to keep your query performance constantly healthy.

Maintaining statistics

Statistics play a critical role in query performance. They provide a distribution of column values to the query optimizer, and that is used by the SQL engine to get the cardinality of the data (estimated number of rows). Thus, it is important to always keep your statistics updated, and particularly when you are carrying out bulk data `INSERT/UPDATE` operations.

In an Azure Synapse SQL pool, we can enable an `AUTO_CREATE_STATISTICS` property that helps the query optimizer create missing statistics on an individual column in the query predicate or join condition.

Statistics can be created with a full scan on sample data, or a range of data. In this section, we are going to learn how to create statistics for different scenarios.

The following command can be run against a SQL pool to validate whether this feature is enabled or not:

```
SELECT name, is_auto_create_stats_on
FROM sys.databases
```

You can configure AUTO_CREATE_STATISTICS on your dedicated SQL pool by using the following code:

```
ALTER DATABASE MySQLPool -- Your dedicated SQL pool name
SET AUTO_CREATE_STATISTICS ON
```

You can create statistics by examining every record in a table or by specifying the sample size. The following code can be run to create statistics by examining every row:

```
CREATE STATISTICS col1_stats ON dbo.table1 (col1) WITH
FULLSCAN;
```

You can run the following code to create statistics by using sampling:

```
CREATE STATISTICS col1_stats ON dbo.table1 (col1) WITH SAMPLE =
50 PERCENT;
```

You can also create statistics on only some of the rows in a table by using a WHERE clause, as illustrated in the following code snippet:

```
CREATE STATISTICS stats_col1 ON table1(col1) WHERE col1 >
'2000101' AND col1 < '20001231';
```

You can create multiple statistics on the same table. While updating the statistics, you can decide whether you want to update all the statistics objects in a table or only specific statistics objects.

The following code can be used to update all the statistics in a table:

```
UPDATE STATISTICS [schema_name].[table_name];
```

The following code can be used to update a specific statistics object in a table:

```
UPDATE STATISTICS [schema_name].[table_name]([stat_name]);
```

In the following section, we are going to learn how to use the correct distribution type for a table in a Synapse SQL pool.

Using correct distribution for your tables

In a distributed table, records are actually stored across 60 distributions, but at a high level, all the records reside within one table. Synapse uses hash and round-robin algorithms for data distribution.

A Synapse SQL pool supports hash-distributed, round-robin-distributed, and replicated tables, outlined as follows:

- **Hash-distributed tables**: A hash-distributed table uses a hash algorithm to distribute the records among 60 distributions. In cases where the table size is more than 2 **Gigabytes (GB)** and the table has frequent INSERT, UPDATE, and DELETE operations, then it is recommended to use hash-distributed tables.

- **Round-robin-distributed tables**: In these tables, data is distributed evenly across all distributions by using a round-robin algorithm. This form of distribution should be used when we don't have a column that is a good candidate for hash distribution, or in the case of a temporary staging table.

- **Replicated tables**: If your table size is less than 2 GB when compressed, then you should try using replicated tables instead of distributed tables. In a replicated table, full data is copied to each compute node so that it can be accessed by any compute node without any latency. Small-dimension tables are the best candidates for replicated tables.

The following section outlines how to use partitions to enhance performance on Synapse SQL pools.

Using partitioning

You have learned so far that a Synapse SQL pool distributes data across 60 distributions for better performance. You should also know that a Synapse SQL pool lets you create partitions on all three table types. Table partitions divide your data into smaller groups of records. Partitions are mainly created for the benefit of easy maintenance and query performance. A query with a filter condition can be limited to certain partitioned data scanning, instead of scanning through all the records in a table.

It is important to decide how many partitions we need to create in a table. We already have 60 distributions, but it is recommended to have 1 million rows per distribution and partition, such that we have optimal performance and compression of clustered columnstore tables. So, if we decide to create 10 partitions, we need to have 600 million rows and 1 million rows in each distribution and partition for optimal performance.

You can use the following code snippet to check the partitions and then the number of records in each partition in a table:

```
SELECT    QUOTENAME(s.[name])+'.'+QUOTENAME(t.[name]) as Table_
name
,         i.[name] as Index_name
,         p.partition_number as Partition_nmbr
,         p.[rows] as Row_count
,         p.[data_compression_desc] as Data_Compression_desc
FROM      sys.partitions p
JOIN      sys.tables    t    ON    p.[object_id]    = t.[object_
id]
JOIN      sys.schemas   s    ON    t.[schema_id]    = s.[schema_
id]
JOIN      sys.indexes   i    ON    p.[object_id]    = i.[object_
Id]
AND    p.[index_Id]    = i.[index_Id]
WHERE t.[name]  = 'TableName';
```

Partitions are mostly created on the `Date` column, but you can decide which will be the best candidate for partitioning your table. A partition can be created while creating a table as well. The following code snippet is just an example of how to create a partition:

```
CREATE TABLE [dbo].[FactInternetSales]
(
      [ProductKey]          int            NOT NULLw
,     [OrderDateKey]        int            NOT NULL
,     [CustomerKey]         int            NOT NULL
,     [PromotionKey]        int            NOT NULL
,     [SalesOrderNumber]    nvarchar(20)   NOT NULL
,     [OrderQuantity]       smallint       NOT NULL
,     [UnitPrice]           money          NOT NULL
,     [SalesAmount]         money          NOT NULL
)
WITH
(   CLUSTERED COLUMNSTORE INDEX
,   DISTRIBUTION = HASH([ProductKey])
,   PARTITION    (   [OrderDateKey] RANGE RIGHT FOR VALUES
                 (20000101,20010101,20020101
```

```
                              ,20030101,20040101,20050101
                        )
               )
       )
```

So far, we have learned different ways to enhance query performance on a SQL pool; however, it is also important to pay attention to the column size while creating a table. In the next section, we are going to learn how to use an adequate column size in Synapse SQL pools.

Using an adequate column size

In most cases, we end up providing a default length for VARCHAR, NVARCHAR, or CHAR data types. We should try to restrict the length to the maximum length of the characters expected in that particular column. There are a few data types that are supported in SQL Server but are not supported in Synapse SQL—for example, the XML data type. We need to use VARCHAR in place of XML data types but keep the length limited to the maximum character length of the XML values. For better performance, we should try to have accurate precision for decimal numbers.

The next section outlines the advantages of using a minimum transaction size in Synapse SQL pools.

Advantages of using a minimum transaction size

In the case of any transaction failure, we need to roll back all INSERT, UPDATE, or DELETE operations. If you are trying to run these operations against a huge volume of data, you may need to roll back all the changes in case of any failure, hence it's better to divide bigger operations into smaller chunks.

You can reduce rollback risk by using minimal logging operations such as TRUNCATE, CTAS, DROP TABLE, or INSERT on empty tables. You can also use PolyBase to load and export data quickly, and we are going to learn more about this feature in the following section.

Using PolyBase to load data

PolyBase is a tool that is designed to leverage the distributed nature of a system to load and export data faster than with **Azure Data Factory**, **Bulk Copy Program** (**BCP**), or any other tool. When you are dealing with a huge volume of records, it is recommended that you use PolyBase to load or export the data. PolyBase loads can be run by using Azure Data Factory, Synapse pipelines, CTAS, or INSERT INTO.

The following screenshot displays **PolyBase** as a **Copy method** in Synapse pipelines for loading the data:

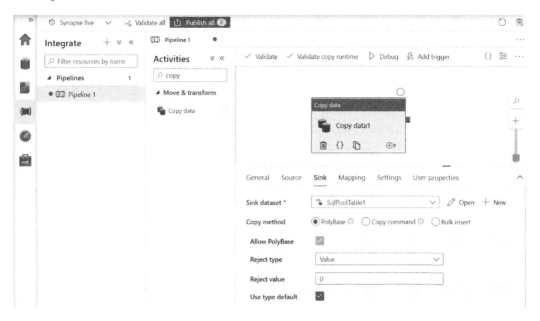

Figure 14.1 – Loading data to a Synapse SQL pool by using the PolyBase copy method within Synapse pipelines

The next section teaches us about index maintenance, which is one of the key ways to keep your indexes healthy and performance optimized for corresponding tables.

Reorganizing and rebuilding indexes

Index maintenance is crucial in keeping your query executions healthy. Sometimes, due to bulk data loading or bad selection of the fill factor, you may end up having index fragmentations, which may lead to bad performance in your query executions. You need to set up a scheduled job to keep track of fragmentation and perform index reorganizing or rebuilding accordingly.

You can use the following SQL code to check for fragmentation:

```
SELECT S.name as 'Schema',
T.name as 'Table',
I.name as 'Index',
```

```
DDIPS.avg_fragmentation_in_percent,
DDIPS.page_count
FROM sys.dm_db_index_physical_stats (DB_ID(), NULL, NULL, NULL,
NULL) AS DDIPS
INNER JOIN sys.tables T on T.object_id = DDIPS.object_id
INNER JOIN sys.schemas S on T.schema_id = S.schema_id
INNER JOIN sys.indexes I ON I.object_id = DDIPS.object_id
AND DDIPS.index_id = I.index_id
WHERE DDIPS.database_id = DB_ID()
and I.name is not null
AND DDIPS.avg_fragmentation_in_percent > 0
ORDER BY DDIPS.avg_fragmentation_in_percent desc
```

If your fragmentation value is more than 30%, consider reorganizing indexes, but if it is beyond 50%, you should rebuild your indexes.

You can use the following SQL script to reorganize/rebuild your indexes:

```
-- To Rebuild you rindex
ALTER INDEX INDEX_NAME ON SCHEMA_NAME.TABLE_NAME
REBUILD;
-- To Reorganize you rindex
ALTER INDEX INDEX_NAME ON SCHEMA_NAME.TABLE_NAME
REORGANIZE;
```

Next, we will see how materialized views can help in gaining better performance on a dedicated SQL pool.

Materialized views

You can create standard or materialized views in a Synapse SQL pool. Materialized views provide enhanced performance by storing data on a SQL pool, unlike with standard views. You get pre-computed data stored in a SQL pool in the case of materialized views; however, standard views compute their data each time we use them. But one thing that we should always keep in mind is that materialized views are storing data in your SQL pool, so there will be an extra storage cost involved when using materialized views. We need to decide the trade-off between cost and performance as per our business needs.

The following code will give you a list of all materialized views in your Synapse SQL pool:

```
SELECT V.name as materialized_view, V.object_id
FROM sys.views V
JOIN sys.indexes I ON V.object_id= I.object_id AND I.index_id <
2;
```

Next, we can see that the syntax for creating a materialized view is similar to that for a standard view:

```
CREATE MATERIALIZED VIEW [ schema_name. ] materialized_view_
name
    WITH (
        <distribution_option>
    )
    AS <select_statement>
[;]


<distribution_option> ::=
    {
        DISTRIBUTION = HASH ( distribution_column_name )
      | DISTRIBUTION = ROUND_ROBIN
    }


<select_statement> ::=
    SELECT select_criteria
```

If you need to improve the performance of a complex query against large data volumes, you can go for materialized views.

Next, we are going to learn how we can enhance query performance by using an appropriate resource class.

Using an appropriate resource class

A resource class is used to determine the performance capacity of a query. By specifying the resource class, you predefine the compute resource limit for query execution in a Synapse SQL pool. There are two types of resource class, and we are going to learn about them in the following sections.

Static resource classes

Static resource classes are ideal for higher concurrency and a constant data volume. These resource classes allocate the same data warehouse units, regardless of the current performance level.

These are the predefined database roles associated with static resource classes:

- `staticrc10`
- `staticrc20`
- `staticrc30`
- `staticrc40`
- `staticrc50`
- `staticrc60`
- `staticrc70`
- `staticrc80`

Similar to static resource classes, you can also use dynamic resource classes. Let's learn about these in the next section.

Dynamic resource classes

Dynamic resource classes are ideal for growing or variable amounts of data. These resource classes allocate variable amounts of memory, depending upon the current service level. By default, a `smallrc` dynamic resource class is assigned to each user.

These are the predefined database roles associated with dynamic resource classes:

- `smallrc`
- `mediumrc`
- `largerc`
- `xlargerc`

You can run the following script on your SQL pool to add a user to a `largec` role:

```
EXEC sp_addrolemember 'largerc', 'newuser'
```

If you need to remove any user from a `largec` role in your SQL pool, you can run the following script:

```
EXEC sp_droprolemember 'largerc', 'newuser';
```

You can refer to the following link to learn more about resource classes in a Synapse SQL pool: `https://docs.microsoft.com/en-us/azure/synapse-analytics/ sql-data-warehouse/resource-classes-for-workload-management`.

In the next section, we are going to learn about workload management in a SQL pool, which is one of the most important features for managing query performance.

Implementing best practices for a Synapse serverless SQL pool

Some of the best practices discussed in the preceding section will be valid even for a serverless SQL pool; however, there are few other considerations for serverless SQL pools. We are going to learn about some of these recommendations in the following sections.

Selecting the region to create a serverless SQL pool

If you are creating a storage account while creating a Synapse workspace, then your serverless SQL pool and storage account will be created in the same region where you created your workspace. But if you are planning to access other storage accounts, make sure you are creating your workspace in the same region. If you try accessing your data in a different region, there will be some network latency in data movement, but you can avoid this by using the same region for your serverless SQL pool as for your storage account.

You need to keep in mind that once the workspace is created, you cannot change the region of a serverless SQL pool separately.

Files for querying

Although you can query various file types in a serverless SQL pool, you will get better performance if you are using Parquet files. So, if possible, try converting **Comma-Separated Values** (**CSV**) files or **JavaScript Object Notation** (**JSON**) files in to Parquet files. Parquet is a columnar data storage format that stores binary data in a column-oriented way. These files enable good compression by organizing values of each column adjacently, which makes the file size relatively smaller when compared to CSV or JSON files.

However, if converting CSV to Parquet is not possible for any reason, try to keep the file size between 100 **Megabytes** (**MB**) and 10 GB for optimal performance. It is also better to use multiple small files instead of one large file.

Using CETAS to enhance query performance

CETAS is an abbreviated form of CREATE EXTERNAL TABLE .. AS. This operation creates external table metadata and exports the SELECT query result to a set of files in the storage account.

The following code is an example of using CETAS to create an external table:

```
-- use CETAS to export select statement with OPENROWSET result
to  storage
CREATE EXTERNAL TABLE population_by_year_state
WITH (
    LOCATION = 'aggregated_data/',
    DATA_SOURCE = population_ds,
    FILE_FORMAT = census_file_format
)
AS
SELECT decennialTime, stateName, SUM(population) AS population
FROM
    OPENROWSET(BULK 'https://azureopendatastorage.blob.core.
windows.net/censusdatacontainer/release/us_population_county/
year=*/*.parquet',
    FORMAT='PARQUET') AS [r]
GROUP BY decennialTime, stateName
GO


-- you can query the newly created external table
SELECT * FROM population_by_year_state
```

CETAS generates Parquet files, so statistics are automatically generated when you use the external table for the first time, which helps in improving performance for subsequent queries.

Now that we have learned how to implement best practices for a Synapse SQL pool, in the following section we will learn how to implement best practices for a Synapse Spark pool.

Implementing best practices for a Synapse Spark pool

As with Synapse SQL pools, it is also important to keep our Spark pool healthy. In this section, we are going to learn how to optimize cluster configuration for any particular workload. We will also learn how to use various techniques for enhancing Apache Spark performance.

Configuring the Auto-pause setting

There are some major advantages of using **Platform-as-a-Service (PaaS)** instead of an on-premises environment, and the **Auto-pause** setting is one of the best features that PaaS has to offer. If you are running a Spark cluster on your on-premises environment, you need to pay for provisioning it even though you may only need to use this cluster for a couple of hours a day. However, Synapse gives you the option to configure the **Auto-pause** setting to pause a cluster automatically if not in use. Upon entering a value for the **Number of minutes idle** field within the **Auto-pause** setting, the Spark pool will go to a **Pause** state automatically if it remains idle for the specified duration, as seen in the following screenshot:

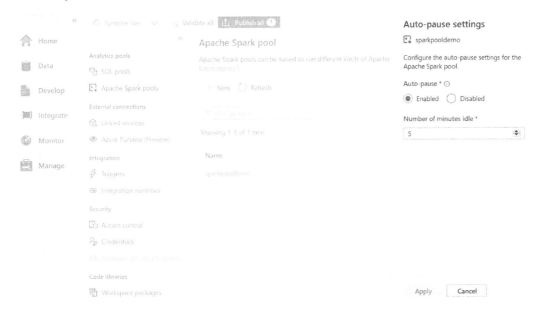

Figure 14.2 – Auto-pause setting for a Synapse Spark pool in the Manage hub of Synapse Studio

When your Spark pool is paused, you are not being charged for the compute power. However, your data is still residing in the storage account even if the Spark pool is paused, hence you are only paying for the data storage.

Next, let's learn some best practices for enhancing Apache Spark performance.

Enhancing Apache Spark performance

In this section of the chapter, we are going to learn how data format, file size, caching, and so on impact job execution performance on the Synapse Spark pool. We will also learn about Spark memory recommendations and how bucketing helps in reducing computational overhead during a job execution on Spark.

So, let's dive into the next section to learn how using an optimal data format can help in getting better Apache Spark performance.

Using an optimal data format

Spark supports various data formats—for example, **CSV**, **JSON**, **XML**, **Parquet**, **Optimized Row Columnar** (**ORC**), and **AVRO**; however, it is recommended to use Parquet files for better performance. Parquet files are the columnar storage file format of the Apache Hadoop ecosystem. Typically, Spark jobs are **Input/Output** (**I/O**)-bound, not **Central Processing Unit** (**CPU**)-bound, so a fast compression codec will help in enhancing performance. You can use a Snappy compression with Parquet files for best performance on a Synapse Spark pool.

The following section will outline the use of caching for better performance on Spark.

Using the cache

There are different ways to use caching in Spark, such as persist(), cache(), and CACHE TABLE. Spark uses Cache() and Persist() methods to store the intermediate computation of a **Resilient Data Distribution** (**RDD**), DataFrame, and Dataset. This intermediate data can be used for subsequent actions.

The following Scala code is an example of using the cache() method with a DataFrame:

```
import spark.implicits._
  val columns = Seq("Id","Text")
  val data = Seq(("1", "This is an exmple of Spark DataFrame
using Cache() method"),
    ("2", "We can replace Cache() with Persist() method in
this example"))
```

```
val df = data.toDF(columns:_*)
```

```
val dfCache = df.cache()
dfCache.show(true)
```

We can replace the `cache()` method with the `persist()` method in the preceding example, as illustrated here:

```
val dfCache = df.persist()
```

The following screenshot displays the execution of the code on a Synapse Spark pool:

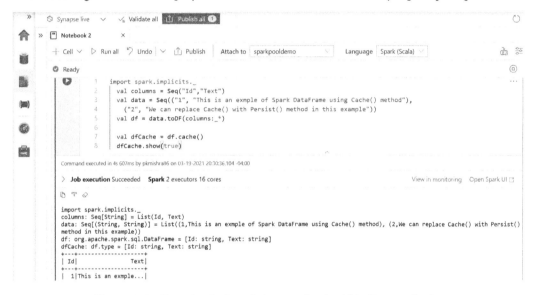

Figure 14.3 – Running Scala code in a notebook within Synapse Studio

We can also use SQL's `CACHE TABLE` command to create a `TableName` table in memory. A `LAZY` keyword can be used with `CACHE TABLE` to make caching lazy. Lazy cache tables are created only when it is first used, instead of immediately.

The following code will create a `CacheTable` for the `TableName` table:

```
%%sql
CACHE TABLE CacheTable SELECT * FROM TableName
```

Similarly, the following code will create a `CacheLazyTable` table:

```
%%sql
CACHE LAZY TABLE CacheLazyTable SELECT * FROM TableName
```

You can validate the records by running the following script in your Synapse notebook:

```sql
%%sql
SELECT * FROM CacheLazyTable
```

The following screenshot displays the records from `CacheLazyTable`:

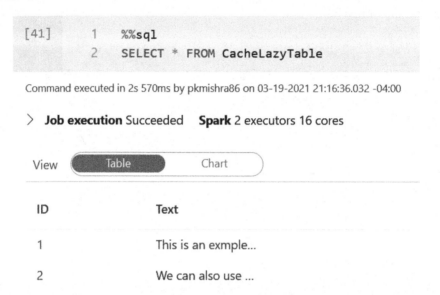

Figure 14.4 – Running a SELECT query against CacheLazyTable using a Synapse Spark pool

Now that we have learned how to create tables in memory for better performance, it's time to learn how to use memory efficiently within a Spark pool.

Spark memory considerations

Spark memory is responsible for storing intermediate state while executing tasks. Apache Spark in Azure Synapse uses Apache Hadoop YARN (where **YARN** is an acronym for **Yet Another Resource Negotiator**) to control the memory used by the container in each Spark node. The main job of YARN is to split up the functionalities of the job scheduling into separate daemons. Apache Spark memory is broken into two segments, namely the following:

- **Storage memory**: Cached data and broadcast variables are stored in storage memory. Spark uses the **Least Recently Used (LRU)** mechanism to clean up the cache for new cache requests.

- **Execution memory**: Objects created during the execution of a task are stored here by Spark.

If blocks are not used in execution memory, storage memory can borrow the space from execution memory, and vice versa.

> **Important note**
> It is recommended to use DataFrames instead of RDD objects to utilize memory in an optimized way.

The following section outlines how you can enhance the performance of your Spark jobs with the use of bucketing.

Using bucketing

Bucketing is a technique in Spark that is used to optimize the performance of a task. We need to provide the number of buckets for the bucketing column, and the data processing engine will calculate the hash value during the load time to decide which bucket it is going to reside in.

Bucketing can be used to optimize aggregations and joins, which we will learn about in the next section.

Optimizing joins and shuffles

Joins play a critical role when developing a Spark job, so it's important to know about optimizations while working with join operations. Let's try to learn about different join types supported by Apache Spark. These are outlined here:

- **SortMerge**: Spark uses the **SortMerge** join type by default, which is a two-step join. First, it sorts the left and right side of the data, and then merges the sorted data from both sides. This join type is best suited for large datasets but may be computationally expensive because of sorting operations. Although this is the default join algorithm in Spark, you can turn it off by setting a `False` value for the `spark.sql.join.preferSortMergeJoin` internal parameter.

- **Merge**: If you are using bucketing, then the **Merge** join algorithm can be used instead of **SortMerge**, and you can avoid expensive sort operations on your dataset.

- **Shuffle hash join**: When the SortMerge join type is turned off, Spark uses the Shuffle hash join type, which works on the concept of map reduce. With a Shuffle hash join, the values of the join column are considered as the output keys, and the DataFrame is shuffled based on these keys. In the end, DataFrames are joined in the reduce phase. It is important to filter out rows that are irrelevant to the keys before joining, in order to avoid unnecessary data shuffling.

- **Broadcast**: In the case of broadcast joins, the smaller table is broadcasted to all the worker nodes, and because of this it is considered to yield maximum performance in the case of little datasets. We can use the following code to provide a hint to Spark to broadcast a table:

```
import org.apache.spark.sql.functions.broadcast
val dataframe = largedataframe.
join(broadcast(smalldataframe), "key")
```

Spark maintains the threshold internally to automatically apply broadcast joins based on the table size; however, we can modify the default threshold value of 10 MB to any specific value by using `spark.sql.autoBroadcastJoinThreshold`.

So far, we have learned about implementing various best practices on a Synapse Spark pool. Now, in the next section, we will learn how to select the correct executor size for Spark jobs.

Selecting the correct executor size

An executor is a process on a worker node that is launched for an application in coordination with the cluster manager. Each application has its own executor, and they are used to run tasks and keep data in memory or disk storage.

The following diagram displays the components of a Spark application:

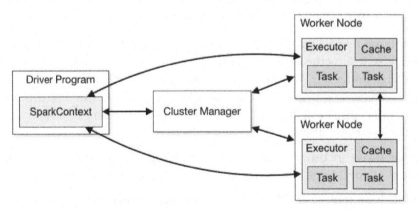

Figure 14.5 – Components of a Spark application

We need to consider the following best practices while working with Spark jobs:

- We should keep the heap size below 32 GB and reduce the number of cores to keep garbage collection overhead below 10%.

- 30 GB per executor is considered the best starting point.

- Increase the number of executor cores for larger clusters.

- For concurrent queries, create multiple parallel Spark applications and distribute queries across these parallel applications.

In this section, we covered the best practices that are common for any Spark jobs, but the list might be even longer based on different specific scenarios.

Summary

This chapter concludes the entire book. In this chapter, we learned about implementing the best practices for Synapse SQL pools and Spark pools. We learned how we keep indexes healthy in a SQL pool such that we gain better performance, and we also learned about using PolyBase and materialized views in Synapse dedicated SQL pools for enhanced performance. This chapter also included the best file type and size to be used in the case of a Synapse serverless SQL pool. Configuring the **Auto pause** setting to help save costs in terms of computational power was also highlighted in this chapter. Last but not least, we learned about memory considerations and bucketing in a Spark pool.

I am thankful to you for traveling with me on this learning journey. Congratulations on reaching the finish line in this book, and I wish you all the best as you continue exploring Azure Synapse.

Hope to meet you again in my next learning journey!

Packt.com

Subscribe to our online digital library for full access to over 7,000 books and videos, as well as industry leading tools to help you plan your personal development and advance your career. For more information, please visit our website.

Why subscribe?

- Spend less time learning and more time coding with practical eBooks and Videos from over 4,000 industry professionals

- Improve your learning with Skill Plans built especially for you

- Get a free eBook or video every month

- Fully searchable for easy access to vital information

- Copy and paste, print, and bookmark content

Did you know that Packt offers eBook versions of every book published, with PDF and ePub files available? You can upgrade to the eBook version at packt.com and as a print book customer, you are entitled to a discount on the eBook copy. Get in touch with us at customercare@packtpub.com for more details.

At www.packt.com, you can also read a collection of free technical articles, sign up for a range of free newsletters, and receive exclusive discounts and offers on Packt books and eBooks.

Other Books You May Enjoy

If you enjoyed this book, you may be interested in these other books by Packt:

Azure Data Factory Cookbook

Dmitry Anoshin, Dmitry Foshin, Roman Storchak, Xenia Ireton

ISBN: 978-1-80056-529-6

- Create an orchestration and transformation job in ADF
- Develop, execute, and monitor data flows using Azure Synapse
- Create big data pipelines using Azure Data Lake and ADF
- Build a machine learning app with Apache Spark and ADF
- Migrate on-premises SSIS jobs to ADF
- Integrate ADF with commonly used Azure services such as Azure ML, Azure Logic Apps, and Azure Functions
- Run big data compute jobs within HDInsight and Azure Databricks

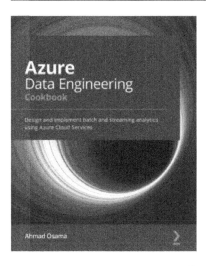

Azure Data Engineering Cookbook

Ahmad Osama

ISBN: 978-1-80020-655-7

- Use Azure Blob storage for storing large amounts of unstructured data
- Perform CRUD operations on the Cosmos Table API
- Implement elastic pools and business continuity with Azure SQL Database
- Ingest and analyze data using Azure Synapse Analytics
- Develop Data Factory data flows to extract data from multiple sources
- Manage, maintain, and secure Azure Data Factory pipelines
- Process streaming data using Azure Stream Analytics and Data Explorer

Packt is searching for authors like you

If you're interested in becoming an author for Packt, please visit `authors.packtpub.com` and apply today. We have worked with thousands of developers and tech professionals, just like you, to help them share their insight with the global tech community. You can make a general application, apply for a specific hot topic that we are recruiting an author for, or submit your own idea.

Leave a review - let other readers know what you think

Please share your thoughts on this book with others by leaving a review on the site that you bought it from. If you purchased the book from Amazon, please leave us an honest review on this book's Amazon page. This is vital so that other potential readers can see and use your unbiased opinion to make purchasing decisions, we can understand what our customers think about our products, and our authors can see your feedback on the title that they have worked with Packt to create. It will only take a few minutes of your time, but is valuable to other potential customers, our authors, and Packt. Thank you!

Index

Symbols

.NET Spark (C#) 192

A

access control 293
Advanced Threat Protection 304
Always encrypted feature 305
Amazon Web Services (AWS) 44
analytical store
  about 134
  enabling, in Cosmos DB 130-132
  full fidelity schema representation 135
  well-defined schema representation 134
anomaly detection
  about 244
  performing 265, 266
anomaly detector resource
  creating, in Azure portal 244-246
Apache Hadoop YARN 47
Apache Spark memory
  execution memory 354
  storage memory 354
Apache Spark MLlib 255

Apache Spark performance, enhancing
  about 352
  bucketing, using 355
  cache, using 352-354
  correct executor size, selecting 356, 357
  joins, optimizing 355
  optimal data format, using 352
  shuffles, optimizing 355
  Spark memory considerations 354, 355
Athena 44
Atomic, Consistent, Isolated, and
        Durable (ACID) 165
authentication mechanisms
  using 94
Automated Machine Learning 255
automatic restore points 272, 273
Auto-pause setting
  configuring 351, 352
Azure
  URL 179
Azure Active Directory
        authorization 295, 296
Azure Blob File System (ABFS) 12
Azure Cosmos DB
  data, ingesting 232-234

S

Made in the USA
Coppell, TX
14 July 2023

19143369R00216